ADVANCE PRAISE FOR
Managing with a Conscience

"Attention all managers! If you believe your most valued asset sits on a pallet in your warehouse, then get off your assets and read *Managing with a Conscience*. The successful 1990s management style will empower, excite, motivate, and reward your organization to set new standards for performance and results."

DEAN F. SHULMAN
Vice President, Sales & Marketing
Brother International Corporation

"A wellspring for productivity and profit....Sonnenberg guides the manager in bringing out the precious creativity that resides within every employee. There is no more important key to success in the marketing and management of a company."

ROBERT W. BELLER
Executive Director
American Marketing Association
New York Chapter

"Sonnenberg presents a compelling analysis of the erosion of values in American business...and a powerful prescription for turning around this serious threat to U.S. competitiveness."

PETER GOLDMANN
Editor
Boardroom Reports

"*Managing with a Conscience* is must reading. Frank Sonnenberg takes a studied look at what separates the long-term leader from the also-ran."

WILLIAM F. DOESCHER
Senior Vice President
Global Communications
Dun & Bradstreet Information Services

Managing
with a
Conscience

Managing with a Conscience

How to Improve Performance
through Integrity, Trust,
and Commitment

Frank K. Sonnenberg

McGraw-Hill, Inc.

New York   San Francisco   Washington, D.C.   Auckland   Bogotá
Caracas   Lisbon   London   Madrid   Mexico City   Milan
Montreal   New Delhi   San Juan   Singapore
Sydney   Tokyo   Toronto

Library of Congress Cataloging-in-Publication Data

Sonnenberg, Frank K.
    Managing with a conscience : how to improve performance through
integrity, trust, and commitment / Frank K. Sonnenberg
        p.   cm.
    Includes bibliographical reference and index.
    ISBN 0-07-059632-8 (hc)   ISBN 0-07-059660-3 (pbk)
    1. Management.   2. Business ethics.   3. Success in business.
    I. Title.
HD30.3.S65   1993   93-30795
174'.4—dc20   CIP

McGraw-Hill

*A Division of The **McGraw·Hill** Companies*

    2 3 4 5 6 7 8 9 0   DOC/DOC   9 9 8 7 6 5 4 3
1 2 3 4 5 6 7 8 9 0   DOC/DOC   9 0 1 0 9 8 7 6

ISBN 0-07-059632-8 (HC)
ISBN 0-07-059660-3 (PBK)

*The sponsoring editor for this book was Philip Ruppel, the editing supervisor
was Frances Koblin, and the production supervisor was Donald Schmidt. It was
set in Palatino by McGraw-Hill's Professional Book Group composition unit.*

Printed and bound by R. R. Donnelley & Sons Company.

This book is printed on recycled, acid-free paper con-
taining a minimum of 50% recycled, de-inked fiber.

To my wife, Caron, and my daughters, Cathy and Kristy, who make everything worthwhile

Contents

Preface   xi
Acknowledgments   xiii

**1. If a Tree Falls in the Woods...: Competing in the
   Age of Intangibles**   **1**

Are We Using Yesterday's Weapons
  to Fight Tomorrow's Wars?   2
The Coming of the Age of Intangibles   3
Deciding What's Important   5
What Goes Around Comes Around   6

**2. From Obedience to Commitment: Building an
   Organization with Passion**   **9**

Why Love a Company That Doesn't Love You Back?   12
A New View: Employees as Assets   17
A New Management Paradigm   19
Management by Principles   22

**3. It's a Good Idea, But...: Building an Innovative
   Organization That Reinvents Itself Every Day**   **29**

Unlocking the Creative Mystique   30
Running the Creative Gauntlet   32

Management Style   32
Operational Style   39
The Organizational Culture   47
Reaching the Winner's Circle   52

**4. Internal Communication—More Than Lip Service:
Building an Organization with Total Concentration
and Focus   55**

Stress to Success   57
Communicating in the Information Age   58
The Role of Leadership   59
The Role of First-Line Management   68
The Flow of Information   73
Honest, Open Communication   79
The New Way to Communicate   80

**5. If I Only Had One Client: Building an Organization
Devoted to Service Excellence   83**

The Q Word   85
The Long-Term Consequences of Your Actions   86
Taking a Holistic View   87
The Road to Quality   88
Conclusion   108

**6. Change—Winning in the Fast Lane: Building an
Organization That Adapts Well to Change   109**

We Must Change the Way We View Change   110
Fallacies about Change   113
Change...Why Bother?   116
The Only Thing We Have to Fear Is Fear Itself   117
Learning...K through Life   121
Learning to Learn   125
Organizational Learning   130
Conclusion   135

**7. When Fast Isn't Fast Enough: Building an
Organization That Responds with Speed   137**

Picking Up the Pace   139
Organizational Effectiveness   141
Management Style—Getting the Most from Others   151
Personal Time Management   158
Conclusion   163

8. Partnering—Entering the Age of Cooperation: Building a Flexible Organization   **165**

What Causes Relationships to Fail?   168
The Anatomy of Relationships   175
When Does the Relationship Begin?   176
Creating the Right Environment for Growth   178
Maintaining the Relationship   180
Making It Happen   184

9. Trust Me...Trust Me Not: Building a Trusting Organization   **187**

Trust—The Miracle Ingredient   190
The Parameters of Trust   191
Winning Trust   192
Conclusion   209

10. Following Your Conscience: A Recipe for Peak Performance   **211**

Notes   237
Index   251

Preface

Results...Results...Results. In the turbulent, frenetic, dog-eat-dog times of the past decade, many believed that the only way to achieve success was to be unscrupulous. Acting like slum lords, corporations let their assets deteriorate by mistreating employees, squeezing suppliers, and taking advantage of customers. What was forgotten in the pursuit of short-term profits, however, was that by such behavior individuals and organizations alike significantly damaged their ability to perform long term.

Managing with a Conscience spells out a better option for improving long-term success: restore traditional values and inject trust and integrity into all business practices and relationships. *Managing with a Conscience* is about replacing the old "we" against "them" mentality with a new perception of "us" that encourages the growth of profitable relationships with employees, customers, clients, suppliers, and alliance partners. It's about stimulating creativity, adapting to change, decreasing time to market, promoting service excellence, communicating in a world of information overload, building trust, and energizing the decentralized work force. In such a culture, people work at a higher level, exceed customer expectations, and ensure that products are flawless and produced on time and within budget. To make this a reality, remember that although the golden rule may be considered a cliché, it still has value. When you act in a way that instills trust, that trust is returned. Acting honorably also does something else: It makes you feel good about yourself—and that is reflected in the way you look and the way other people look at you.

Managing with a Conscience was written to help reanimate those values that count, to restore our ability to find balance. We seem to have forgotten those essential beliefs and values that allow life to bring the rewards—financial as well as personal—that come from living up to a higher ideal of what is right and good. This book is my attempt to say that a return to values now considered old-fashioned, to allowing our consciences to be our guides, will bring both financial and personal rewards.

Frank K. Sonnenberg

Acknowledgments

This book represents the contributions of many people to whom I am most grateful.

First, I would like to thank all the people who took time to review early drafts of this book and provide me with their valuable insights: Alan Hembrough, Gene Papi, Steve Freshman, Mike Haviland, Marlene Salimbene, Joe Fiore, Andy Corn, Richard Welsh, Lisa Galjanic, Tracy Benson, Mark Sandberg, Ed Shulman, Joe Dattoli, Ken Shelton, Brenda Melissaratos, and Philip Ruppel from McGraw-Hill.

I would like to thank my friend and colleague Lee Einhorn for his design consultation for this book. Lee's award-winning talent, care for people, and passion for excellence all make him the outstanding professional that he is.

I would also like to thank Andy Garvin and the world-class information service firm of FIND/SVP for their invaluable research assistance.

There are several individuals I particularly wish to recognize for the impact that they have had on my life and on lessons learned, which are reflected in this book.

Rider College in New Jersey is well known for providing the opportunity of a large university and the personal care and attention of a small school. In all my wildest dreams, however, I would have never believed the impact that an institution—

much less one individual, my good friend Mark Sandberg, Associate Dean of the School of Business—could have on my life. Through DAARSTOC, a leadership development program, and hundreds of hours talking with Mark, and then reflecting on our discussions, I have come to learn some of the most important lessons of my life. First, it is a strength, not a weakness, to admit fault and recognize personal deficiencies. While some are too proud to learn this way, others grow through this process and turn weaknesses into strengths. Second, life is one big learning process. It is possible to learn from every experience and from everyone with whom you come into contact. While some open their eyes and grow to their full potential, others put on their blinders and stagnate. The final lesson is that you must find peace within yourself before you can be comfortable with others.

When I think about leadership, David Tierno, Managing Director, Northeast Management Consulting Group, Ernst & Young, comes to mind. Dave is one of the finest individuals I know, and a perfect role model for others to follow. He has taught me the power of a vision. His emphasis on trust and teamwork in business, his strength of conviction to do what is "right" rather than politically expedient, and his ability to create a working environment conducive to excellence, all make him the very special person that he is. I thank Dave for his years of leadership, his personal counsel, and for his friendship. I am proud and privileged to have worked for him.

My friend, confidant, and editor, Beverly Goldberg, and I have now written two books together. I couldn't have completed either one without her assistance, and I want to thank her for her patience, her energy, and her brilliant and thoughtful insight. When I think about integrity, Beverly Goldberg clearly comes to mind. To give one's word and then adhere to it as if it were cast in stone, to have strong convictions and tirelessly give of oneself to assist in those causes, to sacrifice oneself for the personal gain of others, and to give everything you touch your best effort and then a little more. You're an exceptional individual Beverly; if more people were like you, we would all have a better world in which to raise our children.

My mother and father were role models who instilled the strong set of values in my brothers John, Peter, and in me that are so much a part of this book. We grew up in a household where honesty and integrity presided over all else, where people's worth was measured by their inner strength rather than personal worth, and where people got more joy out of giving than by asking for more. They instilled in us the confidence that we could be anything or do anything, as long as we put our minds to it and worked hard to achieve it.

Being a parent to my daughters, Cathy and Kristy, has taught me that parents can learn as much from their children as children learn from their parents. Through trial and error children learn, and through play they create. When they get older, the rules of society will teach them that asking questions is a weakness, mistakes are bad, and there is only one right answer. A passion for learning and the power to create are abilities all of us are born with, but they must be nurtured or they will vanish. Cathy and Kristy have taught me the importance of having the proper balance in life: to work hard, but set aside time to enjoy the pleasures in life; to recognize the beauty in the simple things that we often take for granted; and to accept the importance of living for the moment while looking to the future.

From my loving wife and best friend, Caron, I have learned that strength comes from maintaining one's own individuality while still being part of a team. It's a wonderful experience building together, growing together, and sharing together. When people sacrifice personal gain for the betterment of the whole; when they join together through a common vision, shared values, and a common purpose; when people share life's ups and downs, the lows are never insurmountable and the celebrations are even more fun. Thank you, Caron, for your encouragement, patience, understanding, and insightful feedback while I wrote this book.

Thank you all.

Be practical as well as generous in your ideals; keep your eyes on the stars and keep your feet on the ground.

Courage, hard work, self-mastery and intelligent effort are all essential to a successful life.

Character in the long run is the decisive factor in the life of an individual and of nations alike.

THEODORE ROOSEVELT

1

If a Tree Falls in the Woods...

Competing in the Age of Intangibles

The 1990s are a time of unprecedented change. The world is in the midst of a transition from the Industrial Age to the Information Age, which is characterized by intangibles that have far-reaching implications for everything we do. Our ability to successfully weather that transition will determine our competitive position in the world market, which will, in turn, affect generations to come.

If we are to succeed as a nation and as individuals, nothing is more important than our ability to identify our priorities and allocate our precious resources. Nothing would be worse than discovering, too late, that the processes we used to make decisions for our future were flawed. When it comes to business, this means that, first, we must decide what investments to make. Then, we must determine the most effective management styles for making those investments pay off, which means we must choose the optimal organizational structures and reward systems for motivating our employees.

Are We Using Yesterday's Weapons to Fight Tomorrow's Wars?

Many people will tell you that such things as empowering your work force, creating an environment that encourages risk and discourages fear, eliminating waste and improving business processes, encouraging continuous education and training of employees, communicating in an open and honest manner, building trust among employees, nurturing long-term relationships with suppliers and clients, working hard to develop an impeccable reputation, living according to sound business ethics, and unifying your organization around a mission and shared values are likely to be among the key determinants of success in this new age. Others will tell you that these are "soft" issues.

What do people mean when they say these issues are soft? Are they saying that they are not effective management practices and that they do not enhance results? Or are they saying that because these things are difficult to quantify and measure, they make them uncomfortable and uneasy? Do they mean that because these practices cannot be isolated from other management practices, as in a scientific experiment, they are not worth doing?

There is a tendency in this country to believe that if something cannot be quantified, it does not exist. This brings to mind the argument associated with Bishop George Berkeley, an early eighteenth-century British philosopher: If a tree falls in the woods, but no one is there to hear the sound, did it make a noise? To put it another way: If someone enhances performance in an organization using an approach that cannot be quantified, did the improvement take place?

This philosophy permeates American life. For example, although there was considerable evidence that smoking was hazardous to one's health, it was only after the Report of the Surgeon General of the United States revealed a direct statistical link between smoking and certain medical problems that people began to heed earlier warnings. Another example is our failure to recognize that the Japanese focus on quality would capture market share in electronics and automobiles until the hard evidence of decreasing U.S. sales made it clear that quality, a "soft" issue, made a difference to customers.

The Coming of the Age of Intangibles

The Industrial Age brought us products such as cars, heavy farm equipment, refrigerators, washing machines, and computers—equipment that could be seen, touched, and demonstrated. The Information Age, in contrast, is characterized by intangibles—those resources that involve the intellect and the ability to gather, analyze, transmit, and synthesize information. The result is the birth of new companies and entire industries, ranging from information services and software to genetic engineering.

Companies in the Industrial Age thrived because of their access to and exploitation of raw materials, standardization of goods and services, and ability to maximize volume. Today, however, the speed with which products are becoming commodities has increased dramatically, and companies are experiencing greater and greater cost pressure from competitors. Now, as soon as new products are introduced into the marketplace, clones marked by similar features appear in months or even in weeks. Unless consumers can see the value in premium brands, many will buy products solely on the basis of price. That is why the only companies that will be able to charge a premium, in the future, will be those that use intangibles—such as product innovation and design, company reputation, and service excellence—to clearly differentiate themselves from their competitors.

The differences in the thought processes between the two periods are evident in the terminology in the table on page 4.

Clearly, the critical success factors of the Information Age are intangibles. And just as you cannot measure liquids in pounds or nuclear fusion in quarts, you cannot use yesterday's measurements of physical inventory to gauge the results of empowerment, brand awareness, creativity, or commitment. Moreover, the unmeasurables include the results of numerous instinctive judgments that are made by executives after years of experience. A senior lending officer for one of the nation's largest banks recently said to me that "today's MBAs just don't understand. Sure, they know the formulas, the financial ratios. They've read all the case studies. They learned all that in business school. But sometimes, it is the gut feel that is the most

Thinking Across the Ages

Industrial Age	Information Age
Capital intensive	Knowledge intensive
Capital expenditures	Education/training
Natural resources	Educated work force
Inventory	Data (information)
Production enhancements	Process enhancements
Hierarchical management	Empowerment
Tangible rewards	Psychic rewards
Issuing orders	Communicating
Top-down planning	Commitment (buy-in)
Inspection	Quality built in
Equipment failure	Employee Turnover
Equipment uptime	Morale
Purchasing	Recruiting
Sales	Customer satisfaction
Laborer	Knowledge worker

important indicator. Some say it comes with experience, and others say it's a sixth sense. But I'm convinced that many problems today are the result of not following these instincts because we cannot logically explain them."

To take another example, Americans are enamored with technology. But they tend to forget that technology in and of itself does not bring results: the way it is implemented does. Unfortunately, some organizations focus only on the purchase of equipment. They do not understand that the way technology is introduced and used—the efforts made to overcome resistance to change, to provide training for those who will use the equipment, and to put methodologies in place to support the technology—is what brings results. As a consequence, new technologies are acquired and then underutilized.

This kind of behavior is not limited to technology; it affects entire companies. A good example of the value of unmeasurable behavior is the case of Johnson & Johnson's Tylenol. Some years ago, a deranged person inserted poison into some Tylenol capsules with fatal results. As soon as the first incident was discovered, Johnson & Johnson pulled all Tylenol off the shelves nationwide without any hesitation and started a massive warning and recall campaign. This decision was far easier for Johnson & Johnson to make because of their commitment to their credo: "We believe our first responsibility is to the doctors, nurses, and patients, to mothers and all others who use our products and services. In meeting their needs, everything that we do must be of high quality."

The speed and certainty of Johnson & Johnson's response allowed Tylenol to make a strong comeback. The existence of their credo and their firm belief in it, something many would call a soft component of their business, made a critical difference to the decision-making process. But the value of a credo isn't usually measurable.

Creativity is another intangible that cannot be measured. The 3M company puts a great deal of effort into creating an innovative climate. How does that climate translate into business? Or, how do you measure the value of brand recognition and customer loyalty? According to research conducted by Total Research Corporation, "Disney World/Disney Land, Kodak, Mercedes Benz, CNN, Hallmark, Fisher Price, UPS, Rolex, Levi's, and IBM" rank highest in perceived value or brand equity.[1] How do you measure the value of CEO Robert Haas's belief in employee empowerment to Levi Strauss? Or the value of reducing a work force with compassion and sensitivity? And how do these things translate into a stronger competitive position? How do you measure the manager who builds camaraderie, trust, and lasting relationships with his team? Or the manager who has a reputation for keeping his word, exhibits strong ethical values, and commands loyalty?

Deciding What's Important

In *Managing with a Conscience*, eight critical success factors for competing in the twenty-first century are examined. You won't find these attributes in an annual report because they are intangible and difficult to quantify. But that doesn't make them any less important to an organization. These critical success factors require that companies:

- Seek to develop employees who will be deeply committed to the organization's mission and values and, most important, who will be passionate about reaching its goals (see Chapter 2)
- Create an environment that stimulates creativity and innovation and reinvents itself every day (see Chapter 3)
- Set priorities that focus the company's efforts and people on the resources that provide the greatest potential return (see Chapter 4)
- Believe that the main reason for the company's existence is to provide service excellence to its clients and customers (see Chapter 5)
- Be able to continually adapt to a changing marketplace (see Chapter 6)
- Recognize that time is both a valuable resource and a fixed commodity and, therefore, that speed provides a competitive advantage (see Chapter 7)
- Build a flexible organization by collaborating with other organizations (see Chapter 8)
- Understand that a foundation of trust between an organization and its employees, suppliers, and clients is what brings and keeps people together (see Chapter 9)

What Goes Around Comes Around

The common thread throughout this book is "What goes around comes around." If you hire the best people and treat them with dignity and respect, invest in them and display confidence in their abilities, motivate them and help them grow personally and professionally, and create an environment conducive to excellence, those employees will reward you by striving for peak performance. Further, if you treat suppliers as part of your own organization, create an environment where everybody wins, build relationships based on trust, honesty, and integrity, your suppliers will reward you with their commitment and with a long, fruitful relationship. Last, but not least, if you view clients as long-term assets rather than immediate sales transactions, develop policies and procedures for the overall impact they have on client service (not for the benefit of your own employees), migrate from mass marketing to niche marketing to personal marketing (carefully listening to and then satisfying the specific needs of your clients), they will reward you with increased market share and profits. Treating employees with integrity increases productivity, encourages loyalty, and promotes passionate performance. Developing relationships with suppliers through a flexible, borderless organization results in quality improvement and the ability to rapidly adapt to changing customer needs. And a long-term focus on service excellence creates a strong customer base, which is especially critical as the production process becomes less of a differentiating factor and everything leading up to, during, and after the sale becomes key.

When companies manage with a conscience, their investment pays tremendous dividends. The winners of the twenty-first century will be those who treat clients, employees, and suppliers according to the golden rule. Reverend Robert Fulghum, author of *All I Ever Really Need to Know I Learned in Kindergarten,* put the rules into language that everyone can understand: "Share everything. Play fair. Don't hit people. Put things back where you found them. Clean up your own mess. Say you're sorry when you hurt somebody. When you go out in the world, watch out for traffic, hold hands and stick together."[2] Soft issues are very like the tree that falls in the woods. In the Information Age, if we don't believe that there was a noise, maybe it is time to get our hearing checked. In the Information Age, if we don't change our view of employees as a necessary evil—if one leaves the company he or she can be replaced by another—we will fail. If we measure employees solely by their ability to increase the quantity of their output, we will lose the best of them. We must learn to encourage employees to create product innovations and design improvements, to be on the cutting edge of technology, and to enhance the company's reputation for service excellence. In the future, in manufacturing companies as in service companies, it will be hard to separate the actual product from those who deliver and produce it. Not only will tomorrow's employees produce products, but their knowledge, experience, and skill sets will be a part of the product. Thus as discussed in Chapter 2, the organization's working environment and its ability to attract, develop, and retain the best and brightest employees will determine its success.

2

From Obedience to Commitment

Building an
Organization with Passion

For the first 100 years of American
history, plantations were one of the primary forms of corporations, mostly located in the southern states and commonly
associated with slavery. The Civil War
and the Emancipation Proclamation
ended slavery and virtually ended the
plantation era, although for many
Americans, plantation management has
continued uninterrupted....

Plantation managers tend to see local
workers as indentured servants who are
born to pick their cotton. [They]...have
no name, no identity, because they are
not real people. You can abuse them, not
pay them fairly, and claim all of the monetary returns on their work.

Modern plantation management
involves the subjugation of people
through more subtle means than slavery,
but the end result is about the same.
People feel like slaves—they feel trapped,
owned, enslaved.   KEN SHELTON
               Executive Excellence[1]

Plantation managers—now as in the days of the Old South—view people as disposable objects. They treat people according to their positions and degree of power: Superiors are treated with respect and dignity, subordinates as worthless beings. Focusing on the bottom line, they have forgotten that everyone has certain inalienable rights.

You can find evidence of plantation management everywhere. Stephen Covey, consultant and best-selling author, tells the story of a manager who bragged to him about his tough management style. The manager said that he told problem employees "to either shape up or ship out." Covey says he then asked the manager "why he didn't tell his customers that if they weren't prepared to buy the goods and services at the prices requested, they should either shape up or ship out. [The manager explained that] he didn't have the same right to do this with customers as he had with his employees."[2]

The problem is that all too many managers really believe that employees are little more than slaves who obey orders, follow the rules, and can't think for themselves. In return for their good behavior, if employees are lucky, they may keep their jobs—and be paid just enough to keep body and soul together. At the same time, according to *Training* magazine, "chiefs who make 100 times the average Indians' pay are no longer rare."[3]

This kind of arrogance has been accompanied by an unhappy trend to quick and easy divorce. Many organizations no longer remain faithful in sickness and in health; instead their relationships with employees are beginning to look more like one-night stands. In fact, "in a recent study by the Conference Board, a New York-based business research organization, more than half of the 216 companies surveyed characterized their relationship with employees as a business financial arrangement rather than a close family one."[4]

When you come to work in a place that doesn't care about you, it's hard to be enthusiastic about what you are doing. It's hard to go that extra mile if you believe that nobody cares whether or not you do. It is hard to see where caring and loyalty and teamwork fit in if the value of your work is measured only in dollars and what you have done for someone that day. Not only is plantation management damaging to the morale of workers and the soul of management, it is a direct cause of the dismal state of American business today and of our low productivity rates and disaffected workers.

To the plantation manager, there is nothing wrong with stealing talented people from well-managed companies rather than making the investment (both personal and financial) necessary to nurture and train the company's own employees. It is not unlike "being a corporate slum landlord. Keep raising the rent while letting the assets deteriorate."[5]

Why then are managers puzzled by employees who are highly motivated outside of work, but show little initiative on the job; people who put in time but no energy; people who spend more time working on their résumés than on the activities at hand? A management style that produces these results obviously won't be enough to compete in today's global economy, especially given changes taking place in the attitudes of workers today. In fact, the result of this plantation-style management is already causing a disastrous collision between the needs of businesses and the demands of today's work force.

According to *U.S. News & World Report*, the 1980s "fast-trackers who floored it to the finish line, hyper achievers who slept, ate, and breathed work, now...are taking weekends off and muttering about personal fulfillment and quality of life."[6] *Fortune* magazine calls it the "boomer backlash. The busters look around the office and observe the 40ish crowd who neglect their families and avocations for...What? By the time the boomers have made it, they've had it. This scares the younger folk to no end." *Fortune* goes on to characterize the new baby-bust generation as people who "want to be happy and fulfilled—socially and culturally—and to progress in the work world to the point where [they're] happy with [themselves]."[7]

This new breed of employees wants to work for an organization that they can feel proud of: an organization that has values and viewpoints compatible with their own; an organization that is oriented toward the long haul, working toward the prevention of ills, rather than only curing symptoms; an organization that cares about morals and ethics, doing what is in the best interests of its clients; and one that cares about the impact that it has on the environment. Employees want this because they recognize that such an organization will also care about them.

They know that this kind of organization conducts a never-ending search for the best and brightest people; that it not only allows but encourages managers to develop their people both personally and professionally; that it recognizes and rewards employees for their unique contributions; and that it gives them real responsibility not just accountability. Today people want to work for an organization where they feel they are making a meaningful contribution; where procedures, policies, and protocol are never more important than results; and where building bonds between people is considered as important as the bottom line. The question is, "Is it possible to achieve this kind of environment and strive for market leadership?" The answer is, "You don't don't have much of a choice."

Why Love a Company That Doesn't Love You Back?

As a leader you must keep in mind all the costs of mistreating employees. Remember that employees can express their dissatisfaction with their jobs in a number of ways—all of them damaging: they can resign, taking important skills and client knowledge with them; they can voice their discontent, thereby hurting morale; they can use every possible "sick day" or constantly show up late; or they can become apathetic, producing only enough to avoid being fired.

"I Quit"

Employees decide to leave an organization for a number of reasons. Among the most common reasons given by employees are that they:

- Do not get along with their colleagues or supervisors

- Believe they could make a stronger contribution if they were given the freedom to do so
- Believe they are not being paid enough or receiving enough recognition for their contributions
- Feel they are personally stagnating and not being challenged
- Feel they don't have control over their own futures
- Disagree with the direction the organization is taking
- Believe the organization has not determined its priorities (They are asked to do one thing today; the exact opposite tomorrow.)
- Are frustrated by the amount of red tape they have to cut through
- Feel they're working in the dark and lack the resources needed to perform their jobs
- Perceive that they are not working in a fun environment

And last, but not least,

- They simply cannot turn down that better offer.

It does not matter why employees leave; the consequences and costs of turnover are the same. The bonds built between them and their clients are severed. Their knowledge of the industry and their ability to network with others within the organization are lost. Replacements have to be found, hired, and trained; then they have to develop the savvy needed to navigate their way through the organization. Moreover, if someone leaves the organization very dissatisfied, and mentions it even discreetly to others, the organization may begin to develop a reputation that can be detrimental to recruiting efforts and to the overall corporate image.

In addition, one day that individual may be in a position to be a potential client, but the person may draw back because of unhappy memories of the organization. Thus, even if it is too late to persuade someone to stay, management may be able to clear the air and improve the mental image they take with them. At worst, it can begin to remedy the problems that are crippling the organization.

"This Is a Terrible Place to Work"

Another effect of plantation management is employees who are unhappy but decide, for any number of reasons, not to leave. Instead, they express their dissatisfaction by voicing their discontent. These are the employees who quickly get the ear of new hires as well as veterans, telling them tales of woe.

Moreover, dissatisfied employees who spend much of the workday expressing their dissatisfaction and unhappiness create an air of dissension, depressing those around them, hindering concentration, and lowering everyone's spirits.

"I Won't Be in Today"

Unhappiness in the workplace also manifests itself in physical and psychological ailments that cause workers to be less productive. People who are unhappy tend to notice minor physical ills more. They can escape dealing with the immediate problem of the job by focusing on their aching back or slight cold. Furthermore, some employees are so distressed by their work situations that they are made seriously ill by them.

According to a *Wall Street Journal* article, "An advertising salesman treated by Bruce Yaffe, a New York internist, screamed so loudly when he argued with his boss that he punctured a lung. Another patient, an office receptionist, had such stress-induced vomiting that she eventually had to quit her job. And a third, a Wall Street broker treated by physician Larry Lerner for hypertension, was so certain his death was imminent that he refused to take his children to the park for fear they would be abandoned when he died. Human resource managers, as well as doctors, psychologists, and pollsters agree that workplace stress is way up. Layoffs—and the persuasive fear of dismissal—are jangling nerves."[8]

Employees can also be so disaffected that they take days off just because they feel they cannot face the office another day. *The Worklife Report* notes that "the more interesting and challenging the work, the less likely people are to be off work. If you like what you are doing, if you feel you are indispensable, you are not as likely to take off without a good reason."[9]

The obvious dollar costs of absenteeism are easy to delineate: loss of productivity, increased costs when temporary workers have to be hired to take the place of absent employees, increased costs of medical benefits, disability payments, possible lawsuits. The less obvious results can also be identified: loss of morale among other members of the organization, loss of productivity as other employees pick up the slack for a "wounded" colleague, and loss of time filling out the paperwork a sick employee generates.

Moreover, an organization faces a kind of contagion if these reactions continue unabated. "A healthy body and a healthy mind" may be a cliché, but clichés contain truths; it is in every organization's interests to consider the analogue: a healthy employee, a healthy organization.

"I Did as Much as I Had to..."

Another way that an individual expresses dissatisfaction—and maybe the most deadly of them all—is apathy because you may never realize that a problem even exists. It is, however, a problem that surfaces in many ways. According to a recent survey, "employee commitment is highest among first-year employees who take up new jobs with enthusiasm and dedication. The level of commitment begins to fall in the second year—and moves even lower by the fourth year."[10]

This loss of commitment is rampant in American business today. When the researchers, Yankelovich and Ammerwahr, examined the situation, they found that the number of American workers who said they were currently working to their full potential was shockingly small—23 percent. They also discovered in their random sampling of American workers that "nearly half (44%) say they do not put any more effort into their jobs than is required to hold onto them. The overwhelming majority, 75%, say that they could be significantly more effective on their jobs than they are now."[11] The implications for productivity are startling.

The problem is a difficult one to remedy because this kind of apathetic behavior is hard to see. You may spot the problem behavior more easily if you think of it as the last stage on a con-

APATHETIC DISGRUNTLED OBEDIENT MOTIVATED LOYAL COMMITTED

tinuum that goes from a high of employee commitment to a low of apathy. If you measure your employees on such a scale, the reason for lack of productivity may become evident—and therefore something you can rectify.

The stages from apathy to commitment are as follows:

- *Apathetic.* These employees are commonly known as deadwood. Their behavior is characterized by a lack of interest and/or caring. These are the employees who sit at their desks shuffling paper, watch the clock, and take every sick and personal day off that they can. They never make a suggestion or volunteer for anything. They take on assignments and hear deadlines with little visible reaction and respond with a shrug if asked if there is a problem. This general air of lassitude and disaffection is as contagious in an organization as enthusiasm.

- *Disgruntled.* These individuals' hopes, desires, and expectations are not being met. However, they still care enough to attempt to change the situation by voicing their discontent. They will show their annoyance when given yet another routine assignment or tell you they'll do something "as soon as they can get to it," and do it in such a way that, if you are listening carefully, you will know something is bothering them. If you don't catch the signals they are sending, they will either reach their limit and leave the organization or become apathetic.

- *Obedient.* These are the employees who do just enough to get by. Whether they are acting out of fear or trying to avoid personal conflict, they are unwilling to do anything that would set them apart in any way. These employees are good soldiers, following orders as they are given, but they have little interest in doing anything to make the organization more successful.

- *Motivated.* Management is doing a good job keeping these employees happy. They are content with their present situation, but that feeling may be temporary. The way that management motivates them today may be taken for granted tomorrow. At this stage, an individual may also care more about personal success than organizational success. The result is that a better offer elsewhere will be very tempting.

- *Loyal.* These are the employees who enjoy coming to work, believe that they make meaningful contributions, believe they are fairly recognized and rewarded, but most of all care deeply about the organization. Loyalty, however, does not always encourage creative and independent thinking, a sense of ownership, and self-initiative.

- *Committed.* These individuals have moved a step above loyalty; they are so deeply moved by the organization's values and reason for being that they constantly look for new ways for the organization to develop and grow. This excitement, passion, and sense of ownership spill over onto others.

The obvious question is, "What do you have to do to inspire commitment?"

A New View: Employees as Assets

It is time for a new style of leadership. Workers do not respond well to micromanagement or to being treated like cogs in a wheel. As part of the search for the best ways to increase work force productivity, management has been taught various theories, techniques, and approaches designed to motivate employees. These approaches are all based on the fundamental premise that it is management's role to do the motivating—that is, management's job is to push employees toward certain behaviors or to control them in a certain fashion. However, great managers know it is much more desirable to attain commitment through an employee's attraction to the organization's beliefs and values.

Successful leaders know that motivational techniques may satisfy employees only long enough to achieve short-term goals. If you supplement today's forms of employee motivation by inculcating employees with a belief in your organization's mission, and a belief in the importance of their contribution to the organization, you bring about commitment—to an organization that they feel proud of, that contributes to society. For tomorrow's employee, being a part of something that will make a difference is much more important than the rewards sought by yesterday's "me" generation.

Doing this, however, requires a very different organizational structure than the traditional hierarchical organization that, according to Robert Haas, chairman and CEO of Levi Strauss, in an interview in *Industry Week*, limits people to "strait jackets of narrow job definitions, rigid functional distinctions, and the mark of not sharing the information that people need to be successful." He added that "the first challenge for all of us is to cut through the ways that we, as managers, inhibit the intelligence, energy, commitment and excitement that already exists in our organizations." He said that in order to succeed organizations must abandon "the myriad policies and procedures that shackle people today, the archaic command-and-control mentality of many managers, the unwillingness to listen and engage in two-way dialog, to value the opinions of people in the workforce [that] is cutting the organization's IQ in half."[12]

In a later interview with *Harvard Business Review*, Haas acknowledged that it is very "difficult to unlearn behaviors that made us successful in the past. Speaking rather than listening. Valuing people like yourself over people of different genders or from different cultures or parts of the organization. Doing things on your own rather than collaborating. Making the decision yourself instead of asking different people for their perspectives. There's a whole range of behaviors that were highly functional in the old hierarchical organization that are dead wrong in the flatter, more responsive, empowered organizations that we are seeking to become."[13]

Only those organizations that can provide employees with the responsibility, the information, and the authority to get the job done will thrive in today's competitive environment. But new structures and policies are only a start; to achieve real success, a new way of thinking must also become a norm. In these organizations, the soft side of business—the beliefs, the values, and the philosophies espoused by management—must reach a peak of importance.

What we are discussing here is social motivation: the controls we impose on ourselves when we work with people with similar expectations and goals. An article in *California Management Review* recently stated that "with formal systems [of control] people often have a sense of external constraint which is binding and unsatisfying. With social controls, we often feel as though we have great autonomy, even though paradoxically we are conforming much more."[14]

The kind of self-motivation that results from a belief structure is in sharp contrast with leadership by command and control. Think of the terms associated with that kind of leadership. In *The Renewal Factor*, Robert Waterman says that it is interesting to "look up the word boss in a book of synonyms. At the start of the list you find manage and direct. Not bad. Then the list continues with control, order, command, take charge, preside over, oversee, supervise, superintend, domineer, dominate, push around, ride herd on, ride roughshod over, trample under foot, and shove around."[15] Obviously, managers who would wear the word "boss" proudly, knowing it carries all of those connotations, do not have the "right stuff" to be leaders in today's organizations, to inspire people to be the best that they can be.

A New Management Paradigm

Stephen Covey, mentioned earlier, has written about the ways leaders can build commitment in an organization. He says that building commitment is a four-phase process:

The first phase, according to Covey, is the scientific management phase. In it, employees are seen primarily as stomachs (economic beings). In such organizations, management motivates employees primarily through use of the carrot and the stick. This is the stage at which managers are likely to say that their responsibility "is to motivate through the great jackass method...the carrot in front to entice and intrigue them, lead them to their benefits, and the stick behind." It says that I, the manager "am in control, I am the authority, I am the elite one, I know what is best, I will direct you where to go, of course the rewards will be fair."[16]

Covey calls the second phase the human relations phase. This is the stage at which management accepts that people also have hearts. They see "that people have feelings....[and thus treat them] not only with fairness, but with kindness, with courtesy, with civility, with decency....[In this] shift from authoritarian to benevolent authoritarian—we still know best. The power still lies with us, but we are not only fair to people but are kind."[17]

The third phase emphasizes human resource principles, recognizing that people have, in addition to stomachs and hearts, minds. Such recognition means that as managers, "we make better use of their creativity, imagination....We begin to delegate more realizing that people are more committed to a goal when they're involved....We begin to explore ways to create an optimal environment, a culture which taps their talents and releases their energy....People want to make meaningful contributions. They want their talents identified, developed, utilized, and recognized."[18]

Covey calls the fourth and final phase the whole person paradigm. This is the best of all worlds. When an organization enters this phase it provides its employees with "meaning, a sense of doing something that matters. People do not want to work for a cause with little meaning, even though it taps their mental capacities to their fullest." In this phase, leaders manage by tapping into "values, ideals, norms and teachings that uplift, enable, fulfill, empower and inspire people."[19]

According to Covey, "the scientific management (stomach) paradigm says pay me well. The human relations (heart) paradigm says treat me well. The human resource (mind) paradigm suggests use me well. The management by principles (whole person) says, let's talk values and goals."[20]

The time has come for business to enter the fourth phase. To do that, leaders must exercise their power by creating a vision and instilling a sense of purpose and mission in those they lead.

In *Leadership Is an Art,* Max De Pree, chairman and CEO of Herman Miller, Inc., points out that "in a day when so much energy seems to be spent on maintenance and manuals, on bureaucracy and meaningless qualification, to be a leader is to enjoy the special privileges of complexity, of ambiguity, of diversity. But to be a leader means, especially, having the opportunity to make a meaningful difference in the lives of those who permit leaders to lead....The measure of leadership is not the quality of the head, but the tone of the body. The signs of outstanding leadership appear primarily among the followers. Are the followers reaching their potential? Are they learning? Serving? Do they achieve the required results? Do they change with grace?"[21]

A recent article in *Fortune,* exploring the exercise of power, discussed the view of John Kotter, a professor at the Harvard Business School, who said that there are five kinds of power: "The first is the power to reward—to give someone a promotion, a raise, or a pat on the back. Its twin is the power to punish, to fire someone;...third is the power that experts call authority. Authority can be specific, and specifically granted—the right to sign $100,000 contracts....The fourth kind of power derives from expertise....Finally, psychologists speak of referent power, which attaches to a leader because people admire him, want to be like him, or are wowed by his integrity, charisma or charm."

The article went on to discuss other views of this theory. Jane Halpert, a professor of industrial and organizational psychology at Chicago's DePaul University, the article said, "points out that the first three—reward, punishment, and authority come with the office. The higher your rank, the more you usually have. But expertise and referent power inhere in the person. The better the leader...the more likely he is to rely on the personal sources of power....Really effective leaders almost never have to put the screws on someone."[22]

Ralph Stayer, CEO of Johnsonville Foods, agreed that "real power is getting people committed. Real power comes from giving it up to others who are in a better position to do things than you are. Control is an illusion. The only control you can possibly have comes when people are controlling themselves."[23]

Management by Principles

More than 200 years ago, our forefathers brought forth a Bill of Rights for the nation. Remarkably, the words they wrote, reinterpreted as society changed, have withstood the test of time. The principles embodied in that document, which have always stood us in good stead as a nation, can be applied to business. Its values can help us move on to that fourth phase of the paradigm—the stage at which leaders grant all employees those inalienable rights that inspire them to be the best they can be.

Before setting forth an employee's bill of rights, it is worth reminding today's leaders that a prerequisite to these principles is embarking on a never-ending search for the right people. That sends a message: that you believe that your employees are your most important asset and therefore must be treated with dignity and respect. Moreover, the greater the effort spent searching for the right people, the more effort that will be spent in developing them, the more their judgment will be trusted, and the more that will be expected from them. It is also an indication that more effort will be made to create an environment that will make it easier to hold on to them. But most of all, making this commitment in the first place sends a strong message to all employees that they are special, thus developing a sense of pride and comaraderie within the organization. All of this will happen if you keep the following guidelines in mind:

An Employee Bill of Rights

Employees have the right to decide how best to achieve their goals. People work best when they know what they are responsible for and have the authority to choose the right path to affect results. Even though they may not determine the direction that the organization is taking, they should have input into the process.

Employees have the right to be treated as part of the engine, rather than as interchangeable parts. People want to be part of something special and to know that they are making a valuable contribution. They want their work to be meaningful—not just busy work—and to be given a clear picture of how their daily activities impact the overall success of the organization.

Employees have the right to be viewed as unique individuals. Every person brings unique talents to the organization. Employees want to spend the greatest portion of their days working in those areas that make the best use of those skills.

Employees have the right to be challenged. Employees should have their strengths utilized; they should be given challenging responsibilities that stretch their potential. Their input should be solicited and contributions valued. They should be encouraged to pursue a philosophy of continuous improvement and know their recommendations will be welcomed.

Employees have the right to be treated with dignity and respect. People should be treated with dignity at all times. There must be recognition of professional and personal needs. Demeaning criticism and temper tantrums must be replaced by civilized behavior and mutual respect. The contributions that every individual makes should be recognized and valued and people should be made to feel that they are part of the same team.

Moreover, many organizations believe that the impact of an action they take falls solely on the individual to whom it is directed, but that is not the case. "For every action there is an equal reaction" applies to personal relationships as well as to physics. It is rare for transfers, promotions, or reprimands to affect only the individual involved. For example, when three people are laid off in a department, management tends to believe that those three are the only people affected by the layoffs. What happens, instead, is that those remaining in the department, and others in other departments, spend a great deal of time speculating about "who will be next," or even job hunting in preparation for the "next round."

Employees have the right to try and to fail. When people don't make mistakes, they're probably not trying anything new. Mistakes, discussed in the next chapter at great length, are an important stage in the learning process. Employees must be confident that trying something new and failing will not have repercussions.

Employees have the right to know their employers have confidence in them and in their abilities. People do not respond well to being second guessed or having every move that they make micromanaged. They want to know that management trusts their abilities and respects them enough to assume they will do a responsible job. Managers who act in this way are likely to achieve superior performance from their employees. In fact, "formal psychological research as well as a large amount of casual empiricism by others leave no doubt that the power of expectation alone can influence the behavior of others. This total phenomenon is called the Pygmalion effect."[24] Studies have shown that the IQ scores of children, especially on verbal and information subjects, can be raised "merely by expecting them to do well....A study showed that worker performance increased markedly when the supervisor of these workers was told that his group showed a special potential for their particular job."[25]

If employees are made to feel like helpless drones, they tend to perform that way. But if they believe that they are essential to the success of the operation, they will respond by accepting greater responsibility, rise to the occasion, and ultimately increase their personal productivity.

Employees have the right to be treated in a fair and honest fashion. Industry Week reported that "while 87% of the workers polled [in a survey] think it is very important that management is honest, upright, and ethical, only 39% believe that it is." It is not surprising that if management condones poor treatment or dishonest dealings with clients and suppliers, employees are given the impression that management is not to be trusted. Moreover, "three-quarters of those polled also indicated that it was very important to them that management truly cares about employees as individuals, but just 27% believe that anything like a caring attitude truly exists."[26] This lack of belief is a result of policies that are not administered in a uniform and consistent fashion and of the failure to extend the same treatment used in dealing with suppliers to employees.

Employees have the right to have their professional standing recognized. For many individuals, it is not enough to perform well in their day-to-day activities. They want to keep abreast of new theories and practices in their field. They want to continue to learn both on the job and through professional affiliations, networking, or formal education. An organization's willingness to support those efforts goes a long way. It not only develops employees personally and professionally, but it also brings returns in the form of increased productivity, loyalty, and commitment.

Many organizations feel that the costs associated with these activities are prohibitive. They fail to consider that these activities ultimately help the organization adapt to change and reduce the rate of turnover. The money that would be spent in recruiting new employees could be redirected into programs aimed at building commitment through training and employee development. (This subject will be discussed in greater detail in Chapter 6.)

Employees have the right to freedom of expression.   Employees should feel confident enough to express their feelings about a subject. They should have their ideas listened to and evaluated, and receive feedback, without recriminations or fear.

Employees have the right to be informed.   Employees should have access to any and all information that helps them perform their jobs. This includes knowing the rationale behind decisions that affect them, rather than merely being expected to follow orders. Furthermore, they should be made aware of *major* events affecting the organization through formal channels rather than through the grapevine or by hearing about them from clients or through reading the newspaper.

Employees have the right to approach management.   Unless they have access to management, employees feel closed out. They do not feel they are valued members of the organization. One way to change this is to announce an open-door policy. But announcing it is not enough. Management must also ensure that employees feel comfortable in approaching them. Ask yourself if you are ever in one place long enough to be approached? Are you available at convenient times or only at 5:00 a.m.? Has your secretary done everything to screen you from outsiders except put barbed wire outside your office?

When a concern was brought to your attention, in confidence, did you divulge any part of the information? Do you really listen or do you just go through the motions of listening? It is up to you to take the initiative and get out of your office to meet with employees. Be seen on a regular basis so people don't think you are avoiding them.

Employees have the right to know that their efforts are appreciated. In an article in *Industry Week,* David Kearns, chairman and CEO of Xerox Corporation, said: "If you have a pot of gold, it's easy to manage. Just keep giving out cash, holding those carrots out. But when that pot of gold isn't there, it's a lot more difficult to manage. That's when the true managers emerge."[27]

Clearly, the first reward for any job is pay. But all things considered, it is far from the only reward employees want. Numerous studies point out that knowing what is most meaningful and important to an individual and then recognizing them for a job well done is usually as important as, if not more important than, salary differentials.

For example, a survey conducted by the Houston-based American Productivity Center reported that "90–95 percent of the responding members said that recognition when I've done a job well is important or very important as a motivational factor. In fact it ranked above competitive salary and pay clearly tied to performance."[28]

Personnel Journal reports that "recognition and praise on the job are so important that one in four workers surveyed by Motivational Systems of West Orange, New Jersey, said they would leave their current jobs—to work at the same salary and benefits—for another company with a reputation for giving special notice and appreciation."[29]

Employee Recognition Programs

As a general rule of thumb recognition programs should meet the following criteria:

- *Be simple enough that everyone understands how, why, and when people will be rewarded.* I'm always amused to hear that an organization launched an incentive program that no one can figure out.

- *Communicate continuously.* I know an individual who won an award from a program she didn't even know existed.

- *Stage ceremonies.* People should be praised in public so that their behavior is then emulated by others. A note of thanks on someone's desk, while nice, is a limited management tool.

- *Mandate senior management involvement.* Senior management's involvement in award giving adds emphasis and significance to any award.

- *Display consistency with major goals.* Recognition should highlight and reinforce the areas most important to the organization. If the program is not consistent with or does not reinforce the strategic direction of the organization, it will be ineffective. For example, rewarding people for length of employment rather than productivity encourages survival rather than results.

- *Provide ongoing recognition.* The best programs offer constant and timely feedback; they do not depend on a formal review process.

- *Ensure informal and formal rewards.* Rewards and recognition should not always be given formally; sometimes the most effective programs are informal and spontaneous. IBM has a recognition program that rewards excellence. It is called "Lightning Strikes" and can be given out anytime at the discretion of management. Recognition can also take the form of creating a sense of ownership. When Apple Computer announces a new development or product, "rather than have a public relations staffer or a senior executive make the announcement, [it] generally has the actual developer or team on hand to discuss the innovation."[30]

- *Have goals that are perceived as realistic and achievable.* If the requirements for winning an award are unrealistic, the program is useless. The opposite—setting goals so low that everyone wins—is just as meaningless.

- *Make rewards meaningful.* Every reward need not be materially significant, it may be just a token. Of course, there must be balance. But I have seen management give out a simple certificate, or the Dale Carnegie Organization give out an inexpensive pen for the best speaker at a meeting, and watched the pleased and proud expressions of the recipients too often to believe that small rewards are unimportant. What is critical is that they be given in a sincere and honest— and timely—manner.

Caring

There is a story told by Fran Tarkenton that sums up so much of what is being said here—and does it so well—that it is worth repeating in its entirety.

A month after my election to the Hall of Fame, I stood in the kitchen of our house in Atlanta with suitcases stacked all around me. The day had arrived for my son to leave home for Princeton University. He left the kitchen for a moment, and when he came back, he had an envelope for each of us.

That's when the realization hit me: My son is saying goodbye to everything he's known. The security of his family, his home...he knows it will never be the same. He's going off to start all over again. And then it happened. He came around the kitchen table to me and I saw the tears. As I put my arms around him, I felt the tears. His tears wet the shoulder of my shirt, my tears spilled freely for the first time in my life. For long moments, we just held each other, saying nothing.

Later, thinking about that moment, I realized that a great change had occurred in my relationship with my son. We really, truly, unequivocally cared. We cared more than macho would let us admit. And when we saw and felt how much good it did, we both knew there was no weakness in letting our feelings be known.

It took strength. Only real men can cry.

The more I think about the mood of business, the problems of management, the more I am convinced that what is missing is tears! Maybe not literally, of course, but certainly what tears represent in terms of personal caring and commitment.[31]

3

It's a Good Idea, but...

Building an Innovative Organization That Reinvents Itself Every Day

When was the last time that someone from your organization came up with a good idea? Do they come from a select few or is it everyone's responsibility to contribute? Do you reward innovation or smother and stifle it with politics, protocol, and procrastination? Do you welcome ideas with outstretched arms or listen because you have to? Do you have a formal plan for stimulating ideas or just allow them to happen? Do senior managers break down old barriers or construct new ones? Do you encourage the exploration of new ideas as a corporate philosophy, or do so only when you are forced to?

In this new age of competitive intensity, an organization's ability to generate and act on new ideas can make the difference between a winner and an also-ran. But just as capital equipment must be properly maintained and repaired to protect its value, creativity—an organization's greatest natural resource—must be nurtured if it is to provide the greatest benefits.

Creativity makes a difference at every level and in every type of organization—whether in the creation of new products and services, managing an advertising relationship, or finding ways to solve longstanding problems that seem unsolvable until someone with imagination throws an old ball with a new twist.

In some organizations, creativity is encouraged by the corporate culture, by the corporation's operational style, and by individual management practices; in others, it is stymied at every turn. The barriers are numerous, and the difficulty of bypassing them depends to a large extent on the level at which they are found. The most difficult roadblocks to creativity are found in organizations where the cultural mind-set encourages playing politics, where there is a caste system, where the organization resists change of any kind, and where failures represent a death knell to an individual's career.

Operational style is a less formidable roadblock because on this level problems can be more easily pinpointed and remedied. The procedures and protocol that dominate, the bureaucratic morass that hinders action, the hearing given new ideas, and the lack of incentives for rewarding people can all be changed to nurture creativity.

The least difficult obstacle to remove is a management style that quells creativity. Removing that barrier requires convincing managers that keeping people in the dark, a dictatorial approach to subordinates, unrealistic timing, and procrastination are not in their own best interests.

Unlocking the Creative Mystique

Many people have little understanding of or have difficulty assessing the creative process. They try to issue orders to stimulate the creative process, put time limits on it, or insist that it conform to preconceived notions. The fact is, the more you understand the creative process, the easier it will be to encourage creativity.

In his intensive studies of creativity, best-selling author Roger von Oech notes that "there are two main phases in the development of new ideas: a germinal phase and a practical one. In the germinal phase, ideas are generated and manipulated; in the practical phase, they are evaluated and executed. To use a biological metaphor, the germinal phase sprouts the new ideas and the practical phase harvests them."[1]

Von Oech warns against concentrating in only one area. Instead, he says, the best thinking comes from playing four different roles—explorer, artist, judge, warrior—at appropriate times. To start you

> need the raw materials from which new ideas are made: facts, concepts, experiences, knowledge, feelings, and whatever else you can find...so, you become an *explorer* and look for the materials you'll use to build your idea....They may form a pattern, but if you want something new and different, you have to give them a twist or two. That's when you shift roles and let the *artist* in you come out....Now you ask yourself, "Is this idea any good?" Is it worth pursuing? Will it give me the return I want? Do I have the resources to make this happen?" To help you make your decision, you adopt the mindset of a *judge*....Finally it's time to implement your idea. You realize, however, that the world isn't set up to accommodate every new idea that comes along...So you become a *warrior* and take your idea into battle...you may have to overcome excuses, idea killers, temporary setbacks, and other obstacles.[2]

Von Oech's interpretation is particularly interesting in light of the common notion that we use different sides of the brain for different kinds of thinking. The thinking that takes place in the left side of the brain is logical, concrete, and judgmental, very specific and consistent. The right side of the brain, in contrast, is capable of abstract thought, of putting various pieces together and coming up with something new; it is the place where intuition flourishes. Thus, the roles of explorer and artist may work best using right-side thinking; judge and warrior, left-side thinking. The difficulty arises when a person who is primarily a right-brain or left-brain thinker is responsible for playing all four roles and has a problem switching gears. An additional difficulty arises when the responsibilities of managing call for the judging role and being on the creative team calls on the artist role; the sides come into conflict when trying to force their different ways of thinking onto each other.

Some companies excel at creativity. Of course, there are pockets of creativity within companies and among managers, but organizationwide creative thinking is more difficult to find. One organization best known for it is 3M, the company responsible for such products as Post-it notes and Scotch tape—a company that strives to get 25 percent of each year's sales from products that are less than five years old. Extolled as "masters of innovation" and "new product champions," 3M offers a perfect example of how to promote the creative spirit among employees.

One reporter examining what makes 3M different, said that "'thou shall not kill an idea' is 3M's 'eleventh commandment.'" This commandment is carried out through establishment of a climate that puts a premium on "patience in the nurturing of developing projects; respect for the ideas of others; a constructive attitude toward failure as a necessary by-product of innovation; and an atmosphere of open communication."[3]

Running the Creative Gauntlet

The first step in encouraging creativity is learning to recognize the roadblocks and the reasons behind them—some of which are unconscious. A good place to start is with those that are easiest to tear down: those created by management because they lack an understanding of the skills required during each phase of the creative process or because they believe that they must maintain control at all times or because of their own inadequacies as managers.

Management Style

In the most creative environments, the line between work and having fun is blurred. People come to work not because they have to but because they want to. Creating that kind of environment is the responsibility of management. As John Welch, Jr., chairman of the board and CEO of General Electric, wrote in GE's 1989 *Annual Report,*

We want GE to become a company where people come to work every day in a rush to try something they woke up thinking about the night before. We want them to go home from work wanting to talk about what they did that day, rather than trying to forget about it. We want factories where the whistle blows and everyone wonders where the time went, and someone suddenly wonders aloud why we need a whistle. We want a company where people find a better way, every day of doing things; and where by shaping their own work experience, they make their lives better and your company best.

Farfetched? Fuzzy? Soft? Naive? Not a bit. This is the type of liberated, involved, excited, boundary-less culture that is present in successful start-up enterprises. It is unheard of in an institution our size; but we want it, and we are determined to have it.

In this kind of organization, employees feel that they are given a proper sense of direction by senior management, that their colleagues are pursuing the same goals they are, and most important, that everyone from the top of the organization to the lowest-level employee is committed to and has a personal stake in reaching the same goals.

In such organizations, management transfers the authority and responsibility for completing work to employees, leaving the process for reaching goals to their discretion. Management's responsibility then is to ensure that employees have the resources they need to do the job and that barriers that might inhibit their progress—such as keeping people in the dark, dictating creativity, setting unrealistic time frames, and procrastination—are torn down.

Keeping People in the Dark

"Why do you have to know so much about what we are doing? All I want are a few ideas." How can someone come up with ideas in a vacuum? The time you invest providing background information in an area often helps ensure that the ideas developed are consistent with your organization's overall strategy. Moreover, such information often becomes a catalyst for the creation of new ideas.

"It's just not right. I can't tell you why, but I just don't like it." Managers who do not take the time or make the effort to carefully evaluate an idea and provide constructive feedback (not just criticism) will be disappointed when employees make the same errors again.

"I know exactly what I want, but can't explain it. When I see it, though, I'll tell you." The inability to provide the proper sense of direction or to verbalize your expectations sets your employees up for failure. Perhaps you need to spend more time figuring out what you want before requesting assistance.

"Discuss the project with Harry, Tom, and Bill. Their input is important." Don't send someone out to get direction from others unless you're sure he will receive consistent input from them or that together they will be able to resolve inconsistencies. Otherwise, the person may end up playing the role of mediator rather than creator. The old adage "too many cooks spoil the broth" applies to the world of business. *The Wall Street Journal* told the sad tale of a speech writer who was told to send a draft of a speech he had written for the company's CEO to some of the company's executives. The writer said that "he received copies of his draft from 24 executives—'with 24 sets of comments.' And the chief executive hadn't even seen the draft. 'Twenty-four people rewrote it from their point of view,'" he lamented, adding that the result was he quit his job.[4]

"Your job isn't to meet with the client. It is to deliver results." The "creative team"—of, say, an advertising agency—should have direct access not only to their clients' management, but to their front line, that is, salespeople and dealers (those closest to the customer). After all, the closer one gets to the actual client, the less chance there is that something will get lost through the filtering process or modified by individual bias.

To ensure that people are not kept in the dark, even unwittingly, management must make a commitment to promote free and open communication throughout the organization, both vertically and across disciplines. That openness is part of the nurturing environment that spurs creativity, an environment in which there is little distrust, one in which everyone pulls together to achieve a common end. In this environment, new ideas are challenged and constructive feedback is offered. Internal communication is not channeled through the eyes of a select few because what seems important to one person may be insignificant to another. Instead, management works hard to break down barriers to communication and create forums encouraging people to exchange ideas as well as to network both within and outside their organization. (A new model for internal communication is introduced in Chapter 4.) In companies known for innovation, communication is constant. *Business Week* notes that "informal information-sharing sessions spring up willy-nilly at 3M—in the scores of laboratories and small meeting rooms or in the hallways. And it's not unusual for customers to be involved in these brain-storming klatches."[5] After all, who knows who will spark the next great idea.

Dictatorships

"Here's my idea; now execute it!"   When you tell people not only what you want, but how to do the job as well, they begin to shift into automatic pilot, stop thinking about a better way to attack the problem, and execute the action as directed. Because your orders seem to indicate a resistance to—and perhaps punishment for—finding new and perhaps better ways to do something, you negate any possibility of someone developing a new approach that might result in greater efficiency.

"Here's my idea; what's yours?"   When managers present their ideas before allowing employees to express theirs, employees with different ideas hold back so they don't seem to be saying their bosses' ideas are not good. This places boundaries and parameters on employee thinking, discouraging independent thought.

"Find me the optimal idea."   When you're looking for only one answer—the best one—it is too easy to stop after reaching a satisfactory one, which may be the easiest but not always the best. Encourage employees to come up with answers until all possibilities have been exhausted.

"Why are you wasting your time doing background research?" Don't let your bias for coming up with ideas influence the processes others use. Remember that someone who uses right-brain thinking likes to explore ideas on the road to new developments; don't let your manager's bias toward left-brain thinking prevent that exploration. The person doing the research knows what works for them. In many ways, "managing talent is like raising children. Talents are children who never completely grow up; managers are people who do grow up, but many of them forget they were ever children. They lose that child-like wonder. They don't know how to relate to children—or to talent. Managers who eliminate the child in their personality can never manage talent well."[6]

"Don't waste your time brainstorming; just come up with a great idea." Remember that many of the best ideas result from a spark that is then built upon. Many innovations have resulted from hearing an idea from another person, industry, or company and then applying it differently to another problem.

"Stop playing around and get back to work." The authors of *The Creativity Infusion* say that "another barrier to creativity often cited is the lack of discretionary time. When you work for an organization, you're generally deemed to be fully employed. Fully employed means that if you're not visibly doing something during all of your hours of employment—and usually beyond—then obviously you don't have enough to do....From another perspective, however, truly dedicated managers will sometimes make sure you can't be creative. They'll pile onto you things that are really unnecessary, again with the theory that if you have your feet up on the desk, you're obviously not fully employed."[7]

"What you came up with is okay, but let's do it somewhat differently." Don't change things by introducing subtle, meaningless changes in order to justify the time you spend reviewing them. Furthermore, it is important to provide recognition for new ideas. When employees know that their suggestions were adopted, they work harder to implement them.

"Here's $3 million to try your idea out." Being too generous can often kill an idea. The size of the investment raises expec-

tations before the idea has had enough time to prove itself. It is often better to test an idea in incremental steps, learning from mistakes, than to increase its visibility and smother it with money.

Managers often turn to a dictatorial style of management out of fear that they will lose control over the situation if they give employees too much latitude. Such managers maintain tight control to avoid having anyone "mess up." They have lost sight of the fact that if you believe in your people they will believe in themselves. Organizations should adopt the philosophy of executives such as Dick Madden, CEO of Potlatch Corporation, who says that it is far better to "think of the boundaries within which your staff operates as you would the walls of a room. Make sure that the walls are far enough apart to give people maximum space, but never so far apart that management can't support people if they stumble. The walls are there to strengthen and guide; they aren't there to neglect or confine. As skills develop, the boundaries can be enlarged."[8]

Unrealistic Timing

"It's only one page. It shouldn't take more than an hour to complete." You can't put a timetable on creativity. If you do, the results will be poor ideas, ideas that are not fully developed, and employees who grow frustrated as they hand in completed work only to have second thoughts about their efforts the next day.

"I know there's no reason to have it tomorrow, but I want it then anyway." Some managers believe they must exert pressure to force creativity, that people respond to such pressure with inspired breakthroughs. Although people often rise to an occasion if they are called upon to do so, pressure or fear is a short-term remedy. Furthermore, if you cry wolf too often, when you do need something extra from your employees, they won't have it to give to you.

"I gave you two days to do this; I can't believe there's a typo in it." By first setting unrealistic time frames and then ridiculing an

individual's best effort, not only do you have a negative impact on employee morale and work, you also reduce confidence, which will negatively affect future work.

Management must resist pressure to raise false expectations by accepting unrealistic deadlines and then forcing them onto their employees. An analysis of a survey of senior managers conducted by the Wharton School points out that "problems arise when senior people's approach to new products does not recognize the learning process....Another problem is impatience. Once management (finally, in the eyes of some) makes the go decision, they want the product out immediately."[9]

Procrastination

"We really do want suggestions. It's not our fault if we're too busy to act on them."   In many organizations, employees are asked for suggestions and then told management will get back to them, but no one ever does. Employees begin to assume no one cares, so they stop trying. The problem is compounded when managers are so overextended that they view a new idea as an annoyance, an attitude that is then communicated to employees.

"I think we've got it now. I only have minor corrections to the eighth draft."   Some managers change things just for the sake of changing them. Others make changes because proper attention was never initially given to the document or idea. A creativity survey reported in *Marketing News* noted that "overevaluation and competitiveness among group members were mentioned by 41 percent of the participants as a cause of failure."[10]

"Thanks for the additional information. Our committee meets in a few weeks, and we'll decide whether to go ahead with it then." Delays cause a loss of momentum. A frequent complaint is that "senior people are willing to entertain new ideas, but tend to drag out investment decisions too long....The hamper to innovation is the analysis process we get into. Rather than use judgment, they'd much rather gather lots more data."[11]

"With all the major problems I have to worry about, you can't expect me to think about that now."   Maybe if you had listened to someone else's idea six months ago, today's problem would not have developed. It takes just as much effort to find excuses not to listen as it does to listen.

Today's competition puts a premium on speed—which is discussed in great detail in Chapter 7. That is why procrastination—waiting until problems are critical before addressing them—creates problems at every turn. You end up spending all your time putting out fires instead of lighting them. Moreover, if you put off dealing with problems until the last minute, you end up setting unrealistic deadlines. Doing so hurts the project by breaking momentum, it creates cynicism among employees about your deadlines, and it dulls enthusiasm.

Operational Style

Every organization is unique in the way that it conducts its day-to-day business. This is evident in the way that it is structured, the rules that people conform to, and the rewards that people receive. It is important to remember, however, that specific rules can be changed to encourage creativity. This is a different proposition than trying to change the corporate culture, which permeates the entire mind-set of an organization.

Formalities and Protocol

"Put it in writing."   This demand stifles creativity in two ways. First, individuals may feel more comfortable and may be more skilled at expressing their concepts verbally, especially when a demonstration is called for. And second, many individuals may lose interest before they have the time or inclination to put their ideas in writing.

"Make sure that your idea conforms to our format."   This is the case of putting boundaries on an idea—style over substance. Why not first evaluate the idea on its own merit before considering its packaging?

"Come up with something really creative, but be sure it doesn't run more than eight pages, has limited text, and uses line art." Injecting your own personal preferences into the creative process and limiting the freedom to express creativity may hinder the process. Or, it may end up changing the basic idea enough that it is no longer valid.

"Don't ask questions, just follow the rules." Every organization needs procedures that organize basic activities; the danger is putting rules into place that stifle creativity and innovation. As Roger von Oech says: "There is a lot of pressure in our culture to follow the rules. This value is one of the first things we learn as children. We are told, 'Don't color outside the lines,' and 'No orange elephants.' Our educational system encourages further rule-following. Students are usually better rewarded for regurgitating information than for playing with ideas and thinking of original uses for things. As a consequence, people feel more comfortable following the rules than challenging them....if, however, you are trying to generate new ideas, then the value 'follow the rules' can be a mental lock because it means 'think of things only as they are.'"[12] In the article in *Business Week* mentioned earlier, the author points out that "the scarcity of corporate rules at 3M leaves room for plenty of experimentation—and failure [which is not considered a death knell of any kind]."[13]

Organizations develop procedures or design standard formats in order to make the organization function smoother—in fact, the absence of any rules would lead to chaos. But many times either the rationale for developing the rule disappears as circumstances change, or procedures take on a greater importance than reaching the ultimate goal. Employees must be empowered to bend the rules when it serves the best interest of the client. When Philip Caldwell was CEO of Ford, he said that "the magic of employee involvement is that it allows individuals to discover their own potential—and to put that potential to work in more creative ways. [It allows people to] develop in themselves pride in workmanship, self-respect, self-reliance, and a heightened sense of responsibility."[14] That is why formats and procedures should serve as guidelines or parameters, but never be so set in stone that they can't be modified. Furthermore, they should be revisited and tested over time to ensure that they still serve their intended purposes.

Bureaucracy

"It's a great idea. Now just get the ten required signoffs and we're all ready to roll."   There are two ends of this continuum. Centralization, where few individuals must sign off on everything, often leading to excessive volume and then to queues. The other end, total consensus, creates a system with so many individuals involved in the decision-making process that quick decisions are close to impossible. The speech writer quoted earlier who had his draft reviewed by 24 executives, noted that the result of taking everyone's suggestions into account was "minestrone." He recalls that "a marketing manager...wanted the speech to tell the audience how certain financial products could be adapted to fit its specific needs. A lawyer wanted to talk about the legislative battle the company was prepared to wage. An economist wanted to focus on trends."[15]

"Run the idea up the flagpole. You need the approval of the five unit heads."   This scenario is all too common. Some comments are inconsistent with one another, one person is on vacation for two weeks, and two others are out of the country for five days—but you have three days to complete the work.

"I personally thought it was a good idea, but when I presented it to my boss..."   Those who created the idea are probably the best salespeople for it. They are in a better position to answer questions and display the enthusiasm needed to gain approval for it. Therefore, when presenting ideas from level to level, try to bring the idea's champion or champions with you to the presentation meeting. After all, one of the greatest incentives is letting employees present good ideas to senior management.

"You can't have him for your new design group...he's in sales."   The authors of *The Creativity Infusion* point out that "it seems

fairly reasonable and logical that if a company's managers are investing in the organization's future survival and growth, they should staff creative projects with their best and brightest. Yet they often do this reluctantly because these folks are so valuable and essential in other important or critical areas. The boss then may be reluctant to volunteer them for a high-risk assignment that takes them away from their already invaluable contribution."[16] The Wharton study mentioned earlier reported that "one product manager said that the biggest problem was that it took 3 months to pull the people out of their existing organization and get them working temporarily on his project. He has continuing problems making sure that these people's bosses recognize the value of their work on the new project so that the people will not suffer in their performance reviews."[17]

The ability to respond to a client's request, to get a new product to market quickly, to be the first to introduce a new idea is key in today's competitive environment. As the 1989 General Electric *Annual Report* mentioned earlier states,

> Being on top of things, controlling them, must give way to sharing, trusting. Most of the bureaucracy that infects business institutions—the reviews, layers, routines and reports—stem largely from a lack of trust...controlling people doesn't motivate them. It stifles them. We've found that people perform better, even heroically, when they see that what they do every day makes a difference. When they see that—when they are allowed to make real contributions to win—they quickly develop increased self-confidence. That self-confidence in turn promotes simplicity—of action, of design, of process, of communication—because there is no longer a psychic need to wrap oneself in the complexity, trappings and jargon that, in a bureaucracy, signify sophistication and status.

When decisions are made only after sending ideas through an elaborate review process regardless of the scope or significance of the idea, the organization will be severely handicapped. This is because very important ideas—not being screened as a priority—will receive just as much attention as lesser ideas, and may die as a result. Furthermore, management, experiencing a significant flow of ideas, will be unable to respond to them on a timely basis. As a result, employees will stop sending their ideas to management knowing that they will never hear back from them anyway. In both cases, the organization loses.

Why then do organizations insist on developing elaborate bureaucracies? In some cases, people are trying to protect their own fiefdoms out of fear that someone will step on their turf. Other organizations impose and maintain a rigid and pragmatic style because those in charge are afraid of losing power or control—or being perceived as having lost it. They review every situation in order to demonstrate their power to the detriment of the organization's ability to innovate.

In yet other organizations, the bureaucratic style develops as managers, afraid of making decisions, pass anything requiring a decision along. Although approvals are clearly needed when decisions involve a lot of money, have major strategic consequences, or require a specialist's review (for example, an attorney), in most cases, those best able to judge whether an idea will fly are those closest to the situation.

Discouraging New Ideas

"I won't have time to meet with you, so why don't you send it in the mail?"   If you want to develop an innovative environment, encouraging new ideas must become a priority. When you find it difficult to review ideas on a timely basis, at least provide an explanation and promise to discuss it at a future date—and keep that promise.

"Sorry, I didn't review your idea yet. But I've already gotten 50 ideas like yours this week."   Everyone thinks their ideas are special. Don't treat them as a number. Next time you ask for ideas, the person you just rejected may be the only one able to come up with something new.

"I personally wouldn't do it, but why don't you try anyway?"   Watch how you phrase your directions. People work best in an environment in which they feel they are making a valuable contribution to the organization. If you grant someone permission to do something, it is important to hold back any

qualifiers that plant seeds of doubt; indicate confidence in them and their ideas.

"Don't come up with ideas, just do your job." It should be everyone's responsibility to come up with new ideas, not only the responsibility of a select few; the person you just discouraged may have the one idea that could make the difference.

"You've got a great idea...now all we have to do is figure out who to present it to." When organizations fail to make it clear who new ideas should be presented to, employees are often at a loss. Innovative companies create a process and designate an individual or a group to whom new ideas are submitted.

"I know that my idea is great, if I only knew a way that I could convince management of that." Many ideas fall by the wayside, not because they are flawed, but because they are not properly packaged and presented. Management could break down this barrier by providing either marketing resources or training to aid the process.

"Why do you bother me with small details." Examining only big ideas is bad business. Innovations resulting in incremental changes in an organization are also important. Besides, that small detail may turn out to be a first step on the road to something big.

The tone of an organization is set through good climate control. Organizations that understand this premise "regard new ideas as wild flowers. They know you do not plant seeds for wild flowers; you find them by searching in many places. They concentrate on preparing the conditions for wild flowers to grow as they push for incremental change everywhere."[18]

This means that organizations must first analyze the internal climate, norms, and personal biases that inhibit creativity and then begin to institute changes that will create an environment where new ideas are welcomed and allowed to flourish; where ideas are evaluated on their individual merits rather than the status of the person introducing them; where people look for "the good" in every idea, trying to add value to it rather than trying to shoot it out of the sky.

The Evaluation Process

"I ran it by the committee, and it didn't fly."   The review process for new ideas should provide the idea's creator with a summary of the decision and a thorough explanation of how it was made.

"Rather than take the time to give you my comments, it'll be easier if I take care of it myself."   Such reactions prevent people from learning by their own mistakes, so the odds are that those mistakes will be repeated. Moreover, by failing to let them do it themselves, you take away the satisfaction most people get from completing an activity.

"I know I asked you to be creative, but this stuff is off the wall." When you rip apart a suggestion and demean the person who made it, you ensure getting more safe solutions in the future. Explaining what was wrong without aspersions is far more productive.

"John, how do you expect me to approve this when you left out...?" This is known as throwing the baby out with the bath water. Be careful not to throw out a great idea because of its packaging or because one element wasn't properly accounted for.

Many times it is not the fact that feedback is negative that stops the flow of future ideas, but the way in which that feedback is presented. Moreover, management must establish an evaluation process in which ideas are not ignored because those reviewing them don't understand their potential but hesitate to raise questions, fearing it will be viewed as a sign of weakness. Furthermore, the reviewers must not be rushed or overextended; they must be able to give new ideas the time and attention commensurate with the effort that was invested in coming up with them. It is also important that those involved in the evaluation process be able to overcome their personal biases.

Incentives

"Why say thank-you? It's his job, isn't it?"   People work for more than money. Most want to be recognized for a job well done and come away from their work with inner satisfaction.

"Why should we broadcast the fact that John had an idea. We want people working, not wasting time generating ideas." By giving John the kudos that he deserves, you create an incentive for him to come up with more good ideas; moreover, you inspire others to emulate his behavior.

"Look at the great idea I just came up with." There is nothing more demoralizing than having superiors take the credit for subordinates' work. As a result of such a breach of trust, people hesitate to present new ideas; furthermore, they are likely to look for a situation in which they will receive recognition for their contributions.

"Why provide incentives or rewards for ideas?" Concrete rewards evoke enthusiasm, dedication, and loyalty to an organization. They also inspire others to emulate the behavior of the person so recognized.

In an article in *Fortune,* Stratford Sherman explains that companies that encourage innovation and creativity "reinforce the fear of stagnation with rewards for success. 'We want our people to focus on the upside,' says GE's Welch, who annually doles out $2 million in special bonuses for extraordinary contributions. Others rely less on money than on ego-boosters. 3M gives prizes—trophies and certificates—while Intel gives its design engineers the gratifying opportunity to present their new products to engineers at client companies."[19] Almost every innovative company has reward systems in place, but perhaps no company does it better than 3M, where the person "who champions a new product out the door then gets the chance to manage it as if it were his or her own business."[20]

Furthermore, at some organizations, dual career ladders have been set up to reward individuals who deserve promotions but are happy doing the creative work that resulted in their recognition in the first place. For example, at 3M engineers who don't want to be managers are not punished. The company's dual-ladder approach says Lester Krough, vice president of research and development "allows employees to go back and forth from management to research. As scientists, they can have the same benefits and monetary privileges as managers."[21]

Indeed, in organizations noted for their creativity, even failures that are the result of unusual effort receive special awards. Managers in such organizations recognize the variety among individuals. They know that some people are less likely to be motivated by money or career advancement than by the inner satisfaction of hatching their own ideas. They make sure that they reward people who take chances by:

- Saying thank-you in public
- Having a variety of methods of granting recognition, including internal newsletters, formal notes, lunches with senior management as well as major gifts
- Making sure that rewards are given soon after the effort is made

The Organizational Culture

A participant in the Wharton School study mentioned earlier in the chapter said, "First you have to learn how to bypass or obliterate or work through the culture to get the product to the market place....A great deal of time is spent selling inside the organization. Then you go sell outside."[22] The most difficult roadblock to overcome is an organizational culture that militates against creativity and innovation, that fights change of any kind, that believes that the way things have been done in the past is the way they should be done in the future. The motivations for such behavior are fear of failure, playing politics, uneasiness with anything new or different (leaving the comfort zone), and a belief in a caste system.

Fear of Failure

"Even though you let me down last time, I'm going to give you another chance." Given this type response, someone wanting to try something new will spend more time fearing reprisal than going all out to follow through on the idea. They will also probably play it close to the vest, hesitating to reveal any part of the idea early on.

"Will you bet your job on it?"   When managers demand assurances of success, employees gloss over problems and overestimate the potential of success, setting up false expectations. Organizations that foster innovation, deter fear by treating mistakes as another step in the learning process. They make it clear that if you're not making mistakes, you're not trying something new.

"I'm afraid that if it doesn't work, we'll look foolish."   Unless your organization accepts the premise that risks are worth taking, it will dampen the impulse toward creative thinking. Everyone must be brought to realize that "the need to be right all the time is the biggest barrier there is to new ideas. It is better to have enough ideas for some of them to be wrong than to be always right by having no ideas at all."[23]

A corporate culture that creates a fear of failure stifles creativity. A participant in the Wharton study said, "One must wonder how many potentially good ideas have not been brought forth because someone did the 'wise' thing career-wise....It is easier to ride the wave than stick your neck out. If you do work on something new, it will be positive or negative—you will succeed or fail. If you fail, you're out. If you succeed, you're only a little bit ahead. It's not worth the risk."[24]

In corporate cultures that stimulate innovation, senior management understands how much you can learn from failure. Ronald Mitsch, senior vice president of research and development at the 3M Company, has said,

> If we gain a lot from each successful program at 3M, we also learn as much or more from every failure. For example, we tried to market a line of suntan lotions that adhered to the skin without being sticky; it protected the skin even after a 30-minute swim. There was nothing wrong with the product's performance; however, we were not successful in the marketplace. The suntan lotions were challenged by those of well-established competitors which offered broad lines of well-known skin care products.
>
> The experience reinforced our traditional wisdom that keeping one foot in a comfort zone enables us to compete more successfully. So we try to leverage our existing marketing strengths as often as we can when we embark on new

products. But we also learned never to give up too easily. Some astute laboratory people kept working on the suntan lotion technology and came up with a successful insect repellent.[25]

Moreover, according to Jack Matson, a University of Houston professor, "There are two ways to fail....One approach, trying out things sequentially [which he] calls slow, stupid failure, is the worst. The process is so drawn out that you get worn out and say the hell with it. The other way, intelligent, fast failure means launching several ideas at once and readying more for the next salvo....Failure is a normal, natural way of mapping the unknown so you want to compress your trials into as small a time period as possible."[26]

A good approach to success, according to Thomas J. Watson, the founder of IBM, "is to double your failure rate."[27] And for that to happen, management must create a comfortable, stimulating risk-free environment where individuals are free to offer speculative, imprecise, sometimes off-the-wall ideas. As Art Fry, corporate scientist at 3M and developer of the Post-it note said, "People need the opportunity to make errors, to explore what looks like blind alleys, and to do so with the same confidence in themselves and the organization."[28]

Politics

"What will the boss think?"   People often look back to the last time they presented an idea. They remember if management was unreceptive. As a result, many ideas never get presented.

"Don't rock the boat...I don't know if it's good politics."   Introducing change is never easy, but in nurturing environments ideas are presented and built upon without fear of someone "getting even."

"I wonder if my idea will offend anyone."   In a corporate environment marked by playing politics, there is good reason to believe that the originator will worry more about what people think than the idea itself. Everyone is afraid there are snipers behind the bushes waiting for them. As a result, ideas may be so compromised that by the time they are presented,

they don't look anything like the original, having been tempered to raise the fewest possible objections.

"I wonder if someone at the meeting will shoot my idea down to get even with my boss."   Where the good of the organization is subservient to the ambitions of its employees, the free expression of ideas takes a backseat to fears of backstabbing.

If everyone in an organization is busily pursuing their own ends, they play games that discourage creativity. Unless the corporate culture can be changed so that everyone pursues common goals and stops the gamesmanship that inhibits the free exchange of information, promoting creativity will be difficult. Encouraging internal and external communications will help eliminate the "us" versus "them" mentality that prevents people from pulling together.

Resistance to Change

"If it's such a great idea, how come no one ever came up with it before?"   Someone probably has, but the idea was shot down either because of inertia, because the person was afraid to present it, or no one ever thought it worth taking the initiative to follow through on it because they knew how hard it was to get anyone in the organization to listen.

"We've never done it this way before."   That may be so, but if it's right for the organization, why not start doing it that way now. Organizational cultures tend to perpetuate themselves by hiring people who "fit in." Secondly, organizations often have a tendency toward inward thinking as a result of either too much success or people living in ivory towers and out of touch with reality.

"We're doing great. If it ain't broke don't fix it."   New ideas are frequently rejected because they are unfairly compared with the great ideas of yesterday. This is particularly true in organizations that have had a long and successful history. But this is a one-way ticket to mediocrity because the outside world changes and what made the company a winner yesterday may not hold true tomorrow.

"How can you say you have a better idea? Don't you realize how long it took us to come up with the present system?" If you fall in love with the present way of doing things, you will become stale and complacent. A mentality that focuses on the past, that likes the reassurance of "we've always done it this way," is bad for business. Instead, learn to question why things are done in a particular way, and frequently ask yourself whether an alternative might be better. Remember that many ideas are discounted because there isn't enough information available to make the decision. And most of all, remember that everybody fears the unknown.

The Caste System

"Why should I listen to you? It's not your area of expertise." It is often possible to be too close to the forest to see the trees. Someone with a different perspective can often find a better way of approaching a problem. In an article evaluating the success of 3M, Thomas Osborn said, "Many of 3M's most successful innovations came from personnel in sales and other departments, not just technical lab people...for example, 3M's most famous consumer product, Scotch tape, was once manufactured strictly as an industrial product, until a salesman got the idea of packaging it in clear plastic dispensers for home and office use."[29]

"Why ask me about that? I'm only a salesman?" It is important to keep employees from focusing only on their area of expertise. According to von Oech, "Specialization can be dangerous because it can lead to the attitude, 'That's not my area.' When this happens, a person may not only delimit his problems to too small an area, he may also stop looking for ideas in other fields."[30]

"Why is everyone sitting around discussing this? That's what we have management for." Surely, the more heads attacking the problem the better. In fact, in a 1988 creativity survey of 150 managers in 27 companies, participants said that they believed "groups surpass individuals for idea quality and quantity.

Seventy-eight percent of the respondents said groups outperform individuals for idea quality, and 91 percent of the respondents said they feel groups outperform individuals on idea
quantity." Furthermore, according to the survey, "Small
groups are preferred for problem solving over working alone
or in large groups. Seventy-one percent said they prefer to
work in groups of six or less to solve problems."[31]

"Why ask Joe, Tom, or Harry for ideas? What do they know?"
Some managers consistently ignore employees because they
are too low on the totem pole. They forget that "any part of
the human body which is not exercised properly starts to atro-
phy. This is true too, of the various parts of the human mind,
and particularly true of imagination."[32] They have never
escaped the ancient Roman belief that creative individuals
were "endowed by the gods with transcendental intellectual
and/or artistic powers...geniuses were born, not made."[33]
Managers forget that deciding who is creative may prove a
self-fulfilling prophecy; it may also mean that if the "creative
type" doesn't come up with ideas, nothing can happen.

Organizations with cultures based on an "old-fashioned
snobbery of the kind that took for granted that the common
man was incapable of creating anything...[that] the universe
functioned according to a cosmic pattern in which everything
and everybody had a place," are organizations that will not survive in today's competitive, rapidly changing, technology-dri-
ven world.[34] Such a condescending culture must be changed if
an organization is to meet the demands of modern competition.

Reaching the Winner's Circle

It is not enough, however, to simply remove the roadblocks to
creativity and innovation. Internal communication, the subject
of Chapter 4, must be viewed as an avenue to release the creative genius in an organization. Furthermore, you must also
encourage everyone in your organization to look at things
through new lenses. Remember that most people have been

educated in the American school system, which emphasizes—and rewards—rote learning. Try to encourage your employees to be broad thinkers and not to have tunnel vision. Let your employees know that their jobs are not just a series of tasks but that they are responsible for finding new and better ways of doing things. Let them know that coming up with a new idea that fails is not regarded as a personal failure, and perhaps most of all, let them know you value creativity. Tearing down the roadblocks to creativity is the only way to achieve victory.

4

Internal Communication— More Than Lip Service

Building an Organization with Total Concentration and Focus

Over the past 10 years, the world has changed dramatically. The enormous increase in global competition has forever altered the way we conduct business. Time is now so compressed that where it was once a victory to launch a product in two years, today the competitive environment dictates that the same task be done in months. This means employees need information today, not tomorrow, and to make matters even more difficult, the amount of information available is steadily growing. In fact, according to Richard Wurman in *Information Anxiety*, information now doubles every five years. "The weekday edition of *The New York Times* contains more information than the average person was likely to come across in a lifetime in 17th century England."[1]

Add to these changes the avalanche of takeovers, restructurings, downsizings, divestitures, and leveraged buyouts, and you have the makings of a confused and anxiety-ridden work force. The challenge that faces us all is to find ways to increase employee loyalty, build bonds between people, and improve productivity during a period of unprecedented change coupled with information overload.

In an article for *Training and Development Journal,* behavioral scientists reported that "individuals prefer to exert control over their environments...particularly...in stressful situations such as an organizational acquisition. Because information increases an individual's sense of control, open and honest managerial communication can help employees gain a feeling of personal control."[2] This is totally consistent with the findings of a study conducted by the Columbia University School of Business and Dunhill Personnel System Inc.: "When 225 middle managers were asked the top on-the-job stress points, 43 percent of the respondents pointed to a lack of information while 31 percent of the respondents cited conflicting information."[3] This need for information can be seen everywhere. For example, there is the case of the major multinational corporation that installed a free 800 number to provide a daily recorded update of company news to the media. Much to their surprise, they discovered that most of the calls were from their own managers in the United States and throughout the world who wanted to know what was going on in their own company.

Employees are saying that they need information today, because it will be obsolete tomorrow; they are saying that it must be customized to meet their specific needs or they're just not interested. What brought about this fierce desire to know more and know it now? It is driven by the belief that in an age of abundant information and rapid change, you can't be productive by waiting till the end of the month to get a generically written, watered-down newsletter that doesn't provide relevant information. While that may have been satisfactory in the past, when everything wasn't so time sensitive, in today's global economy, it just isn't enough.

Stress to Success

Think about your organization's communication effectiveness. If you randomly selected 50 of your employees and asked them basic questions about your organization, how similar would their answers be? For example: What is our organization's mission? What factors are most important to our future success? How does someone get ahead in our organization? Who are our competitors and how do we differentiate ourselves from them? What are our major initiatives this year? How do you think our industry will change over the next few years, and how will our company respond to those changes? Unless you get common answers to these most basic questions, waste, redundancies, inefficiencies, confusion, and anxiety are likely: the result—employees working at cross purposes.

In *Innovative Employee Communication,* Alvie Smith, former director of corporate communications at General Motors, compares communication to the cardiovascular system of the human body: "The management organization is the prime top-to-bottom link with employees. It represents the network of arteries which hold the corporate body together. And communication is the lifeblood which draws its informational strength from various sources, recasts it into digestible forms, and transmits the revitalized materials to every part of the corporate body."[4]

In fact, a majority of the 132 CEOs surveyed in 1987 by IABC [International Association of Business Communicators] and Johnson and Higgins said that "employee communications directly influences job satisfaction, improves employee commitment and increases productivity. A full 71 percent said communications directly affects the bottom line."[5]

To succeed in today's competitive marketplace, organizations must give internal communication the priority that it deserves. They must view it as an avenue to release the creative genius of an organization, not as a bothersome chore. After all, communication acts as a powerful agent of change, a source of continuous improvement, and a catalyst for moving the organization forward. And finally, organizations must address their internal and external audiences with a single voice to avoid sending mixed messages to the marketplace.

Unfortunately, those trying to establish strong internal communication programs must compete for an organization's limited resources. This includes time and money spent communicating to customers, shareholders, employees, and the local communities in which they reside. Internal communication is usually one of the first things to be cut in tough times; it is treated as a stepchild compared with external communication. Furthermore, organizations consider internal communication something that they have to do, rather than something they want to do.

In the next decade, organizations will have to focus on winning employees back; building trust, respect, and teamwork between people; being receptive to and then acting on the best ideas; and once again instilling employees with pride in and commitment to the organization. Internal communication will be a major force in achieving those ends.

Communicating in the Information Age

Internal communication has to keep up with the changes taking place in the world. Where the bimonthly newsletter was considered a preferred source of information for 45 percent of employees in 1980, today, according to an IABC study, it is listed as helpful by only 16 percent of employees.[6] As a vehicle to keep employees informed it is as out of place in today's new organization as the adding machine. Where employee communication was once produced by the professional, it will now be developed by the layman. Where it was once broadcast from the ivory tower, it will now be transmitted through the grapevine. Where the purpose of internal communications was once to report on the completion of an event, it will now plant seeds that will grow into new ideas. Where communication was once infrequent, it will now become constant. Where there was once lag time in reporting an event, communication will become instant. Where formal mass communication was once commonplace, customization and personalization will become the norm.

Everyone in the organization must face the fact that internal communication is a philosophy, not an activity. There is no longer room for statements such as, "We should communicate more with our employees, so let's put up bulletin boards," or "Morale seems a little weak this month; let's hold some meetings." There is no room for believing in the efficacy of a magic communications wand that will make problems go away. Instead, organizations must make a commitment to an ongoing process of communication that exists on three levels. The first is between the organization's leadership and its employees, the second is between first-line managers and those who report to them, and the third is between colleagues.

The Role of Leadership

In the past, the leader's role was controlling the information employees needed to make day-to-day decisions. Leaders who continue along that path will become frustrated as they lose the confidence of employees whose desire for timely, customized information is not satisfied. Furthermore, employees will increasingly demand communication that is multidirectional, participatory, comprehensive, credible, open, relevant, and delivered in a timely fashion. They will use electronic bulletin boards, voice mail, and other forms of technology in addition to networking to bypass formal communication vehicles.

Instead of trying to control information that will be obsolete before they have the chance to send it, tomorrow's leaders will provide employees with a different message. General Electric's Jack Welch once said, "Leaders—and you take anyone from Roosevelt to Churchill to Reagan—inspire people with clear visions of how things can be done better. Some managers, on the other hand, muddle things with pointless complexity and detail. They equate it with sophistication, with sounding smarter than anyone else. They inspire no one."[7]

Tomorrow's leaders must communicate a clear and compelling vision that reinforces the beliefs and values on which the organization is based. They must provide a consistent direction, clarify the rationale behind the policies that exist, and

enroll everyone in a common cause by creating rituals and ceremonies that help establish heroes to emulate. And they must do
this not only with words but with consistent actions that vali-
date those words.

Creating the Vision

In a 1989 study of 400 managers and professionals, Robert
Kelley, business professor at Carnegie-Mellon University, discovered that almost two-thirds of those surveyed felt that their
company's leadership failed to give them a "clear understanding of a corporate vision, mission and goals....Only about one
in five company executives were identified as having the skills
to motivate employees and to implement a vision successfully
enough to result in high performance....Only one in three workers feels tied into the company's destiny and its performance
goals."[8]

Leaders must create a shared vision that shapes the way
employees feel about their organization. They must accept
responsibility for making "the company," "our company," a
place where people work together instead of "doing their own
thing." The vision may be precise or it may be vague; it may be
a specific goal or it may be a dream of a better future. What is
critical is that it present a clear and concise view of the future
organization that is realistic, believable, and attractive, and
even more, that it promise a better future than prevailing conditions in visible and important ways.

But the vision cannot be so far from the reality of the organization, or so difficult to achieve, that no one takes it seriously.
The shared vision, shared sense of purpose, and operating values must be integrated so that they mesh with the day-to-day
actions of the organization. Peter Senge explains this process in
his book *The Fifth Discipline* by asking us to "imagine a rubber
band, stretched between your vision and current reality. When
stretched, the rubber band creates tension, representing the tension between vision and current reality....There are only two
possible ways for the tension to resolve itself! Pull reality
toward the vision or pull the vision toward reality, which
occurs will depend on whether we hold steady to the vision."[9]

A shared vision must also connect with the personal values and desires of each and every individual. Here, a useful metaphor is the hologram, "the three-dimensional image created by interacting light sources....If you cut a photograph in half, each part shows only part of the whole image. But if you divide a hologram, each part shows the whole image intact. Similarly, as you continue to divide up the hologram, no matter how small the divisions, each piece still shows the whole image. Likewise, when a group of people come to share a vision for an organization, each person sees his own picture of the organization at its best. Each shares responsibility for the whole, not just for his piece. But while the component pieces of the hologram are not identical, each represents the whole image from a different point of view. It's as if you were to look through holes poked in a window shade; each hole would offer a unique angle for viewing the whole image."[10]

Creating the vision is not, however, enough. The vision must be brought to life and then imbued in the corporate culture. The vision must be so omnipresent that employees old and new assimilate it as part of their personal and corporate belief structure, and then communicate it to customers and suppliers and even the world at large. Moreover, it must be articulated clearly and frequently throughout the organization, so that it becomes ingrained in the organization's culture. Then the corporate structure and management style must be shaped to lend credence to the picture created by the vision.

When the shared vision is embedded in the corporate culture, internal politics and game playing starts to come to an end. As people begin to buy into the organization's vision and exhibit confidence in its future, not only do they begin to work in unison rather than at cross purposes, but they discard their self-interest and work for the common good.

Promoting the Beliefs and Values of the Organization

Because beliefs and values form the heart of an organization's culture, great leaders never miss an opportunity to reinforce them. They know that once internalized, these beliefs and values become the norms that influence everyone's day-to-day actions, providing guidance about what is important, reinforcing appropriate behavior, and changing attitudes.

However, if these norms are to hold firm, management must support them by clear and visible action; management must believe the values not only in their heads, but in their hearts. Otherwise, they are likely to be inconsistent in applying them, or worse, fail to promote them in times of stress. If leadership's commitment to the organization's values is perceived as rhetoric without substance, the organization will not succeed.

According to Terrence Dean and Allen Kennedy in *Corporate Cultures*, there are a number of clearly visible "signs of a culture in trouble; weak cultures have no clear values or beliefs about how to succeed in their business; or they have many such beliefs but cannot agree among themselves on which are most important; or different parts of the company have fundamentally different beliefs; the heroes of the culture are destructive or disruptive and don't build upon any common understanding about what is important; the rituals of day-to-day life are either disorganized—with everybody doing their own thing—or downright contradictory—with the left hand and the right hand working at cross purposes."[11]

Leaders make certain that everyone has a consistent picture of the organization's beliefs and values and is ready and willing to act on them. They do this through their own actions and by creating heroes, establishing rituals and ceremonies, and encouraging storytelling to create myths that set the tone for the organization.

Heroes.   The heroes of an organization are those individuals who are placed on a pedestal so that others can emulate their behavior. There are two kinds of heroes. The first serve as day-to-day role models for everyone to follow. They personify the values of the organization. Although they may not be at the helm of the organization, they are frequently those who are placed in fast-track programs, are in visible positions, are involved with turning around an unsuccessful operation or championing a successful product. They are employees who have gone the extra mile to service the needs of a client, won back the business of a client that was vulnerable to a competitor, or led change within an organization.

The second kind of hero is a legend—those who built the organization and made it great—like Thomas Watson, Henry Ford, and Thomas Edison. These heroes are like the forefathers of this country; their histories should be written down and their words deeply embedded in the enterprise. They are the immutable source of inspiration. And because of that they serve as role models.

Rituals and Ceremonies. Rituals are the day-to-day activities that demonstrate the cultural values of an organization, and cere- monies are the spectacles that are almost larger than life. Each serves an important function. If there are too many ceremonies, they soon become extravagant rituals with little meaning. The annual Veteran's Day parades held in many localities are rituals that allow us to say thank-you and we remember. A spectacular ticker-tape parade welcoming returning heroes is a ceremony cele- brating the nation and its accomplishments in the course of which the contributions of veterans are honored. In business, ceremonies are a celebration of the heroes and myths that stand for the organi- zation. Rituals encompass everyday activities that are often taken for granted: there is no spotlight shining on them, and they are part of the unconscious mind-set of employees.

As nice as ceremonies are, however, they do not constantly remind employees of the importance that the organization places on values nor do they reinforce those values. Rituals, the embodiment of the organization's culture, are the everyday events that reinforce the beliefs and values of the organization. They run the gamut from the way meetings are conducted to how many are held each year, from the way an individual's promotion is announced to how a large new sales order is cele- brated, from the way someone is introduced into the organiza- tion to the tone displayed when they depart. Rituals set the cli- mate of the organization and mold the actions of its employees.

Storytelling. In *Leadership Is an Art,* Max De pree points out that "every company has tribal stories. Though there may be only a few tribal storytellers, it's everyone's job to see that things as unimportant as manuals and light bulbs don't replace them."[12]

Stories are nonthreatening, they expand perception, they show alternate possibilities and different ways of working, they engage the imagination, and they make difficult concepts more interesting and engaging. Stories help us deal with complex feelings, open us to new relationships, and call us to action. But to be effective, stories must include aspirations achieved, dreams fulfilled, goals reached.

There are any number of common story types. One type involves helping employees understand what will happen if they do their jobs right. It addresses the questions people have about the organization they work for. Stories can provide information about a company's reaction to someone who breaks rules or to someone who notices a higher-level person breaking the rules and reports the transgression. There is a pattern to these stories. According to an article in *Administrative Science Quarterly,* these stories send a message saying that "everyone should have to obey the rules; everyone is human; anyone should be able to rise to the top if he or she is sufficiently competent and hardworking. In the positive versions of these stories, these equalities do emerge. In negative versions, they could emerge and their failure to do so reinforces the inequality."[13]

The authors of the article go on to tell two classic tales that illustrate this point. The first, which took place at IBM, and the second, which happened at the Revlon Corporation, are considered by those who worked at those organizations good reflections of their very different cultures:

> A twenty-two year old bride weighing ninety pounds whose husband had been sent overseas and who, in consequence, had been given a job until his return...was obliged to make certain that people entering security area wore the correct clearance identification. Surrounded by his usual entourage of white-shirted men, Watson [a former IBM Chairman] approached the doorway to an area where she was on guard, wearing an orange badge acceptable elsewhere in the plant, but not a green badge, which alone permitted entrance at her door. I was "trembling in my uniform, which was far too big," she recalled. "It hid my

shakes, but not my voice. 'I'm sorry,' I said to him, I knew who he was all right. 'You cannot enter. Your admittance is not recognized.' That's what we were supposed to say." The men accompanying Watson were stricken; the moment held unpredictable possibilities. "Don't you know who he is?" Someone hissed. Watson raised his hand for silence, while one of the party strode off and returned with the appropriate badge....One possible message or moral of the IBM rule-breaking story for higher status employees is: "Even Watson obeys the rules, so you certainly should." For lower status people there is another moral: "Uphold the rules, no matter who is disobeying....Another type of organization is possible, one where bosses break rules with impunity and lower level employees do not dare challenge the infraction."[14]

The second story tells of the behavior of Charles Revson, head of the Revlon Corporation.

[Revson] was worried that employees were not coming to work on time, although Charles himself seldom arrived much before noon. Therefore, as late as 1971,...everyone was required to sign in in the morning. Everyone. Even Charles signed in. One day, when Revlon was in the process of moving from 666 Fifth Avenue up to the General Motors Building, in 1969, Charles sauntered in and began to look over the sign-in sheet. The receptionist, who was new, says "I'm sorry, sir, you can't do that." Charles says, "Yes, I can." "No sir," she says. "I have strict orders that no one is to remove the list; you'll have to put it back." This goes back and forth for a while with the receptionist being very courteous, as all Revlon receptionists are, and finally, Charles says, "Do you know who I am?" And she says, "No sir, I don't." "Well, when you pick up your final paycheck this afternoon, ask 'em to tell ya."[15]

Storytelling can also be used to establish the boss as a "real" human being. The story must first reinforce the boss's position within the organization—revealing status, usually through the title, say, CEO; then the story must afford the boss an opportunity to perform an act that we usually would not expect someone in a high position to perform; and finally, it must be clear that the human act performed does not in any way cause the performer to lose status.

A few years ago, the director of a major nonprofit organization agreed to let two members of the staff, who had plans to eventually open a catering service, provide the meal at an important planning meeting. The night before the meeting, the city was hit by a major snowstorm. Many of the attendees who came from different cities had been housed at a hotel across the street from the organization's headquarters. The meeting went on as scheduled, but one of the young women who was to cater the meal lived so far away from the city, she couldn't get in. The director, a noted gourmet and a fair cook himself, slipped out of the meeting from time to time to help the lone caterer.

When the lunch began, he announced to those assembled that since he was one of the cooks for the day, he wouldn't be able to join them at the table till later. Because one of the waiters had also failed to make it in, the director helped serve. Once the main course was served, the director took his place at the head of the table and joined the conversation. His guests teased him about getting them refills, and they asked about his availability if they were in need of such assistance. It turned out to be a lunch they all remembered.

It is easy to see why senior people at that organization roll up their sleeves to get the job done; why the whole staff stays late when work has to get done in a hurry, with all hands pitching in to meet a deadline. Helping cook and serve a meal in no way diminished the director's power; instead, it showed that he considered any work that helped the organization important.

Stories also help address questions and dispel rumors. In a company that is downsizing, for example, a major concern of employees is whether or not they will be fired and, if they are, what assistance the company will provide. If precedents have already been set, and there are stories about people who were retrained for other jobs or who were assisted through an outplacement program or who received generous severance packages, premature departures or time lost due to gossip behind closed doors are less likely.

Stories can be communicated to employees through the grapevine, recounted in the few minutes before a meeting begins, incorporated into speeches, or disseminated through newsletters when appropriate. There should be stories about rewards earned by those who perform above and beyond the call of duty. And there should be stories about those first-line managers who create an environment where work is more enjoyable and rewarding and who motivate others to higher levels of productivity as a result.

Organizational stories should be perpetuated because they reveal important information about the organization and influence employees by pulling them rather than pushing them toward their goals. Moreover, by providing information on past actions that indicate a likely course of future action, they give employees a sense of control. Among the questions people hesitate to ask, but that can be answered by stories, are:

- Does the company value ethical behavior over short-term business? If it's the last day of the sales month, and the numbers look lousy, are people still encouraged to do what is in the best interest of the client or are they asked to tread that fine line, selling something for the immediate gain even if that transaction may jeopardize the long-term relationship with the client?

- Are people rewarded only for the bottom line or for the development of their people as well? There should be stories about how individuals made it to the top of the organization and still kept the best interests of others in mind, rather than stepping on those in their way.

- Are people trustworthy, living up to their promises? Was a promise made and kept to a client even though circumstances have changed in such a way that such an agreement would now be prohibited? This sends a message to all employees, as well as customers, that the organization can be trusted.

- Are relationships lasting or made out of convenience? Are there stories about people who are always there to support you when you work for them, but when they get promoted seem to say to you, "I don't need you anymore so don't bother me. You have a new manager."

- Are employees treated with understanding when they have to take care of sick or elderly parent or child?

- What happens to someone who was once the star performer but is now having a streak of bad breaks?

Remember, however, that stories about actions that do not cast your organization in a good light are as likely to find their way into the common currency as are those you choose to emphasize. Stories that communicate an uncaring, hard, cold organization that considers employees unimportant cogs in a wheel are particularly damaging. No organization can long survive a multitude of stories about, for example, the person who worked for the organization for 16 years and then was fired because of a downturn in business. Rather than treating her with dignity and respect and thanking her for her contribution during all the good years, she was told she was no longer needed and escorted to her office to pack up, while someone stood guard and then escorted her out the door. That sends a message for all that stay. The story communicates the inhumanity of the organization.

The Role of First-Line Management

While leadership enrolls everyone in a common cause, first-line management should act as facilitators making sure that barriers to communication are removed. To do this, they must pay more than lip service to communication, training employees not only to become better presenters of information, but also better receivers. They must develop an environment that is conducive to building open, trusting, caring relationships between people—an environment that encourages new ideas and welcomes constructive feedback, and one in which management actively serves as a catalyst, first nurturing and then helping to disseminate new ideas.

The job of first-line managers is to be conscious of all the things that can create barriers to communication so that the organization can avoid them.

Barriers to Communication

Rigid Adherence to Organizational Charts. Managers must recognize that organizational charts may be misleading and inhibit communication. Although these charts are necessary to an organization, no organization should adhere to them so rigidly that they prevent the communication of ideas across departments, functional areas, and units.

Therefore, it is important that management realize that "organization charts in a company neither define relationships as they actually exist nor direct the lines of communication. If the organization does not exist in the minds and hearts of the people, it does not exist. No chart can fix that. An organization's function is simple: to provide a framework, a format, a context in which people can effectively use resources to accomplish their goals."[16] The problem is that organizational charts make it look as though communication should only flow vertically. Communication must flow across organizational and functional units as well.

Management Isolation. All too many managers do not communicate with employees, isolating themselves in various ways. Some CEOs do it by appearing in their offices infrequently because they spend so much of their time serving on boards of other organizations or making appearances at gatherings. First-line managers do it by spending most of their time in meetings with other managers, attending association meetings, and engaging in other outside activities.

If those managers guilty of isolation would think back to the fantastic productivity of small start-up companies, where five or so people work closely with the founder of the company, all giving enormously of themselves, they might rediscover the connection between productivity and communication. They might remember that if employees have to go through two secretaries to make an appointment that is then canceled and rescheduled, saying the company has an open-door policy is meaningless.

Managers must also keep in mind that creating impressive executive floors, having their secretaries construct what amounts to barbed wire enclosures around their offices, establishing perquisites—the corner office, parking spaces, separate executive floors, private washrooms, dining rooms, limos, lear jets, even flying first-class—that loudly proclaim who is the boss, all increase personal distance, lead to suspicion, and ensure that people are in awe of their leaders and feel that they are unapproachable.

The Development of Caste Systems. The caste system is also a barrier to communication. Think of the response of the employee "walking in from the back parking lot, through the snow, in zero-degree temperatures, [who] just before entering the building, sees one of the bosses pull his car into that sacred parking place....The employee thinks why doesn't the son of a bitch have to find a parking place like the rest of us? When that happens, the executive parking lot has just moved the business backward."[17]

There are other artificial barriers that create levels in the organization that inhibit internal communication. For example, does your organization encourage clear language, or are jargon and "insider" variations the norm? Are there opportunities for people at different levels of the organization and in different functional groups to spend time getting to know one another, or is there socializing along status lines only? Encouraging participation in a softball league or volunteering for such organizations as the Special Olympics all help to break down barriers between people.

The Existence of Physical Barriers. I wrote in my earlier book, *Marketing to Win*, that "distance poses another kind of problem in the workplace. Because people communicate most with those physically closest to them, people who are assembled in groups to work on special projects but spend most of their time in their usual workplaces tend to communicate less. Thomas Allen of MIT notes that 'beyond a distance of 25 or 30 yards, personal interaction drops off markedly.' That is why it is important for management to try to bring together as much as possible those who work together."[18] This can be done by providing meeting rooms or assigning people to different locations on a temporary basis.

The Ambiance Surrounding Meetings. Managers must be aware that the actual process of setting up a meeting and the non-verbal messages during the meeting often communicate as much as the content of the meeting itself. The answers to the following questions, for example, reveal an enormous amount about an organization's culture. How often are meetings held? Are people early or late for meetings? Where are meetings held? What is the layout of the room? Who gets invited? What is on the agenda? How is the agenda prepared? What is the order of the subjects on the agenda? What time is allotted to each subject? What time is the meeting held? Who is sitting next to the boss? Who introduces the speakers? Is the tone of the meeting formal or informal? What questions are asked at the meeting? How much dialogue is there? Is there give and take?

Consistency of Words and Actions.   Are the actions of your organization consistent with its policies? Does the organization, for example, say that it cares about innovation, but promote those who don't rock the boat? Does it say that it believes in rewarding high performance, but give across-the-board raises? Does it say it rewards creativity, but have such long, drawn-out approval processes that anyone with a new idea is quickly frustrated?

A glaring example of the failure to match words and actions was reported by Thomas Schellhardt in an article in *The Wall Street Journal*. Schellhardt pointed to an annual report issued by Utilicorp United that said that "behind its growth 'have been the dedication and professionalism of our employees.' Yet except for a picture of its chief executive, the report has only drawings of workers."[19] Consistency also means continuously reinforcing the message at appropriate times; for example, at one company, when "management invited small groups of employees to 'no holds barred' discussions to talk about company culture, goals, and the selling process [they discovered]...that employees hired within the past five years—more than 50% of the company's total population—believed their mission was to increase business, even if that meant neglecting existing accounts. In concentrating on expansion, management had not taken adequate steps to define and reinforce key cultural values for its new workforce. Rapid growth had weakened the company's culture at a critical time in its development."[20]

Political Warfare.   Some people hoard information for personal gain. They believe they increase their power when they know about a given subject and others are in the dark. Organizations must work to combat the idea that playing politics with information will bring personal gain. Organizations marked by politics, turf battles, and staff infighting lack adequate communication.

Listening. Everyone in the organization, from the top to the bottom, must communicate more effectively. In *Marketing to Win,* I pointed out that according to research, we spend seven out of every ten minutes that we are awake communicating, and that communication time is devoted 9 percent to writing, 16 percent to reading, 30 percent to speaking, and 45 percent to listening, and when report cards are given out for how well we listen, very few of us would receive passing grades. The barriers to listening include assuming a subject is uninteresting and tuning out, focusing on how something is said rather than what is said, reacting too quickly before the message is completed, picking up on emotional words and not hearing anything past that, listening only for facts rather than trying to absorb ideas, allowing yourself to be distracted, and avoiding hearing about subjects you don't understand. Everyone must learn to overcome these barriers.[21]

Effective Internal Communication

The most difficult barriers to communication are erected by those who do not acknowledge that communication in the future will take different forms than it has in the past. Thus, management must find ways to encourage the use of new technologies and support different forms of communication. It must view information as a competitive weapon, not as a threat; it must support knowledge and learning at every level. Effective internal communication must be:

- Multidirectional—upward, downward, lateral, diagonal
- Objective—expressing all sides of an issue
- Comprehensive—both in breadth of subject and depth of content
- Relevant—expressing issues that are meaningful, for example, providing the rationale behind policies

- Credible—expressed by those in the know
- Inviting—cutting through the information clutter
- Honest—truthful, factual, and error free
- Open—a fair and open exchange of ideas, bad as well as good news
- Thorough—contain more rather than less information
- Prioritized—ranked in importance so people don't feel bombarded
- Timely—so that they don't have to go to other sources to get the information
- Consistent—actions consistent with words
- Appealing—easy to scan and understand
- Frequent—disseminated at regular intervals
- Reinforced—through multiple mediums
- Coordinated—in line with other communication elements
- Participatory—involve the audience
- Measurable—undergo regular evaluation to determine effectiveness on target audience

The Flow of Information

Rather than thinking that communication only flows downward or upward in an organization, conforming to organization charts, it is everyone's job to encourage it to flow laterally and diagonally as well, breaking down the compartmentalization of knowledge. In this scenario, information sharing would exist between different levels, departments, and business units of an organization.

Downward Communication

According to an A. Foster Higgins & Company survey, "more than one third (34%) of the CEOs indicated that they communicate with other CEOs daily or weekly. Forty-three percent said that they communicate with customers daily or weekly. Fifty-nine percent communicate daily or weekly with professional and technical staff; and fully 98% communicate daily or weekly with other top managers. Yet only 22% of the surveyed CEOs reported that they communicate daily or weekly with their company's rank-and-file employees."[22]

According to another study, while "top executives are a preferred information source for 62 percent of employees, only 15 percent of employees tell us that they are currently receiving information from their organizations' leaders."[23] Even when the form of communication is formal, involving a review, some 33 percent of employees don't believe that their last performance appraisal helped them to understand what was expected of them.[24] Downward communication is just not working.

Leaders can dream up all sorts of excuses for failing to communicate: "I don't have the time." "Why ask them anyway? I know how they feel." "I don't think they'll be able to handle negative information; it will just demoralize them." "They won't understand the implications of the decision, so why bother explaining." "It's sensitive, and I'm afraid that someone might spill the beans." And sometimes executives just aren't confident enough to address the group: They are worried about being asked questions that they might not be able to handle. And, of course, there is always the potential for disagreement.

Then there is the problem of the executive who pays visits to various offices of the organization. The visits include arriving with an entourage, flying through the offices so quickly that no one is ever sure that he came, except for the fact that in anticipation of the visit employees have been tidying up the office for the prior two weeks. Executives all too often fail to realize that because their position alone intimidates employees, they must overcompensate for that reaction.

And even if employees find access to management easy, "too many bosses don't know how to talk to employees and too many employees are afraid to talk to their bosses. As a result, both groups are left stranded on the opposite banks of the same river, struggling toward a common goal but separated by a current of unshared information, stymied good intentions, misunderstandings, and fear."[25]

Upward Communication

First-line managers can create an open environment where employees are willing to share their hopes, ideas, feelings, fears, criticisms; all it requires is that they be sensitive and empathetic to the needs of employees. According to a study of 5000 workers nationwide surveyed in 1987 by the Boston-based Wyatt Company, only 40 percent said that management seeks their input on important issues; about 25 percent said they had no freedom to express opinions.[26]

A good example of the success that can be achieved by working together is found in this story told by Jack Shewmaker, former vice chairman and CFO of Wal-Mart. Shewmaker said that he

> remembers when in 1975, 14 out of the 100-plus stores were doing poorly, and management decided to confront the problem at the grass roots level. Sam Walton, chairman and founder and the rest of the management team visited all these stores....On our visit to each store we simply said, you're doing lousy. We may have to close this store, though we've never done it before (or since for that matter) for lack of performance. We know you don't want us to do that, so tell us what we should do to be more successful.
>
> At first, the suggestions were seemingly minor, such as moving a clock from one wall to the next, or installing a new clock. In my own mind I wondered what difference does it make? So we'd either move the clock, or go out and buy a new one and mount it on the wall. We went through three or four suggestions of the same scope. Then all of a sudden, they began to talk about what they could do to change the store. It wasn't a question of what management had to do, because management was receptive and attentive. It was what they had to do. Ten years later, management returned to those same 14 stores, which Wal-Mart had considered closing. All but one were among the top 10 percent as profit producers.[27]

There are many ways to encourage the kind of upward communication that made Wal-Mart such a success. For example, you might try management by walking around. In some organizations, executives randomly select a cross section of their employees to have breakfast with. In other organizations, advisory councils are set up and selected employees from all areas of the organization serve on them for a specified period of time. Others have one-day meetings to address a timely problem or to spur new life into a project. Other organizations have various programs to encourage employees to communicate.

> Suggestion systems and speak out programs are increasingly common. IBM uses a mail-in system, 'Speak up,' which allows employees to get individual responses to questions from high-level managers while maintaining their anonymity. Employees indicate their names and addresses, but these are removed by the 'Speak up' director and kept separately. When an appropriate executive has supplied an answer, it is mailed to the employee's home. Alternately, the employee may request a face-to-face or telephone response. Many large companies, including Anheuser-Busch and Eastman Kodak, now have similar programs.[28]

Other kinds of programs include setting up telephone hot lines, holding focus-group meetings, and having skip-level meetings where managers meet with employees two levels under their direct reports.

In order for these programs to work effectively, every question or idea must be taken seriously. The results of the initiative must be reported to management and to employees. The program should include a plan for action. Many programs fall short because management only looks for big ideas rather than for ways to make big strides from incremental gains.[29]

Lateral Communication

Employees must know and understand how their actions affect others in the organization, and they must be held accountable for the impact of their decisions on other areas of the firm. Changes must be communicated among peer levels, within and between departments, and between shifts. Keep in mind the story of the new CEO who on one of his first days on the job asked for a copy of every report used in management. He said that "the next day, 23 of them appeared on my desk. I didn't understand them. The manufacturing reports were written in manufacturing language, the finance reports in finance language, and the sales reports in sales language....Each area's reports were Greek to the other areas, and all of them were Greek to me. Since we had to start cutting costs and products, we were going to have to do a lot of talking, but until we had a single market-driven language, we weren't going to have any common management information to talk about."[30]

The emphasis placed on vertical communication often overshadows the importance of lateral communication, which includes sharing information with those on the same level as you, but in different departments, or business units. But, "according to a recent survey, more than 60% of employees in a variety of organizations say that lateral communication is ineffective. More specifically about 45% say communication between peers within departments is inadequate, and 70% claim that communication between departments must improve."[31]

When employees don't share information, efforts are duplicated, deadlines are missed, redundancies occur, rework increases, and interdepartmental relationships deteriorate. When coworkers don't communicate with one another, people become task oriented and forget to take other departments into consideration. These problems also occur when employees become so focused on achieving their own departmental goals that they don't want to be bothered by problems that they believe don't really concern them. In such cases, work delegated laterally doesn't get done because everyone is looking to optimize their own personal interests even at the expense of the organization. Furthermore, inaction occurs when employees are accountable only to their supervisors and not at all accountable to their peers.

Regular information exchanges between employees about projects they are working on, processes they go through, and problems they encounter are important. But in many organizations, employees communicate laterally only when a crisis or problem develops. As a result, they often don't understand the products being sold in other business units around the organization, the effect their work has on others, or who to contact for information in other departments.

There are many ways to foster communication within an organization. For example, there is the planning process. Plans are far easier to implement when employees take part in the planning process. Rather than have some staff group or consulting firm far removed from the day-to-day action develop plans in isolation, management should see to it that employees are involved in the strategic planning process. In addition, drawing groups from different parts of the organization into the planning process fosters comaraderie and helps gain employee buy-in. In addition, planning sessions provide an opportunity to meet with colleagues in different areas of the organization and gain a better understanding about the problems and issues others face. Other ways of providing healthy forums for communication across departments, functional areas, and units include establishing temporary task forces, job-rotation programs, and organizationwide training programs.

Diagonal Communication

In order for diagonal communication to flourish, employees must be free to contact and network with anyone who has the information necessary to accomplish an activity, without regard to level, business unit, or other artificial boundary. This should include external networking. Management must actively develop forums encouraging employees to get to know people, build shared values, discuss emerging issues, and solve joint problems.

By dividing knowledge, you fail to allow people the opportunity to see the big picture. The only way to succeed is for communication to flow downward, upward, lateral, and diagonal. Each plays an important role, and if all coexist, you end up with the kind of organization described by John Young, CEO of Hewlett-Packard, who said that "communication is pretty fundamental....We have the kind of company that is one team. There's no them-and-us managers or workers, and even though we have 40 companies around the world, 55 operating divisions, we think of the company as a single enterprise and everybody's a member. So good communication is a centerpiece of the way we approach employee relationships."[32]

Honest, Open Communication

Does your organization run on the need-to-know principle, because you are afraid to communicate with your employees out of fear that the information you give them may fall into the hands of a competitor? Donald E. Petersen, former chairman of the Ford Motor Company, says: "One of our fundamental objectives is to establish trust with our employees. One avenue is by communicating with them honestly on the facts about the company, its actions and its points of view. This must include our problems and controversies, as well as our attributes and achievements....Good news and bad."[33]

Petersen's approach is very different from the philosophy of sharing only enough information with employees to enable them to do a specific job. Organizations subscribing to such an approach say that they don't think their employees would understand more, that their employees can't be trusted with sensitive data, or that their employees are not productive when time is spent communicating. This is typical of many companies. In *Rude Awakening: The Rise, Fall, and Struggle for Recovery of General Motors,* Maryann Keller says that American companies "tend, fundamentally, to mistrust workers. There is a pervading attitude that if you give them an inch, they'll take a mile, because they don't really want to work....More than anything else, GM's philosophy on people has contributed to its loss of the competitive edge. There is no trust. No respect."[34]

Communication serves as an important coordination function, and access to information is so fundamental to doing our jobs properly that it must not be considered a privilege but a right. At a time when we need new ideas from our employees, the information that we give them serves as the fundamental building blocks and catalysts to stimulate those new ideas.

When in doubt, it is always better to err on the side of providing too much information than too little. People who don't provide needed information forget how much time people lose second-guessing other people's intentions and the costs of gamesmanship, politics, and maneuvering to get information. The irony of it all is that these are usually the same people who say they can't understand why their organization isn't one happy family.

Wal-Mart sees open, honest communication as a key to success. Jack Shewmaker explains that

> the Company was not afraid to challenge a widespread assumption on the part of management that holds that it's risky to tell company employees too much about the business for fear that competition will find out. We decided that it was important that every single person associated with our company understands our mission, understands our direction, understands our progress or lack of it, and understands his or her role in making Wal-Mart a better company tomorrow than it is today.
>
> By withholding information from Wal-Mart's employees, we were penalizing the very people who needed some way of measuring their contribution to the company, he says. Today, Wal-Mart issues monthly operating data, including every loss, every charge for every operating division of the company. It comes out a few days after the end of every month. Every department manager, every sales clerk gets finite data on his or her department compared with everyone else's in that particular store, in the district, in the region, in the industry. Not only do they get the information, we expect them to understand it and make use of it.[35]

The New Way to Communicate

Internal communication has gone through several phases. The first phase was similar to the military model: Orders were given and obeyed. There was no opportunity to provide input into the process. The second phase of communication involved the bilateral flow of information. Instructions were still communicated down to employees, but feedback was possible through formal means and selected channels. The third phase of communication encouraged two-way communication. The value of listening to employees was recognized and mechanisms for doing so were created. The fourth phase of internal communication recognized the value of multichannels. Just as some communication vehicles are more efficient and cost effective when communicating to the external environment, some mediums are better when communicating internally; very sophisticated techniques were applied to employee communication. In the fifth phase, intimacy is introduced but even with timely mediums like daily video broadcasts, employees' information needs still aren't being met.

It is the sixth phase, the one at which the control of communication is abandoned, that organizations must strive to reach. In this phase, communication is continuous, the responsibility not of any single individual but of everyone within the organization. It is at this phase that good organizations stop dealing with only the "tip of the iceberg" as far as communications are concerned. They no longer send a flurry of memos, letters, reports, and policy statements. "We think that 90 percent of what goes on in an organization has nothing to do with formal events....Even in the context of a highly controlled meeting, there is a lot of informal communication going on—bonding, rituals, glances, innuendos, and so forth. The real process of making decisions, of gathering support, of developing opinions, happens before the meeting—or after. In a strong culture, the network is powerful because it can reinforce the busy beliefs of the organization, enhance the symbolic value of heroes by passing on stories of their deeds and accomplishments, set a new climate for change, and provide a tight structure of influence for the CEO."[36]

Networking, or the grapevine, is at the heart of the sixth phase. It will be enhanced and formalized as a result of the changes that are taking place in technology and the comfort level of today's workers with those advances. After all, the baby boomers, having grown up with electronics, are very comfortable communicating through that medium. For example, Alvie Smith, formerly of General Motors, writes that "at Tandem all employees, except factory assemblers, have an electronic work station on their desk. They are hooked into the company's worldwide network. Through it they can communicate both business and social information. One employee told me 'You can take away everything, but don't touch my computer.' Helping people communicate directly with each other rather than through a hierarchical protocol builds trust."[37]

Of course, networking is not likely to replace other forms of communication overnight, but people will turn to it and to small-group interaction more and more because they are highly personal. In networking, the message is usually delivered by someone you know and trust, as opposed to someone who may be trying to give you the company line or who is far removed from the issue. The message is never discussed in generalities, but is always customized. Furthermore, you always have the chance to discuss the implications of what is said. Such personal communication is expressed with passion and received with great interest, but on the downside, the information is not always accurate.

Accessible, affordable, easy-to-use technology, which is the means to formalize networking, will help create an open, honest environment, especially when combined with the elimination of communication barriers and the commitment of great leaders who seize every opportunity to communicate the guiding principles and the beliefs and values of the organization. For just as the stars were used to navigate ships in the night, these guiding principles dictate what is important, how decisions are made, how people are rewarded, who gets promoted, what kinds of people join the organization, and how they communicate with one another. One value that should be communicated to employees is the company's main reason for existence: to provide service excellence to its clients and customers, as we shall see in Chapter 5.

5

If I Only Had One Client

Building an Organization
Devoted to
Service Excellence

*If I only had one client, if my whole busi-
ness and livelihood was solely dependent
on that one client—boy, would I treat
that client differently than I treat my
clients now. That client would really be
special to me.*
OVERHEARD IN AN ELEVATOR

Even though your company may have hundreds or even thousands of clients, some large and some small, each deserves to be
treated as your only client. In all too many companies, however,
no client is treated as special. Why do companies make it so difficult to do business with them? Why do offices look drab and
dirty? Why are proposals filled with typos and promises broken
with regularity? Why are customers ignored, talked down to,
and treated as inconveniences? Why are employees indifferent,

careless, even rude? Why aren't employees well trained, why don't they know their own products, and why can't they even answer basic questions? When problems surface, why are customers passed around the office like hot potatoes? And why is the typical reaction to a customer: "I know it all and you know nothing," "It's not my job," or "I'm right; you're wrong."

This attitude has become all too typical in business. *AdWeek's Marketing Week* reports that "from 1966 to 1983 the Lou Harris polling organization found that the number of Americans with 'a great deal of confidence' in professional institutions fell precipitously. In medicine, it fell from 61% to 36%. A recent Gallup poll found that two of every three Americans believe doctors are `too interested in making money.' Another recent Harris poll revealed that only 13% of Americans have 'a great deal of confidence in lawyers,' the lowest rating among 13 separate categories...." The mom-and-pop law firm and the laid-back family doctor who had time to sit and chat no longer exist, says Samuel S. Smith, chairman of the American Bar Association's commission on outreach: "One doesn't really get the chance to establish the kind of relationship you'd like. You've got 20 other cases waiting for attention, and you're expected to charge hundreds of dollars an hour for your time."[1]

The impact of such low levels of service is staggering. One reason this problem is often neglected is that today's accounting systems do not accurately reflect the true costs and benefits of client relationships. For example, they ignore cash flows over the lifetime of the relationship because accounting practices do not reflect the fact that it is easier and five times cheaper to keep an existing client than to recruit a new one.[2] As a result, many people think of each sales transaction as an isolated event, rather than as an investment in building a lifelong relationship with a customer; they believe if a transaction is handled badly, the cost is the loss of a single sale.

Unfortunately, the costs of this short-term thinking go even deeper than a loss of unhappy customers: a Technical Assistance Research Programs study says that the average person who has been burned by a company tells nine to ten colleagues about the experience, and 13 percent of dissatisfied customers will spread the bad news to more than twenty people.[3]

The *Q* Word

Overcoming the tendency to treat customers poorly—and the costs of doing so—will require a new focus on quality service. In fact, providing quality service has been shown to lead to market expansion and even makes premium pricing possible. In a Forum Corporation survey of 2374 customers from 14 organizations, more than 40 percent listed poor service as the number one reason for switching to the competition, while only 8 percent listed price.[4] And, according to the Strategic Planning Institute's Profit Impact for Marketing Strategy (PIMS) database, companies rated highly by their customers for service charge on average 9 percent more than those rated poorly.[5]

Until recently, however, the term *quality* primarily applied to manufacturing. When people talked of quality, they referred to the workmanship of a product and to the number of defects found in products coming off the assembly line. Companies were able to differentiate their products and their organizations based on manufacturing prowess. It has finally become clear, however, that while the manufacturing process is important, it is only part of the quality equation. Due to global competition, companies have placed so much emphasis on, and have made such great strides in, the production process that, in the future, it will be very difficult to differentiate products solely on the basis of workmanship. The difference between products will be so infinitesimal that much more will be needed to win the loyalty of the marketplace. As discussed in Chapter 1, there will be growing emphasis on intangibles as a way to satisfy customers.

This emphasis is even more important in the services industry where the products themselves are often intangibles and where precise specifications cannot be set and where production and consumption of many services are inseparable. There, quality will be defined universally as meeting and exceeding the expectations of customers—that is, everything leading up to, during, and after the sale. Customers will feel that the cost of the service is measured not only in dollar outlay, but in psychological costs such as convenience, cachet of the organization and of the product, and risk associated with the acquisition, which will be discussed in greater detail in Chapter 10.

Since superior client service is as much a mind-set as it is an activity, it is important to discover just what kind of culture produces that mind-set. Ask yourself:

- Is your organization willing to make policy changes to make your life or a client's life better?

- Does your company tend to take clients for granted because they've been clients for a long time?

- Do your company's employees do their best work only after the competition has made inroads?

- Do your company's employees know that their first and foremost job is to service clients?

- Are your company's policies geared to the long-term success of your clients or only to your firm's quick profits?

- How well do you really understand your clients' businesses? How much do they know about yours?

- Do you know why clients are happy or unhappy with your company's services? What steps have you taken to find out?

- Are you accessible when your clients need you?

- In what areas do you treat your clients differently now than you did when you were courting them?

- Are you so concerned about losing your clients that you stop making innovative suggestions?

- Do you encourage and reward employee performance that is in the best interests of clients?

The Long-Term Consequences of Your Actions

If organizations are to deliver service excellence, their employees must learn to recognize the value of building long-term relationships with clients and understand the consequences of not doing so. They must abandon the view that clients represent no more than immediate sales transactions and a quick way to increase commission checks. Instead, they must treat clients on the basis of potential business that they may receive over the years. They must learn to see themselves through their customers' eyes rather than focusing inwardly. They must go beyond playing a selling role and offer advice and information that provides added value to buyers and recognizes their ongoing needs. They will concentrate on building ongoing relationships with a few clients instead of endlessly searching for new prospects and then losing them as they focus on yet new leads.

Taking a Holistic View

Many organizations are divided into separate profit centers that market their services to clients as though each profit center were an entirely different company; they forget that, from the perspective of clients, they are part of one company. When important clients of one division of an organization receive calls from a representative of another who treats them as a first-time buyer, the client thinks the organization is disorganized.

Furthermore, when organizations fail to really think about the needs of their customers and to tailor or cluster services to meet those needs, they provide inadequate levels of service. For example, travel agents planning clients' vacations try to make their trips as pleasurable as possible. They help them select and then book hotels; choose the best means of travel, from direct flights to scenic routes to car rental specials; and arrange their itineraries. They deal with all the specifics of their vacation, sparing them time and trouble.

This kind of holistic approach aids in building long-lasting client relationships. When a business or service fails to approach problems in this way, they perform a disservice to their clients. For example, when individuals are ill, they often undergo many tests to determine what is ailing them. When patients see several specialists who fail to coordinate their findings, it becomes the responsibility of sick patients to describe the test results to each doctor they see, adding a needless burden at an already difficult time.

A holistic approach can be demonstrated by sales representatives who understand the inner workings of their own organizations. If there is a problem, clients assume that salespeople will know who to go to for answers. When a customer has a question or a problem, it is a mistake to say, "I am in sales, speak to someone in service" or "The person who originally helped you isn't here now" or "Since the merchandise was purchased from a different branch it has to be returned there." Only when organizations view themselves from the perspective of their clients will they build lifelong customer loyalty.

The Road to Quality

According to the book *Delivering Quality Service,* there are 10 factors that customers use to measure service quality:[6]

1. Tangibles—Appearance of physical facilities, equipment, personnel and communication materials
2. Reliability—Ability to perform the promised service dependably and accurately
3. Responsiveness—Willingness to help customers and provide prompt service
4. Competence—Possession of the required skills and knowledge to perform the service
5. Courtesy—Politeness, respect, consideration, and friendliness of contact personnel
6. Credibility—Trustworthiness, believability, honesty of the service provider
7. Security—Freedom from danger, risk, or doubt
8. Access—Approachability and ease of contact
9. Communication—Keeping customers informed in language they can understand and listening to them
10. Understanding the customer—Making the effort to know customers and their needs

These 10 critical factors will be used as the framework for the discussion that follows.

Tangibles

Customers gain their first impression of your organization by the way their phone calls are handled and from the advertisements that your organization runs. When they visit you for the first time, they notice whether your building is attractive and whether the people are friendly and appropriately dressed. They notice whether the technology you use is obsolete or leading edge and whether your new business proposal was professionally prepared. After they buy a product, customers measure you by the service they receive and how easy it is to understand your billing.

Pride in Your Work. Spelling the client's name wrong, preparing a report without checking that all the data is accurate, or providing an estimate with numbers that do not add up leaves a bad taste in your client's mouth. Everything must be read and proofread before it goes out the door. As soon as a typo appears, even in a cover memo, clients feel you are careless and sloppy and lose confidence in your ability to deliver; they fear that lack of care and precision may carry over to the work you do for them.

It's Not Enough to Be on When You're on Stage. Some people feel a proposal can look sloppy as long as the final product will be of high quality, that being late for meetings is all right as long as they are on time when they are really needed, that an implied promise doesn't have to be kept, but "real" ones do. They believe that as long as they are conservatively dressed at business meetings with clients, they can dress any way they want to when they meet with clients after hours. The fact is that trust is a result of accumulated impressions and experiences, and a customer's lack of confidence in one area can easily spread to another.

The Small Details. There is no way to overemphasize the point that every impression is an important one. In *Customers for Life,* Carl Sewell and Paul B. Brown point out that clients look at everything in your organization as a sign of its quality. They ask themselves questions such as, "If that's how they take care of their restrooms, how'll they take care of me?"[7] If the flip-down trays in an airplane are dirty, are the airplanes properly maintained? Clients notice whether phone calls are answered promptly and whether those who answer the phones take the time to find the right person for them to talk with. They learn to trust organizations that send them directions before their first visit and take the time to include descriptions of places to see and restaurants to go to. And they appreciate congratulatory notes on a job promotion, the birth of a child, or even a postcard from a vacation. It is not the expense of the items, but the indication that you remembered them that builds relationships.

Providing What the Client Needs. Clients don't buy products; they buy solutions. Never tell a customer that your product is the best until you know how they plan to use it. Rosabeth Moss Kanter wrote in *Harvard Business Review* that "products derive their meaning and value only from the uses to which customers put them."[8] Many companies are so close to their products that they compare product features with those of their competitors and wrongfully conclude that their products are best for everyone. It is important to determine how products will be used and compare only those particular features that address specific client needs. Kanter went on to explain that a "senior executive was widely quoted as saying, 'if customers don't like our solutions, they have the wrong problems.'"[9]

Friendship Should Never Be a Substitute for Quality. Getting to know your clients and nurturing your relationships with them is good business, but friendship should never be substituted for good work. People often believe they can provide inferior products or cut corners if they wine and dine their clients. If the products you deliver are inadequate, or if you don't provide products that address customers' needs, how nice you are won't matter.

Pricing. As Sewell and Brown said in *Customers for Life*, "You can shear a sheep for many years, but you can only skin it once."[10] As a general rule of thumb, don't charge customers for anything that you wouldn't charge a friend for. According to an article in *Manager's Journal*,

> All too often "the client is charged for the conversation in which he explains the problem to the senior partner....The client is charged for the senior telling the junior what the client told him....The client is charged for the junior calling

the client to clarify some points....The client is charged for the senior reviewing the work of the junior....The client is charged for the time the senior uses to explain the work to the client....The client is charged for all the time it takes the involved lawyers to figure out how much time they should bill the client for the work....The client is sent the bill, and two months later, the client is sent another bill for xeroxing, telephones, delivery, etc...."[11]

A client treated in such a manner will soon find someone else to work with.

Stay within Budget.   Be sure to get approval before you spend a dime of your clients' money. Submit a written estimate and update it if the scope of the work changes. If it exceeds budget, make sure you promptly notify your clients in writing. Even when the changes that increase the cost of projects were asked for by clients, notify them; they may not realize the cost implications of their requests.

Reliability

When customers see advertisements or product literature claiming a product will perform in a specified way, they want to know that there is no fine print. They want to know that if your organization claims merchandise can be returned if it does not provide complete satisfaction, they can return it without a hassle. Customers want to know that you will keep your word. When you make a promise and say, "You'll have it by Friday" or "I'll get back to you early next week" or "I'll put it in the mail today," they want to know it will happen. Furthermore, customers want to know that you can follow instructions, that work will be performed right the first time, and that they can be assured of consistency; they want to know that the service will be delivered the same way every time.

Be Organized.   It is often a mistake to let your paperwork fall behind in an effort to complete additional work for your client. Misunderstandings often develop because discussions were not put in writing. Furthermore, clients want you to have answers at the tip of your tongue; they do not want to hear "I'll get back to you," because you don't remember the details about their accounts or can't find their files because of the clutter on your desk. Finally, clients want your record keeping to be up to date, and they want to be billed promptly, not three months after work is completed.

Be Prepared for Meetings.   Be sure that you go into meetings with formal agendas and goals. Don't wait till the eleventh hour to finish your work and then fumble around during a presentation because you don't have the materials ready. Make sure that you have rehearsed your presentation and eliminated any redundancies, the slide projector is in good working order, you have an extra light bulb for the projector in case the original one burns out, the group next door won't be noisy, and you know where the light switches are and where the thermostat is.

Provide Service "Above and Beyond the Call of Duty."   In *Close to the Customer,* James Donnelly points out that "there are some conditions in every service encounter that operate primarily to dissatisfy customers when they are present. However, the absence of these conditions does not create or build strong customer satisfaction...that is, when they are not present, the best you can do is achieve no dissatisfaction among customers."[12]

This concept is known as expected service: it involves a level and kind of service that is expected and taken for granted. For example, no client will ever get excited if you show up at a meeting on schedule, if a project is produced within budget, or if billing is accurate. But if you're late for a meeting, go over budget, or produce billing errors, it is fairly certain that the client will get upset. It's like being responsible for the payroll of a company. No one ever says thank-you when a paycheck is correct, but the phone rings off the wall if there is a problem.

On the other hand, according to Donnelly, there are some conditions in every service encounter that, when present, can build high levels of customer satisfaction. If these conditions are not present, they do not prove highly dissatisfying to the customer. In these cases, while the absence of any action goes unnoticed, action can result in satisfaction. For example, when you bring in your car to be serviced and the mechanic not only fixes your problem, but finds something else wrong and fixes it at no charge, you are extremely pleased because you didn't ask for it. But if they didn't address the problem, you would never know it. Other examples include a doctor calling you up a week after a procedure to see how you are feeling, a teacher calling a parent to find out how a former pupil is doing, or a computer salesman calling up two weeks after a product purchase to see if you are experiencing any problems.

Donnelly says that it is important to "concentrate first on identifying and then eliminating the causes of dissatisfaction because, as we mentioned, these are what cause customers to leave....Having eliminated opportunities for dissatisfaction, you can devote resources to satisfying and delighting your customers after you have determined that such opportunities exist and what they are."[13]

Responsiveness

Customers want to know that their business is valued and that you will be helpful and responsive to their needs. They don't want to see three people chatting behind a desk while they wait in line. They don't want to be told that you don't have the time to meet with them as promised because a "big" client is coming in that day.

Timeliness. Time is one of our most valuable resources. Being late shows a lack of respect for everyone else's time. Think about how you feel when you have a 10 o'clock meeting and the person you are meeting arrives 20 minutes late—and then doesn't even offer an apology. Of course, there are occasions when it is impossible to be on time—planes are delayed by weather, children and spouses become ill, a truck delivering an item breaks down. When such delays occur, your response is important to your future relationship. The least you should do is call clients and warn them that you are running late. Remember that clients also appreciate being given regular updates when there are delays in a large project or in fulfilling an order.

It is also important to respect your clients' time and answer requests in a timely and responsive fashion. Keep in mind that, according to *The Journal of Services Marketing,*

The perceived value of time is key in evaluating customers' waiting experiences. Time, then, like money is a scarce resource to be allocated among competing uses. When two customers who value their time differently experience the same service wait, they are paying different prices....Expectations of waiting for service are also related to the amount of choice that the individual perceives he or she has in the situation. Lack of control creates stress which may intensify if continued....When customers feel the purchase decision is forced on them, as in buying necessities and making routine purchases, the lack of control over the situation can make waiting time unbearable.[14]

There are a number of ways to ease the burden of waiting. For example, theme parks such as Disney World make the wait a part of a positive experience, with entertainment. Waiting can also be made more comfortable by acknowledging how long the wait will be: "This plane is fourth in line for takeoff." Waiting is also made easier when concern is displayed. The idea is to ease the perception of delay. For example, if a report is taking longer than expected to produce, even if the problem is the result of changes requested by the client, getting the covers to the client "hot off the press" makes the waiting period easier. The client knows that progress is being made.

Make Certain That Your Company's Policies Do Not Cost You Clients.   Companies often place policies and procedures ahead of clients. When employees are told to follow the rules or else, when they are given no leeway to use common sense, customer relations—and company reputations—suffer. Everyone can recount experiences that caused frustration. For example: You purchase a computer and discover faulty software. You call up the company you bought the computer from to see if they can send you a new copy of the software overnight. They explain that company policy requires returning the software to the nearest software dealer (a 30-mile drive) or mailing it to the manufacturer, which will send you a replacement (in three to four weeks). If the company stopped to examine the problem, it might make an arrangement with the software vendor to make such exchanges themselves.

Or, take the story Jim Donnelly tells in *Close to the Customer:*

I was browsing in the fabulous Water Tower Place, a collection of some of the finest stores in the world. I spotted a sweater in the window of a department store that I wanted very much. Unfortunately, I was informed by a salesperson that the store was out of stock in all sizes and would not be getting any more in. Disappointed, I left the store. As I walked past the window display and took one more glance at the sweater I wanted so much, I was delighted to see that it was my size. Excited, I returned to the store and found the same salesperson.

'It might be a bit hard to reach,' I said, 'but the one in the window is my size.' 'Oh sir,' the salesperson informed me, 'we never take anything out of the window.' 'Never,' I asked. 'Do you mean that that sweater will be in the window for the rest of my life?' She informed me that it was company policy not to take anything out of the window.

I pleaded that since there were none in stock in any size and no additional stock was coming in, all this policy could possibly result in was one lost sale and more disappointed customers like me. And she could avoid all of these problems by selling me this sweater. I've had to learn to live without the sweater.[15]

Unfortunately, when employees are forced to choose between the best interests of clients or doing what management wants, they often do the latter. That is why management must empower employees to break rules when it is in the best interests of clients. For example, if the cashier on the express line has no one waiting, he should be able to take the next person on an adjoining line with more than the limited number of items. An employee who is allowed to make such judgments will learn to spot problems that arise and then act on them.

Resolving Client Problems.   When customers call with problems, many employees who can't resolve them simply transfer them to someone else. They don't take the time to find out who the right person is. They forget how frustrating it is to be bounced from person to person. In these situations, employees should be taught to remain on the phone with customers until they resolve the problem or find the right person to transfer the caller to. Employees might also take callers' numbers, do the legwork, and then promptly get back with answers. Employees must be taught that they represent the entire organization and that customer satisfaction is everyone's responsibility. Passing the buck and transferring clients from person to person only results in the loss of customers.

Accepting Blame When a Problem Occurs. Instead of pointing fingers at another part of their organization or even blaming the customer, employees must learn to acknowledge problems and solve them. When clients complain, it is important to first understand their problems and then resolve them as quickly as possible. After the problems are satisfactorily resolved, the cause must be uncovered, not to cast blame, but to make sure the problems don't happen again.

In fact, the way a problem is handled often shows how much you care about the client. Surveys show that you can win back between 54 percent and 70 percent of clients by satisfactorily resolving their complaints. Indeed, about 95 percent of dissatisfied clients will become loyal customers again if their complaints are properly handled. But be careful; do not assume that you are hearing all of the complaints. According to a Technical Assistance Research Programs study, "On average 1 in 4 customers is unhappy enough with customer service to leave an organization. But of all those that are unhappy, 26 out of 27 will not complain."[16] Indeed, a study by the U.S. Office of Consumer Affairs reveals that consumers don't complain because they believe complaining is a waste of their time and effort (no one wants to hear about their problems); moreover, they report that they do not know how to complain, especially, where to lodge complaints.[17]

Competence

Customers want to know that employees are properly trained. They want employees to know their own product lines, be able to answer questions, and know their own organizations well enough to solve customer problems. Customers also want to be certain that employees are up to date about new product developments and advances in their fields.

Trainees. Many companies use the term *trainee* to describe new employees going through an extensive training period to learn the company philosophy, the product line, competitive offerings, and so forth. Employees shouldn't feel that once they have completed their initial training programs they can stop learning. It is just as important to keep up with new products and competitive offerings two years after joining the organization as when you start. In fact, employees should never stop learning.

Product Knowledge. When customers meet employees who cannot answer questions about their products, they assume that the company hasn't properly trained them or that they don't care about the impression they give customers.

Product training can be accomplished through such methods as formal internal training programs, laboratories where employees have hands-on experience with competitors' products, providing employees with new products before announcing them, or working with clients to discover how they actually use products.

Courtesy

Remember that every client wants to feel special. No one likes to be treated like a number, or receive letters addressed to "Dear Customer," when they have been a loyal client for years. When clients hear you are canceling your meeting with them because something "came up" with another client, or feel they are receiving poor service because they are considered a small client, your relationship with them is in jeopardy. Every customer expects employees to be pleasant, to know their personal nuances, and to offer explanations in a clear and noncondescending manner. And perhaps most important, clients do not want to be taken for granted just because they have been clients for a long time.

Respect. Be courteous to everyone you work with, not just the person who signs your check. No one wants to spend time with people who make them feel uncomfortable or inadequate. You should never underestimate the influence someone may have; for example, many secretaries have tremendous power because of their access to the boss.

Admit Fault.   Poor service is all too commonplace, but that does not make it acceptable; customers deserve an apology every time they receive less than adequate service. For example, an airline captain who apologizes for a delay and adds, "Sorry we are late in arriving, but our policy is safety first," soothes the ire of a late passenger. When was the last time that a dentist apologized for keeping you waiting? Or the maitre d' of a restaurant apologized because your table wasn't ready and offered you a complimentary glass of wine? Don't be afraid to admit mistakes. Sometimes saying "I'm sorry" or adding a simple "Thank-you" goes a long way. No one is perfect and your clients appreciate someone who is straightforward and sensitive to their needs.

Use Your Clients' Products.   Clients want to know that their suppliers are loyal. Make sure that you don't insult a client by using a competitor's product. Doing so says that you don't believe in them, and leads them to ask if they should continue giving you their business.

Be Careful about Hiring Clients' Employees.   Never hire someone who works for a client unless the client approves it in advance. Even if you handle the situation tactfully, however, you may find that the person you hired, while competent, has a poor relationship with people in his or her former organization.

Use Special Care with Out-of-Town Clients.   There is nothing worse than traveling out of town to visit a client and then demonstrating that you are anxious to leave as soon as you get there. For example, be careful not to ask them to confirm your travel arrangements for the trip home as soon as you arrive. Moreover, when you visit a client, you should make it clear that you are available as long as they need you. You should also try to arrive the evening before a morning meeting to be sure you are not late for the meeting or exhausted because you left at the crack of dawn.

Be a Good Sport.   If you are asked to join activities when visiting a client, do so. And if you play tennis or golf with them, be a gracious winner or, more important, a good loser.

Don't React When You're Angry. Every relationship has its ups and downs, and as adults, we must know how to manage both. Don't let emotions get the best of you. Don't send out a letter or make a call when you're angry; you may eventually regret that you sent it out—count to 10.

Let Your Client Say Thank-You. Sometimes clients want to say thank-you for doing good work. This may include inviting you to their house or picking up the tab for a drink. Don't make them feel inadequate by always insisting that you do the entertaining and pick up the tab. And accept thanks for a job well done graciously, not disparaging your own achievements.

Credibility

Companies care about the reputation of their suppliers because it indicates whether or not they will live up to their guarantees. They also prefer working with a company that has been in business for a while because of the likelihood they will continue to remain in business; no one wants to be in the middle of a large project with a company that goes out of business or buy a product from one that won't be around to support it.

When to Walk Away from a Sale. There are many times when the best thing for you to do is walk away from a sale. Don't accept business unless you can handle it properly. Do not sell your services if you are not 100 percent sure that you can satisfy your customers' needs. Never perform a service when you feel that clients won't receive sufficient value for their money. Lastly, never give away business just to get your foot in the door because the long-term costs may lead you to resent the client later.

Honesty. Honesty isn't the best policy; it is the only policy. There are two forms of dishonesty: the first is marked by a conscious attempt to deceive, whether by being outright misleading, exaggerating your claims, or withholding information; the second is unintentional, often the result of an honest mistake or a misunderstanding due to poor communication. But both are equally damaging and should be avoided at all costs. After all, it takes a long time to win confidence and trust, but both can be quickly destroyed if you do not live up to your claims. (Chapter 9 is devoted to this subject.)

Integrity.   People do business with those who have a high degree of integrity. They avoid suppliers who charge different prices for the same merchandise. They avoid suppliers who have a reputation for talking about other clients with outsiders, whether that involves disclosing confidential information or not speaking well of them. They avoid suppliers who claim other people's ideas as their own or who take advantage of a relationship by overselling.

Loyalty.   Every salesperson has dual loyalty—to clients and to the organization to which they belong. It is important that your first loyalty is to your organization. That doesn't mean, however, that you should avoid fighting internally for those things that allow you to better serve your clients. It does mean that, even though you may have occasion to be unhappy with your company or your boss, you should never discuss those problems with your clients. Never say, "It's not my fault; I only work here" or "What do you expect from my company?" or "If you saw what really goes on here, you would never do business with us." All are inappropriate comments that will make your clients feel uncomfortable with you.

Living the High Life.   It is never appropriate to put on special airs for clients; as a general rule, clients want to work with suppliers who are not too different from themselves. Learn all you can about the culture of your clients' organizations through their publications. Try to find out how their offices look, how they dress, and where they take guests to dinner. Set your tone by theirs. Going out of your way to try to impress your clients with your success can backfire. Clients may end up perceiving you as someone who squanders money and lives the high life by their standards (for example, by working in extravagant offices or driving expensive— and frequently different—cars every time you meet them); if they do, they may come to feel that they are supporting your life-style.

Gifts.   Many large companies have policies that prohibit employees from accepting gifts. Don't put clients in an awkward position by violating company policies. A client should use your services because of the value that you provide—nothing else.

Security

Clients should not have to think about security—during any stage of the business relationship. They want to know that they can confide in you and never regret it, that any information they give you will not get into the hands of their competition, and that you will see to their personal safety during site visits. They also want to know that you are taking the necessary precautions to protect important information that you collect from them.

Confidentiality. Once you breach a confidence, even of a friend, your relationship is damaged. No matter how much you apologize to clients or how often you assure them that it won't happen again, there will always be an element of doubt in their minds. This applies to personal information or information about their organization; moreover, to avoid suspicion about your trustworthiness, avoid breaching your own organization's wall of confidentiality. Once you violate confidentiality, clients will wonder when you will do the same to them.

Technological Security. In the course of switching from a paper-intensive office to a computer-intensive office, a set of processes that were in place may fall by the wayside. For example, carbon copies of important correspondence were always sent to clients. Today, a single copy of a letter is run off and the computer serves as backup. In addition, information critical to running business operations has grown exponentially; for example, a direct-mail house may hold all a company's lists on its computers or a service organization may prepare a company's payroll. Since these records are not in clients' hands but are essential to their businesses, they want to know that you back up all computer files, make multiple copies of important documents, keep them in different locations, and have a comprehensive disaster recovery plan.

Safety. No client will fault you for having facilities in disadvantaged areas, but they do expect you to ensure their safety when they visit you. This may mean having someone meet them at the airport to show them the best and safest way to your office or having an ample security force guarding the parking lot.

Access

In an increasingly competitive marketplace, customers ask themselves many questions before renewing long-term commitments. For example, they ask, When I had to reach my supplier, was it hard to get through to them? Are their hours convenient? Do they have a toll-free number? Did they return my calls promptly? Are they conveniently located? If I had a problem and my usual contact wasn't there, could I find someone else to help me? When they went away on a business trip were they accessible?

Be Available. Make sure you don't put off client meetings because you are too busy with other clients, and always return telephone calls promptly. When that is not possible, have someone call back for you, asking whether someone else can help; it assures your client that you care. Furthermore, when you meet with clients, make sure you give them your undivided attention and avoid constant interruptions. Your mind must be on the meeting, not somewhere else.

When you have to be away for an extended period of time, prepare your clients for your absence. Let them know who is handling their accounts and what work is being done in your absence. Reassure them that in a real emergency, your office can and will reach you.

Be There When You Are Needed. People always seem to be around when things are great, but disappear when things go wrong. Be a foul weather friend. Be available, even reach out, when clients need you: when they are having work-related or family problems and can use a sounding board; when there is a sickness in their family and they need advice or need to let off steam; when they lose their jobs and need names to call and ideas to pursue or an office to hang their hats in while they are in transition. You can't do these things effectively and sincerely if you expect to get paid back; you must do them because it makes you feel good.

Communication

You should always look for better ways to communicate with clients. Ask yourself if you speak in language that your clients understand. Do you address your clients' needs when you present products or demonstrate those features you find most important? Do you keep clients informed about new developments? Do you speak to your clients' senior management, but cut others out of the loop, even when they are responsible for getting the work done?

Too Close to the Forest.   Because we have a thorough understanding of our products, we often forget that our customers don't. We forget the problems that we faced when we first began using the products ourselves. Be careful to explain your product to your customers, take time to show them how things work, and gauge the response you get. Even more important, remember how frustrating it can be to deal with the unfamiliar; be careful to neither intimidate nor speak down to customers because they ask fundamental questions. A little patience and empathy can go a long way toward educating your clients to the benefits your products provide.

Presenting to Your Client.   Customers do not buy your products or services because of their features; they buy them because they offer solutions to their problems. It is also important to try to explain the benefits of new products or services in person; it allows you to answer questions and to highlight the features you think your clients will find most interesting.

Reporting—Formal and Informal.   It is very important to be in touch with your customers on a regular basis. One of the ways that this can be achieved is through call reports. Since misunderstandings and miscommunication lead to losing clients, written confirmations of your discussions give clients an opportunity to correct misunderstandings. Furthermore, you can use these reports to follow up on outstanding items that need to be pursued and to communicate within your own organization.

Another important way to communicate with clients is through progress reports. Send each client a list of all the projects that you are working on for them on a regular basis. It's a good way to let them know the scope of your activities and also highlights obstacles. Such reports provide a good forum for follow-up discussions.

It is also important to keep your clients informed about events in your own organization. When they hear about new hires, new product introductions, employee dismissals, pricing changes, client gains, or even mergers through the press or through the grapevine instead of directly from you, clients may wonder about your relationship.

Out of Sight, Out of Mind. It is very important to maintain continual contact with your clients. It isn't enough to get an assignment, disappear, and show up later with a completed work product. It is important to establish certain milestones along the way and gain approvals at every juncture. This prevents the client from becoming apprehensive; it ensures that you are moving in the right direction (and allows the client to change direction before you complete the activity); and it helps reinforce a client's appreciation of you and your work.

Furthermore, make sure that your clients know you are thinking about them—out of sight means out of mind. Be proactive: bring fresh ideas to them even when they aren't asked for and send them information that may be of interest to them. But be careful not to waste your clients' time or overload them with unnecessary information just to prove you are thinking of them.

Managing Uncertainty. Uncertainty creates dissatisfaction. A client may not really understand how you are going to tackle the job, who will do the work, how long it will take, how much it will cost, or whether it will work. Because you have been through the process 500 times before, it is easy to forget that clients may be novices: keep them informed, don't make any assumptions, give them all the information that you have, and be sensitive to their needs. Let customers know what you are doing behind the scenes to service them; they aren't mind readers. Sometimes clients can be reassured by estimates or best guesses. Furthermore, remember that clients are often accountable to others in their organization and must provide them with answers.

Managing Expectations. A precept that will never get you in trouble is underpromise but overdeliver. Always try to do just a little more than the client expects. You can do that only if you understand how expectations are established. Sometimes they are based on hearsay; for example, a client may get a rave review about you or your organization from friends. Sometimes expectations are a result of promises made in your advertising. Sometimes they are based on prior experience: "Vendors have always provided me with terrific service." Other times they are the result of personal expectations.

Once you understand how expectations are created, you can manage them:

- Carefully examine the situation for all possible problems before making promises about timing, costs, performance of the product, or service.

- When marketing intangibles, fully describe your end product so clients know what they will receive (and can avoid surprises).

- If clients make changes that translate into additional costs, be sure to spell them out as they are incurred to minimize the shock when the bill arrives.

- Explain that delays in getting approval may translate into longer delays at the end of the project.

- When you know of delays or problems, don't wait till they compound; bring them to the clients' attention at the earliest possible moment.

- Be conservative in your estimates rather than promising the world each time and falling short on your promises.

- Don't be afraid to be human—to say that you can't deliver when it's not possible.[18]

Promises.   You must be careful about promises that you make. "You can't promise your customers sunny weather, but you can promise to hold an umbrella over them when it rains."[19] Problems arise when promises can't be met. It doesn't matter what size the promise or how important. There are no degrees of promises; every promise is equally important because the person who is disappointed by your failure to keep a promise, is likely to think: "If they can't be counted on for small things, I sure won't trust them on large ones."

Surprises.   Customers do not like surprises. Make sure that you let clients know about problems, even small ones, before they discover them themselves. Even though your intentions may be admirable (for example, you may really believe the problem will be solved and that by not telling your clients you are sparing them needless worry), if clients discover the problem themselves, they will wonder if there are other problems you are hiding.

Understand the Customer

Just as you cannot develop a long-term friendship with someone you don't know well, you cannot develop relationships with clients unless you understand their needs. How much of an effort do you make to understand their needs? Do you spend your time dominating discussions or actively listening? Do you understand your clients' political sensitivities? Are you flexible in delivering your services to your clients or very set in your ways?

Knowledge of Client's Company and Industry.   It is very important to learn as much as you can about a client's company and industry. This includes understanding the corporate culture, especially its nuances; knowing what criteria are most important in their decision-making process; understanding former vendor relationships; and learning why they chose to do business with you. Many vendors falsely assume that, if they are doing work with one company within a particular industry, others are similar. They also believe that all industries are the same; if you can develop an advertisement for a consumer products company, you can do the same for an industrial concern. Moreover, taking the time to discover why clients use some of your products and not others, how they use your products, and if they are taking full advantage of them allows you to learn how you can be of greater assistance to them and perhaps even improve the products themselves.

The knowledge you build up about a company or industry over the years gives you an advantage over potential competitors. Clients recognize that trying to teach someone else the nuances of their organization will be costly, and they usually factor that into their decision making before changing suppliers, which gives suppliers they have successfully worked with an advantage.

Identify Those Things That Are Most Important to the Customer. Because giving customers what they want is the only thing that matters, it is very important to understand what customers consider excellent service. Provide as many opportunities for feedback as you can: conduct account reviews, periodically meeting with your clients to discuss the relationship and how it can be improved; hold focus-group sessions; conduct surveys; establish dealer councils; set up 800 numbers.

Anticipate Customer Needs. In today's competitive business climate, it isn't enough to be responsive to your clients' needs; you must be able to anticipate them. One of the best ways to improve client service is to actively search for new ideas both from inside and outside your industry, and then find ways to adapt those ideas to your organization.

Listening. Pay attention not only to what your customers' say, but also to those things that are left unsaid. Listening helps you uncover customer wants and needs, allows you to identify new product opportunities, and prevents misunderstandings. Make it easy for customers to complain to you. Encourage customers to be open about problems by making them feel comfortable with you, and let them know when you act on their recommendations. It is also important to respond to concerns held by very few, explaining why you are not making the changes they requested.

Objectivity. Organizations hire outsiders to serve as their eyes and ears, giving them a clear picture of what is happening, a picture not colored by position or politics or personal gain. To do this, it is necessary to maintain your objectivity at all times. In addition, because of your role as an outsider, their employees, distributors, or clients may feel more comfortable speaking to you than to them when there is a problem.

Make Your Client Look Good. Your job is to make your clients look good—to stay in the background and let them take credit for good work, even if you did it. Avoid making it clear, even indirectly, that you believe you are invaluable, that the work would never have been completed without you. Your role is not to be a star but to create one by whispering ideas into their ears. You were hired to help them do a job, and you succeed when you help them. Their way of thanking you will be to ask you to continue to do work for them.

Conclusion

Treating each client as your only client brings far more long-term rewards than does the "love 'em and leave 'em attitude." Not only will you improve market share and reduce your marketing costs, but you will also improve employee morale. In the end, you will feel good about yourself and know that your clients feel good about you.

Being responsive to clients today but falling short tomorrow because you are not changing with the times is bad business. Chapter 6 discusses how organizations can continually adapt to an ever-changing marketplace.

6

Change—Winning in the Fast Lane

Building an Organization That Adapts Well to Change

*The future...is coming toward us like
enormous waves of change. Set after set
they are getting bigger and coming
faster....Things will never get back to
"normal" because unpredictability and
change are normal. There is no going
back. Get used to it. Change will be fol-
lowed by more change. That's one thing
that isn't going to change. The waves in
this ocean won't flatten out, they're only
going to get bigger and come at us faster.*
ROBERT J. KRIEGEL AND LOUIS PATLER
If It Ain't Broke...Break It![1]

We are living in a time of unparalleled change, turbulence, and
uncertainty that is transforming our lives at work and at home.
In the course of two years, the superpower that inspired us to
build a great military machine turned into a cluster of poor
nations needing economic aid to survive. Business takeovers
have disappeared from the front pages of our papers, replaced

by "the permanent disappearance of middle management" and tales of 20 percent layoffs due to "downsizing." New technologies have become part of our everyday lives: VCRs, microwave ovens, and voicemail are eliminating fixed viewing times, hours in the kitchen, and the need for answering machines.

Can you remember the last week that your favorite news magazine or news show did *not* tell you about a startling new development? The speed of new developments that seemed to have reached the upper limits in the 1980s has not abated. In fact, according to General Electric's Jack Welch, "The pace of change in the nineties, will make the eighties look like a picnic, a walk in the park."[2]

In a world in which change is an everyday occurrence, business as usual is a guaranteed recipe for failure. To succeed, tomorrow's company must go beyond coping with change; it must embrace it. Rather than react to change; it must learn to anticipate it. Those who cling to the past will meet change with apprehension and anxiety. Only those prepared to meet the challenges of change will be rewarded with unparalleled opportunities. The payoff will go to those employees who are not only committed but ready to lead the effort.

We Must Change the Way We View Change

In the past, management choose from among six strategies to overcome resistance to change. These strategies for dealing with resistance to change, described in a 1979 *Harvard Business Review* article, were (1) education and communication; (2) participation and involvement; (3) facilitation and support; (4) negotiation and agreement; (5) manipulation and co-optation; and (6) explicit and implicit coercion.[3]

The first of these, education and communication, is an approach that gets people to accept change by educating them about its benefits before implementing the change. The theory is that by explaining why change is needed, you help people accept it—and its effects. The article warns, however, that "some managers overlook the fact that a program of this sort requires a good relationship between initiators and resistors or...the latter may not believe what they hear. It also requires time and effort, particularly if a lot of people are involved."

The second strategy hinges on participation and involvement of employees in some elements of the change process itself. The article warns, however, that the "participation process does have its drawbacks. Not only can it lead to a poor solution if the process is not carefully managed, but...when the change must be made immediately, it can take simply too long to involve others."

The third strategy, facilitation and support, requires management support for employees who are facing change, because, as the article notes, change efforts "can be time-consuming and expensive and still fail." The fourth approach, negotiation and agreement, involves offering incentives to employees who are against change. Here, the article warns, the greatest problem tends to be cost.

Manipulation and co-optation, the fifth approach, requires managers to resort to "covert attempts to influence others. Manipulation, in this context, normally involves the very selective use of information and the conscious structuring of events....[but] if the people feel they are being tricked into not resisting, are not being treated equally, or are being lied to, they may respond negatively." The sixth strategy is explicit and implicit coercion. Employees are threatened, either explicitly or implicitly, with penalties for failure to accept change.

Although these solutions may have worked yesterday, they are not likely to be enough today. The first three strategies require time, an asset no company can afford to waste in today's highly competitive marketplace. Furthermore, when companies rush to implement change, as evidenced in the last three strategies, they end up creating animosity, increasing anxiety, building resentment, damaging trust, and in the end, hampering competitiveness.

There are two factors that render yesterday's change management approaches obsolete. First, change is no longer an occasional event but rather an everyday occurrence; it has become so constant that companies can ill afford the length of time between the development of an idea and its implementation. Almost as soon as new approaches are introduced, they are on the way to becoming obsolete. Just as manufacturers search for faster ways to bring new products to market, companies must search for better and faster ways to bring about change in their organizations. They must create a working environment where employees change and renew themselves everyday. Second, the way companies are managed has itself changed. In an age in which the work force is becoming empowered and layers of management are being dismantled, companies can no longer afford to have a few select people making all the decisions for the company. In the past, once decisions were made by management, employees were expected to conform. Today, such attempts will cost the commitment of employees, something empowered companies cannot afford.

Peter Senge points out that, as "one seasoned organization change consultant once put it, people don't resist change; they resist being changed."[4] To reduce the time for getting people to change, companies try to force change rather than secure the involvement of their employees—an approach that often backfires. In fact, the authors of *Management by Participation* say that "considerable research has demonstrated that, in general, participation leads to commitment, not merely compliance."[5]

Companies must tap all of their employees, encouraging them to be catalysts of change rather than reactors to it. Instead of employing change management techniques in response to change, then waiting for the next wave of change to arrive, the ability to change must become an everyday occurrence—it must become part of every employee's mind-set.

The truth of the matter is that being reactive rather than promoting change will be the downfall of many companies in the 1990s. In order to succeed, change has to occur as new ideas are born. Companies must move forward in a synchronized way, with different leaders taking the helm as different parts of the operation move ahead; the motion should be like that of an amoeba rolling forward to a new destination.

Fallacies about Change

One of the reasons why many change management efforts fail is a lack of understanding of the change management process. That leads to so-called solutions that exacerbate rather than solve problems. Until companies view change management as a continual process involving commitment, learning, and understanding, they will be unable to lead their companies into the future. Some of the fallacies about change that lead to failure are:

"The best way to address tomorrow's problems is to see how they've been handled in the past." People like to define future events based on extrapolating information from the past or to determine what will happen tomorrow by examining today. The problem with that approach is that there are too many events for which there are no precedents.

"I don't have the time to focus on trivial things." Many companies only recognize large problems; they ignore small ones that could be easily remedied, because they do not understand their accumulated impact on a company. They forget that, as Peter Senge says, "for almost all of our collective history as a species, the great threats to our survival have been sudden dramatic events: a volcano erupting, a sabretooth tiger attacking, or an army marching over the hill and wiping out our tribe, for instance. All that has changed. Today, the major threats to our survival as a species are slow, gradual processes. They are systematic phenomena that unfold gradually the way environmental decay has. We have no idea how to deal with systematic threats because all of our notions of ensuring our survival have to do with getting rid of external threats, with fighting something—with fixing our attention on an adversary." This runs counter to a modern world in which the threats are systematic and require, according to Peter Senge, "learning to use the tools and methods of systems thinking and translating them into action."[6] Today, it is necessary to focus on the small steps that will enable us to advance as a whole company, with every employee moving in tandem.

"Let's have a meeting and think about change." You shouldn't think about quality only when you're in a quality meeting; you shouldn't think about learning only when attending a seminar; and you shouldn't think of change as a once in a while occurrence, a separate function from everyday activities. Change is as much a mind-set as an activity. It is not a special program or an event, but something that must be incorporated into everything you do.

"Let's send them to a seminar to learn the information they need to be successful." A critical element of successful change management is education. The American educational focus, however, has always been on specific skill sets; today, when skills become obsolete every few years, we must devote as much effort to learning how to learn as we spend focusing on learning specific skills or techniques. For example, an article in *Harvard Business Review* says:

> Most people define learning too narrowly as mere "problem solving," so they focus on identifying and correcting errors in the external environment. Solving problems is important. But if learning is to persist, managers and employees must also look inward. They need to reflect critically on their own behavior, identify the ways they often inadvertently contribute to the organization's problems, and then change how they act....Put simply, because many professionals are almost always successful at what they do, they rarely experience failure. And because they have rarely failed, they have never learned how to learn from failure. So whenever...strategies go wrong, they become defensive, screen out criticism, and put the "blame" on anyone and everyone but themselves. In short, their ability to learn shuts down precisely at the moment they need it most.[7]

"The best way to stay on top of your industry is to study the competition." Too many companies focus only on their competition. They forget how important it is to learn by looking outside their field or industry and then applying those principles to what they do. If you do nothing but follow in your competitors' footsteps, you may catch up, but you are unlikely to move ahead. It is, according to Kriegel and Patler, "a strategy that automatically puts you in second place trying to catch

up, at best gaining a small, short-term advantage."[8] Applying approaches, technologies, and processes used by excellent companies outside your field gives you an opportunity to leap ahead of your competitors.

"Visions and dreams are soft issues; we should focus on hard goals." The difference between a dream and a goal is that the dream supplies meaning, while the goal is an interim milestone. Visions lead us to change the way we perceive our roles, and they inspire learning. When you follow a dream or strive to make a vision a reality, you think long term and "out of the box." The problem, according to Kriegel and Patler, is that "goals...limit you....When we live and die by the short-term numbers, it's easy to lose perspective. Everything is exaggerated. Small victories are cause for celebration and small setbacks become huge catastrophes. Minor annoyances take on major importance. As a result, the mad-dash rat race to make the short-term numbers hinders our creativity, our motivation, our spirit."[9]

"If we don't change our first-line employees, we will never be successful." To succeed, a company must change people at all levels; it must change the company's culture, opening it to continual learning. Unfortunately, according to Peter Senge, a strong proponent of the learning organization, "There is a tendency in the United States, especially in the quality movement, to assume that the changes that need to take place should occur down low in the organization. The idea that people at the top need to lead the change by changing themselves is novel to many U.S. managers.... [In America, workers on the lowest level get the most training, mid-level employees get a little less, and the top level gets a] briefing. In Japan, by contrast, it is exactly the opposite. This is very significant symbolically. The leaders are the learners."[10]

"We don't need employee commitment in order to succeed." Employees who are forced to accept change give the effort no more than lip service; they just go through the motions. They quietly resist the change, using techniques such as disparaging remarks and slow learning; they may even sabotage efforts to bring about change. In an article in *Quality Progress,*

Brooks Carter notes: "If an individual publicly announces that he favors something, but he doesn't entirely believe what he has said, he will be in a condition of cognitive dissonance. To resolve this dissonance, the individual will change his attitude to be more congruent with the statement he has made. However, if he is coerced to make the statement, his attitude will not change. Under coercion he can justify his statement by the coercion."[11]

Change...Why Bother?

It is very easy to look at a situation and ask, "If it isn't broken, why fix it?" After all, *inertia* creates comfort, and changing requires breaking old habits, which creates discomfort. The article in *Quality Progress* mentioned above notes:

> Managers' habits resist change, are based on education and training, and are embedded in the culture of their organization....These habits produce enough short-term successes to justify continuation year after year....For instance, if you hold enough people accountable, some will succeed. This is sufficient to maintain the habit of holding people accountable. If you set enough goals, some will be reached. This is sufficient to maintain the habit of setting goals....[Indeed,] management methods that achieve short-term success, perceived or real, will often establish management habits, in spite of the fact that the long-term consequences of these management habits can be destructive.[12]

The major reasons, in addition to inertia, for resisting change are:

- *Procrastination.* We all have a tendency to put off till tomorrow what is difficult or uncomfortable. Unless there is a problem that forces people to change immediately, there's always time to think about change tomorrow. (Procrastination will be discussed at length in the next chapter.)
- *Lack of motivation.* Unless the personal benefits gained from change are clear, most people will decide that changing isn't worth the effort.

- *Fear of failure.*   If change requires us to learn a new skill, we may evade change because we are not emotionally ready to deal with a setback.

- *Fear of the unknown.*   What we don't know, frightens us. The very thought of leaving our comfort zone and facing uncertainty creates enough anxiety and paralysis to make us avoid change. Even when things are not functioning well, people are still more comfortable with the known.

- *Fear of loss.*   We all worry that a new approach may reduce our job security, power, or status.

- *Dislike of the initiators of change.*   It is much more difficult to accept change when we lack confidence or distrust the people trying to bring it about.

- *Lack of communication.*   If we do not understand why change is necessary, misunderstand the initiator's intent, or receive our information in bits and pieces, we are more likely to resist it.

The Only Thing We Have to Fear Is Fear Itself

One of the most destructive forces in any company is fear in the hearts and minds of employees. Just as pollution damages the environment, an air of fear is toxic to companies. Although playing Russian Roulette with prisoners of war violates the Geneva Convention, in many companies today, a form of Russian Roulette is commonplace, with the pink slip serving as the bullet. Fear discourages people who want to "do the right thing," destroys creativity, and shatters loyalty and commitment. While some managers use fear to get people to stop doing something, fear never inspires people to perform at their best. Furthermore, although some people feel they do nothing to create fear, they forget that fear can be caused by actions directed at someone else, because we place ourselves in their position.

When people believe they lack control over what happens to them, they become fearful. These fears can be real or they can be perceived or imagined. Fears arise over things that are concrete and immediate, such as loss of a job, as well as things that are more ephemeral and long term, such as personal embarrassment or damage to personal credibility or career mobility.

When people play it safe rather than sail uncharted waters, they fail to recognize opportunities and often put off decision making. For example, Lee Iacocca is quoted as saying that the "key to decision making is that at some point you have to rely on your gut instincts, which causes lots of sleepless nights for people who want to play it safe....Unfortunately, research shows that the overwhelming majority of Americans (85 percent) are reactive and static, not action- or dynamic- or instinct-oriented" as a result of this desire to play it safe.[13]

Moreover, fear instills a real sense of powerlessness, making it less likely that people will challenge the status quo, openly question things they think are wrong, or confront someone. When people are afraid to make suggestions, feel they can't say what's on their minds, or think that speaking up is a waste of time, innovation and creativity die. An *Industry Week* survey of employees in 22 organizations around the country revealed that "70% of them say they 'bit their tongues' at work because they feared the repercussions of speaking out. And 98% of their responses indicate that fear has negative effects on them or their work."[14]

Fear also causes people to withdraw, to cover mistakes, and misrepresent facts. It teaches them to play it close to the vest and discourages them from sticking their necks out, because trying something new may leave them open to criticism. It makes them hesitant to discuss problems with others, for fear they will leave themselves open to ridicule.

In fact, it has become clear that companies that promote fear destroy creativity, commitment, and confidence. The result is a work force that has been described by Judith Bardwick as: "Narcissistic: I'm watching out for number one. Paranoid: I think everyone is out to get me. Territorial: I'm grabbing my turf and surrounding it with barbed wire. Rigid: I'm hanging on to what I know. Cynical: I'll believe it when I see it. Political: I'm keeping my eyes open."[15]

At the same time, fear may cause some to procrastinate, some to go into automatic pilot, and others to go into superdrive, running around making themselves look busy for fear of losing their jobs. It reminds me of the white rabbit in *Alice in Wonderland* who ran around saying, "I'm late, I'm late for a very important date. No time to say hello-goodbye. I'm late! I'm late! I'm late!" Only this time it's no fairy tale.

Fear is instilled in the work force in many ways including taking away someone's work, slowly but surely, until the person doesn't have a job left; not sending communications to them or excluding them from important discussions; cutting them out of the information loop; constantly looking over their shoulders; insulting, openly criticizing, or challenging their competence or ridiculing them in public; giving them impossible deadlines; or transferring or firing them.

Fear, which creates a horrible background noise in companies, is transmitted in the workplace in many ways. Kathleen D. Ryan and Daniel K. Oestreich have described a cascade of techniques that produce fear in their book *Driving Fear Out of the Workplace:*

> Silence—pausing and allowing the pause to continue, especially if it is accompanied by direct, deadpan, or cool eye contact, can be extremely intimidating....
>
> Glaring Eye Contact: "The Look"—Some people can look at others with sufficient power to wither the brightest flowers of confidence. This is more than just eye contact. The look is a testing, evaluative glare....Combined with silence, the look is a powerful way to shut down communication—all without saying a word.
>
> Brevity or Abruptness—This behavior is what one research participant described as "short, sharp answers" to questions or comments, using words that have a clipped, cold feel to them.
>
> Snubbing or Ignoring People—This behavior separates people into castes: "I'm up here. You are down there." It can take the form of simply not talking to people, leaving them out of meetings important to their jobs, or reminding them of their "place"...put downs, in-crowd conversation, sitting in the power seats, turning one's back on someone at the meeting, stubbing out a cigarette in front of someone at the table. In general, making sure everyone knows they are very, very important.
>
> Insults and Put-Downs—These represent the commonly cited fear-provoking interpersonal behaviors: cutting

remarks, direct or implied, that attack a person's credibility, self-esteem, or integrity. They often take the form of labeling, making jokes at someone's expense, ridicule or sarcasm, and racist, sexist, and other discriminatory remarks of all kinds. The impact of these comments is a combination of both fear and anger, permanently engraving the remarks in people's memories.

Blaming, Discrediting, or Discounting—These behaviors place responsibility for the problem on someone else. The process is one of labeling or fixing blame in a way that traps or targets the other person.

An Aggressive, Controlling Manner—People described this autocratic behavior as demanding, intense, "my way or the highway."...This type of behavior easily blends with a micro-managing, high surveillance approach to controlling people, such as requiring time logs for every task. Sometimes this behavior is calculated and manipulative. It is at this point on our behavior scale that abrasive behavior can become abusive.

Threats about the Job—Comments like "I'll remember this. You are undermining me," and "I can replace you" put the employee's job security on the line. Threats can be either implied or direct. Performance criticisms related to a particular project can include an unstated threat of job loss....

Yelling and Shouting—Next to put-downs and insults this category, the loud voice or loud argument, was the most frequently cited interpersonal behavior that causes fear. Sometimes, people said, someone's voice was loud enough to be heard "all the way down the hall" or "all over the building," as if the venting was intended to widely publicize a failure and to humiliate the employee....

Angry Outbursts or Loss of Control—This behavior represents an explosion. It is the point at which people throw things in their offices or resort to exaggerations.

Physical Threats—Physical threats are only one step away from patently criminal behavior.[16]

In a company where this kind of environment is allowed to flourish, behaviors become ugly. It is much like the picture William Goldman drew in *Lord of the Flies,* where civilized children became savages and cannibals to protect themselves. In the same way, people will do just about anything to save their hides, including finger pointing and engaging in witch hunts.

More time is spent covering up tracks than it would take to do the work in the first place. Passing the buck and copying everyone on memos become cultural norms. No one goes out on a limb or reports problems for fear of being labeled a troublemaker, and minor disturbances soon grow into major problems. And no one will accept responsibility. Everyone spends their lives in meetings and on committees in order to avoid making decisions. Inaction is justified as not rocking the boat or maintaining the status quo. And perhaps most important, in an age of rapid change, the inaction, procrastination, or wasted time that result from fear keep employees from learning new skills that are vital to a company's success.

This kind of behavior will prevent many companies from becoming market leaders. According to General Electric's Jack Welch:

> The individual who typically forces performance out of people rather than inspires it: the autocrat, the big shot, the tyrant [is no longer useful]. Too often all of us have looked the other way...[because these types of managers] "always deliver"—at least in the short term. And perhaps this type was more acceptable in easier times, but in an environment where we must have every good idea from every man and woman in the company, we cannot afford management styles that suppress and intimidate. Whether we can convince and help these managers to change—recognizing how difficult that can be—or part company with them if they cannot, will be the ultimate test of our commitment to the transformation of the Company and will determine the future of the mutual trust and respect we are building.[17]

Learning...K through Life

In a turbulent business environment, organizations must renew themselves every day. When people are forced to think about change in the world around them and in the environment they work in, the general tendency is to reject what they see out of hand. They either ignore the signals, discount the relevance of the message, or end up shooting the messenger. Indeed, it often takes a crisis to create the sense of urgency necessary to alter thinking, modify strategy, or embrace change, but by the time the crisis is recognized, the damage is done. It is like the "motivational speech I heard years ago. An indignant employee was saying, 'But how can they lay me off? They need me. I know my job inside out. I have thirty years of experience.' Answer: 'No, you don't. You have one year of experience repeated 30 times.'"[18] The danger for America is that, like most civilizations that have fallen, we will not recognize the crisis we face until it is too late.

For business, the challenge is to create a working environment that strives toward bringing the personal views of employees closer to those views needed to succeed in the marketplace. In order to survive, businesses must become learning organizations; places in which everyone learns to do things better in an age of uncertainty.

Establishing the Learning Environment

In order to prosper in the future, companies must view change as a source of opportunity. Everyone should be encouraged to promote learning and continuous improvement rather than allow fear of failure to dominate. To accomplish this, companies must foster an environment of trust, loyalty, and commitment, qualities that free people to devote time and attention to learning instead of covering their tracks and hiding errors.

Furthermore, in this new environment a new kind of leader will emerge. Walter Kiechel III, who has written extensively on this issue, presents these two examples:

> Neal Thornberry, a professor at Babson College and an expert on so-called self-directed work teams uses the term "unleader" in summarizing what successors to today's managers will and won't do. The unleader will take team development as his primary charge. He'll be an expert in adult learning, of course, understanding that different team members learn in different ways. But he will also know the ins, outs, ups, downs, and general convolutions of group dynamics—how teams form, reach agreement or fail to, act

in concert or fall apart. So armed, he'll be equipped to help the team along, mostly by asking questions: "Have you considered the legal aspects of this?"...If he does his job right, he'll end up serving not as facilitator...but as a catalyst."...

Jim Kouzes, a consultant with the Tom Peters Group, [who] offers an only slightly fanciful version of correct managerial technique in the learning organization: Subordinate calls up and says, "I have a problem." Manager replies, "That's terrific, just why I hired you," and hangs up. Subordinate tries again, maybe a couple of times, and gets the same response. If the subordinate finally convinces the manager he needs help, the assistance will largely take the form of more questions: "If this problem is solved, what will the solution look like? Let's generate some ways to get there. What are the strengths and weaknesses of each approach? So which one did you choose?...You're teaching people a problem-solving process."[19]

Once the organization embraces this new environment, any successes that result must be used as a springboard for additional success, not as a capstone. In other words, rather than sitting back and relaxing once a goal is reached, employees in the learning organization will go on to ask how they can do even better tomorrow.

In the learning environment, everyone looks forward to the next challenge. It is much like the response of James Michener when "asked to name his favorite book among those he had authored. 'My preference, among the thirty-five books I've written,' he said after a long pause, 'is always the next one. I'm an old pro. And the job of an old pro is to move on to the next task.'"[20]

Accepting the Risks That Accompany Change

In learning organizations, risk is understood, and differing views are not only tolerated but encouraged. The slogan of such companies could be the old adage: Nothing ventured, nothing gained. Kriegel and Patler expand on that thought, explaining that "risk taking is natural. In fact, it is unnatural not to take risks. Can you imagine a baby thinking, 'I don't know if I should try to stand. I know I'll fall. I know it will hurt. Maybe

I'll wait a few years until I'm bigger and stronger'? If that were the case we'd all end up on our hands and knees."[21] Many companies discourage risk taking by reprimanding people for errors and stigmatizing those who try something new and fail. Instead, management should present problems as learning opportunities, praising innovative attempts even if they are unsuccessful. After all, the fewer negative costs associated with risk taking, the more employees will try something new.

Companies can also encourage learning by rewarding rather than shooting messengers who bring bad news. The messengers aren't the ones who created the problems; they are part of the solution. To ensure that employees feel free to surface problems, companies should publicize and celebrate the efforts of those who identify problems that are then corrected. To promote this open environment, companies should also encourage people to admit mistakes rather than sweep them under the rug, because that yields several benefits. For example, when errors are openly acknowledged, small mistakes can be corrected before they become large problems. In addition, hiding mistakes from decision makers only compounds errors, because decisions are then based on faulty information. Moreover, openly discussing problems allows colleagues to jointly participate in resolving them.

It is not only risk taking, or discussing mistakes that is important, but the effort an organization makes to learn by them. Joe Paterno, coach of the Penn State University football team, once replied when "asked...how he felt when his team lost a game,...that losing was probably good for the team since that was how the players learned what they were doing wrong."[22] Paterno's comments highlight the advantages of an environment in which mistakes are viewed as an opportunity to learn. Soichiro Honda, founder of Honda, reinforces that idea when he says that "many people dream of success. To me success can only be achieved through repeated failure and introspection. In fact, success represents the 1 percent of your work which results only from the 99 percent that is called failure."[23]

Not only can an organization learn by its mistakes, but individuals can as well. Management must promote the importance of personal growth through the acceptance of feedback. In fact, in an open environment, one where there is honesty and trust, people ask others for feedback, and then follow up on their suggestions.

Since open and honest communications are essential elements in creating an atmosphere of learning and change, management must accept the responsibility of fostering this kind of environment. After all, people are more willing to embrace change if they understand what it is, and why it is necessary, and if they are prepared for the change rather than surprised by it. It is useful for senior managers to communicate their enthusiasm and support for change and to give employees road maps that contain milestones that make the journey clear. If a visionary leader communicates the long-term need for change, employees buy in more quickly.

Changing to a more open and trusting environment requires letting go, unlearning many management practices of the past. But that is not easy, and it does not happen quickly. It requires that managers leave behind many skills, sources of status and power, and implicit assumptions about the workplace that were formulated during past experiences. Dr. Tineke Bahlmann notes that "learning only happens in a simple structure...without too much hierarchy, where there is room for individuals, where a collision of opinions is cultivated, because only then emerging strategies and creative interactions with the environment can happen."[24]

Learning to Learn

Encouraging people to learn is necessary for instituting the kind of change that will make companies competitive in the future. The more you learn, the more you are open to change; the more people in a company are open to change, the easier it is for the company to forge ahead. The first thing research into this subject area reveals is that learning can take many forms, and a philosophy of one size fits all is not an appropriate strategy. Alan Mumford explains that "researchers have identified four types of learning styles: activists, who learn best from activities while they are engrossed in them; reflectors, who learn from activities which they have had the chance to review; theorists, who benefit from activities when they are offered as part of a concept or a theory; and pragmatists, who learn best when there is a direct link between the subject matter and a real life problem."[25] It is important to keep these learning styles in mind when constructing formalized training programs. It is also critical to know your employees' optimum learning style, so that the informal learning that takes place during meetings, feedback sessions, and on-the-spot training will be effective.

Recognizing that people learn in different ways, companies might want to recognize teaching models that have proven successful with children. Lucia Solorzano noted several learning styles in a report in *U.S. News & World Report:* "'Manipulative' learners [who]...need to get more physically involved in their lessons to remember them. Hands-on projects, such as model building or play-acting, are useful learning tools. [While] 'visual' learners...retain information best by seeing it. Films, educational TV and museum exhibits help them learn. 'Informal' learners...thrive in less structured study arrangements. Beanbag chairs may make a better workplace, for example, than a desk and straight-backed chair. 'Walkman' learners...use background noise as a screen for better concentration....'Dyadic' learners...work best with a partner, rather than alone or in a group—small or large....'Mobile' learners...need to move about and take breaks while studying."[26]

There are, of course, numerous other factors involved in learning. For example, some people learn on a need-to-know basis, finding the time and concentration only when necessity drives them. Some systematically assess the gaps in their knowledge and skills and then take courses to fill them in. Others use free time for reading, highlighting and filing away material, while others attend lectures or go to conferences. For some, learning involves active participation, doing things by trial and error. Others learn by exchanging information and debating issues with people from other companies or departments. Some spend a great deal of time observing and collecting information through constant assessment of what they hear and see going on around them; they are always open, looking beyond the boundaries of their own companies and then contrasting what they see in one place with what they see in another.

All of these methods, including the ones described below in greater detail, are effective.

Curiosity

The desire to investigate and learn is part of human nature. Children are notorious question askers, wanting to know everything about the world around them. They ask questions ranging from why the sky is blue to why there is no sun at night. But as we grow older, we are inhibited by a fear that we will look stupid if we ask questions. Even more dangerous, we begin to assume that the things we have already learned are set in stone. The problem is, as the Greek philosopher Epictetus said, "It is impossible for a man to learn what he thinks he already knows." That is why we must all learn to continually examine what we take for granted, regaining that childlike ability to question and requestion. We must not allow old information to cloud our judgment, and we must learn to abandon the familiar to discover and savor what is new.

Making Data Meaningful

Data is only meaningful when it can be attached to ideas. For example, it is not enough to collect financial statistics without understanding what they mean and the context in which they exist. It is the accumulation of data and the connections we draw between different kinds of information that provides knowledge. It is important then to have diverse interests, because in order to make data relevant, you make connections between what you already know and the new concepts that you are learning. Without that knowledge base, you might lose interest because you don't know how to apply the data.

There are a number of methods for helping others make the connections between seemingly unrelated concepts. Metaphors are a very good way to explain the unexplainable, and analogy is yet another powerful tool. Keep in mind that, as Richard Wurman says, "facts are only meaningful when they relate to a concept that you can grasp. If I say an acre is 43,560 square feet, that is factual but it doesn't tell you what an acre is. On the other hand, if I tell you that an acre is about the size of an American football field without the end zones, it is not as accurate, but I have made it more understandable."[27]

Seeing Patterns

It is important to take the time to see emerging patterns in the world, rather than seeing events in isolation. When you have two things to compare, you can see differences; when you have many, you begin to see patterns. People learn when they look at the things that are happening around them, draw conclusions, and then apply what they learn. Any fact in isolation is a bit of data; a lot of data is information; a lot of information is the beginning of knowledge. The more of the big picture employees have, the more they can make connections and learn.

Active Participation

Active participation is a more powerful learning device than spoon feeding. Not only are we more likely to remember something when we discover it ourselves or learn through trial and error, but we are more likely to value it. We file away what we hear, but we test what we discover, which makes us more likely to use it. Abstract concepts do not lead to action the way experience does.

The Socratic Method

One of the best ways to learn is through a directed question and answer dialogue, a form of conversation that was used by Socrates as he taught his disciples the principles of logical thought and analysis. Socrates was using a formal version of the oral tradition typical of most primitive cultures. As Peter Senge points out, "most native American cultures just sat in a circle and talked for hours or even days. No purpose. No leader. No agenda. Just talk. Then the group would disperse and people would go about their work attuned to what everybody else was doing and thinking. Dialogue let them understand collectively a deeper pattern of reality than any one person could understand."[28]

One of today's equivalents is the "brainstorming" session, in which a group of employees get together to look at issues and suggest ways of tackling them. If facilitated properly, such sessions become free and open forums for inspiring out-of-the-box thinking. Through such exchanges, companies can help employees broaden their perspective of the world around them. And that understanding, in turn, translates into an acceptance of the need for change.

Reflection

It is also important that companies understand that learning requires more than the accumulation of knowledge. It is not enough to collect information; we must absorb it, internalize it, and connect it to concepts that we already understand, thus making what we learn our own before we use it. Anyone can memorize the fact that two plus two equals four. Without thinking about what it means, how do we come to understand that two oranges and two apples are four pieces of fruit? It is only when we have time to think about what we are told, to make patterns out of information, to test ideas, that we truly learn.

Companies that push employees to work at top speed all the time, to try to generate creative ideas on command, will never foster the kind of environment in which creativity and innovation flourish. Unless we have time to step back and learn from our activities, we will never be able to evaluate whether we are moving in the right direction or just creating motion. Senge points out that "in the west we have a cultural predisposition toward action to the exclusion of thinking....In a Japanese organization if you were to see someone sitting and doing nothing, you would never think to interrupt because obviously that person is thinking. It's perfectly acceptable, however, to interrupt an active person. In the west, we are exactly the opposite."[29]

Play

Sometimes learning takes the ability to abandon preconceived notions about how to solve problems. Playing games often allows us the freedom to think in more original, innovative ways. Jeremy Campbell writes that "under the guise of play, new forms of behavior can be invented with impunity and thus it becomes an inspiration to innovation."[30]

Formal play is also a useful way to build relationships and stimulate communication between employees. For example, the communication and comaraderie that result from participation in a company volleyball game or bowling tournament provide exchanges of ideas that can generate new thinking. If these relationships cross functional lines or operating units, they also help spread information about what is happening in different areas of the company.

Mentoring

Sometimes it is easier to learn from observing others than from reading books, attending lectures, or through trial and error. For example, one can learn aspects about leadership that cannot be found by reading books because there are subtleties that no one thinks to put down on paper. Learning how to manage employees is easier when you can emulate someone who does it well, and even better if that person spends time watching you do it and provides insights about your approach. Learning how to behave in certain business situations, for example, dealing with a difficult employee, meeting a major potential client, or responding to an irate customer are all unique situations that often get lost in the translation: you have to be there. It is much like the apprenticeship system that once governed the learning of skill sets. A blacksmith was trained by watching another blacksmith, then helping him, then doing the job under close supervision.

Organizational Learning

Not only do companies have to ensure that individual employees are provided opportunities to learn and grow, but they themselves must find new ways of operating that encourage learning and enable change, such as those discussed below.

Redundancy

Ikujiro Nonaka wrote in the *Harvard Business Review* that "to Western managers, the term 'redundancy' with its connotations of unnecessary duplication and waste, may sound unappealing....[but deliberate] redundancy is important because it encourages frequent dialogue and communication," which spreads knowledge throughout the organization.[31] For example, while assigning two groups the same problem may seem like a waste of time, there are numerous advantages to such a process. If they both come up with the same answer, you can be confident that the solution is probably right. If they come up with different solutions, the arguments over them throw new light on the project—and often leads to a third solution that is better than either of the originals. "In this case it is not that one wins and another loses, but they take the best angle from each team to derive the best product."[32]

Competing against Yourself

Companies that experience great success often continue along the path they have been following rather than reexamine what they do. The problem is that if the marketplace shifts, they will be left behind. One method that can be used to overcome the tendency to remain complacent is to develop a task force that develops ideas on how they would compete against their own organization. Through this process, of looking at what they could do differently, a company can incorporate new information into their current plans.

Contingency Planning

Unexpected events will always occur; in fact, they occur much more often and with much greater rapidity than expected. Companies must therefore prepare for these unexpected events rather than resist them or play catch up when they arrive.

Christopher Knowlton says in *Fortune* that "you can't control the unexpected, but you can control your response to it. Practitioners of Aikido, a form of martial arts, know that they may get thrown if they resist an attacking force. So they learn to blend with the force and use an attacker's energy for their own advantage."[33]

One of the ways that an organization can prepare for that eventuality is to promote a "what if" mentality among employees. This encourages them to think "out of the box" and explore the unexpected. What are the most likely scenarios? What events do we have control over? What are our options? How will we react to the situation? Knowlton points out in the same article that "war gaming helps Shell prepare for the unexpected...they study and debate detailed scenarios developed by the planning department that sketch reasonable but contrasting alternatives for how the world may look in ten years. Each region and each operating company [then] uses [these scenarios] to formulate strategy."[34]

Collective Insights

The more information that is shared across a company, the more everyone learns. No one unit of the company or single person should have information that is solely their own. Nonaka said in his *Harvard Business Review* article that "in an economy where the only certainty is uncertainty, the one sure source of lasting competitive advantage is knowledge. When markets shift, technologies proliferate, competitors multiply, and products become obsolete almost overnight, successful companies are those that consistently create new knowledge, disseminate it widely throughout the organization, and quickly embody it in new technologies and products. These activities define the 'knowledge-creating' company, whose sole business is continuous innovation."[35]

In the article, Nonaka goes on to explain that there are different types of knowledge and that knowledge has to be built upon before it can benefit the organization. He says that "the centerpiece of the Japanese approach is the recognition that creating new knowledge is not simply a matter of 'processing' objective information. Rather, it depends on tapping the tacit and often highly subjective insights, intuitions, and hunches of individual employees and making those insights available for testing and use by the company as a whole."[36]

Knowledge, he explains, is not often easily shared:

> Explicit knowledge is formal and systematic [so] it can be easily communicated and shared, in product specifications or a scientific formula....Tacit knowledge [however] is highly personal....It consists of mental models, beliefs, and perspectives so ingrained that we take them for granted, and therefore cannot easily articulate them.
>
> Sometimes, one individual shares tacit knowledge with another....They become part of her own tacit knowledge base...[but because that] knowledge never becomes explicit, it cannot be leveraged by the organization as a whole....[In another case,] an individual can also combine discrete pieces of explicit knowledge into a new whole. For example, when a comptroller of a company collects information throughout the organization and puts it together in a financial report, that report is new knowledge in the sense that it synthesizes information from many different sources. But this combination does not really extend the company's existing knowledge base either.
>
> In the knowledge-creating company, all...these patterns exist in dynamic interaction....First she learns the tacit secrets....Next, she translates these secrets into explicit knowledge that she can communicate to her team members....The team then standardizes this knowledge, putting it together into a manual or workbook and embodying it in a product....Finally, through the experience [they] enrich their own tacit knowledge-base....This starts the spiral all over again....[37]

Evaluation Techniques

Over the years, many techniques that provide information about how well an organization is doing have been developed. These techniques, which allow companies to compare themselves to others, reveal strengths and weaknesses. By studying the results, companies can discover ways to learn and grow and change.

Best Practices. The process of measuring best practices involves looking at various companies in order to discover basic principles of management that can be transferred to your own company. Moreover, because the companies studied are often in unrelated areas, the findings are evaluated more objectively and adopted with less disruption and defensive reactions. A good example is GE's Best Practices project, which asked the question "What's the secret of your success?"

The answers were surprisingly similar, as explained in a recent *Fortune* article:

> Almost every company [studied] emphasized managing processes, not functions; that is, they focused less on the performance of individual departments than on how they work together as products move from one to the other. They also outhustled their competitors in introducing new products and treated their suppliers as partners....
>
> The implications of the Best Practices study were earthshaking. GE realized it was managing and measuring the wrong things. The company was setting goals and keeping score; instead, says business development manager George Zippel, "we should have focused more on how things got done than on what got done."...
>
> The Best Practices findings [were turned] into a course...[that] teaches three essential lessons. The first is that other companies have much to teach GE....Second is the value of continuously improving processes, even in small ways, rather than taking big jumps....The third lesson is that processes need owners—people whose responsibility and authority reach through the walls between departments.[38]

Benchmarking. Sometimes it is important to measure specific functions against the way they are performed in other organizations. To do benchmarking requires not only determining who does similar functions but who does them as well as, if not better than, we do. One approach is to measure a specific functional department, say, marketing, against the marketing groups of other organizations. What new hardware and software seem to be coming into use? What services do they provide their internal clients? Are their users happy with the level of service provided? Benchmarking allows an organization to focus on improving one area at a time in very specific ways.

Performance Measurement. Have you set up systems that tell you how well your customer hot lines work? Do callers get through to someone knowledgeable quickly? Do your employees do everything possible to help customers? One critical step to building an environment marked by continuous improvement is visible and reliable measurement and reward systems. Measuring and rewarding employee performance promotes a belief among employees that performance matters. And if there are rewards offered for innovation and improvement, employees will be motivated to learn more and do more.

Studies. By participating in comparative studies, you can compare specific characteristics of your organization against those in other organizations. Moreover, the very act of answering the questions involved can teach employees which areas need attention.

Customer Surveys. You can learn from your customers, using them as beta sights, soliciting their input on the likes and dislikes of your products. These surveys, which can be formal or informal, also provide valuable information on new services or products that customers want.

Conclusion

The creation of a learning organization serves a number of purposes. First, learning helps employees remain sharp and enthusiastic, increasing their value to the organization. When new skills are practiced every day, efficiency increases and people are willing to accept more responsibility. Second, learning leads to greater fulfillment, because employees are more challenged and know that their skill sets are at the cutting edge. This translates into greater loyalty to the company. Third, and most important of all, employees who know the value of learning are not afraid of change. In fact, they often tend to keep an eye out for new developments and become catalysts for the rest of the company.

The message is that learning and change go hand in hand. Without a focus on learning, change is slow and costly to implement, something no organization can afford in the world we are living in today. Chapter 7 discusses the impact that time, a valuable resource and a fixed commodity, has on companies today.

7

When Fast Isn't Fast Enough

Building an Organization That Responds with Speed

Standing next to a conveyor belt as beautiful creamy white cakes roll by, Chaplin sprays on the frosting, adds a rose or two, puts the cake in the box, and puts the box on a shelf. Everything is working fine and he is enjoying himself immensely. Then the belt speeds up. In his haste to keep up, he begins moving with the famous Chaplin hyperspeed. As the cakes fly by him, the icing gets sprayed all over, the roses look like Rorschach's ink blots, and the cakes go ker-plop! on top of each other, forming a sweet white mound on the bakery floor. Chaplin foreshadowed our current "modern times." We used to laugh at this scene; now we live it.

ROBERT J. KRIEGEL AND LOUIS PATLER
If It Ain't Broke...Break It![1]

The 1980s were a time of abundant resources. We could squander them and still succeed. If some employees weren't doing their jobs effectively, there were others around who could get the work done. If marketing programs missed the mark, everyone shrugged and began developing new ones. If you had problems to solve, you could spend days contemplating solutions. In fact, if you floundered half the time, there usually was enough slack to achieve your goals. Because of the tremendous resources available, there was far less emphasis on allocating them properly. Everyone seemed to have time and money to burn.

Times have changed, however. Where once, customers waited a week to have a roll of film developed, today they expect to get it back the day they bring it in. Where once, you made corrections to a report before lunch and were lucky to get it back before a day went by, today you make the corrections yourself in minutes. Given the tremendous value placed on time, we depend on overnight delivery, when we absolutely, positively must have it overnight; we use cellular phones, faxes, and laptop computers to maximize our time on the road; and we look to automatic teller machines and 24-hour grocery stores to make life more convenient for two-wage-earner families. The emphasis on speed permeates every aspect of the world we live in. For stock traders and foreign exchange dealers who make decisions based on real-time information, a minute can be a lifetime. In the world of health care, time can mean the difference between life and death. For a busy accountant or attorney, lost time represents money; for a sales representative, it translates into lost sales opportunities; and for a new product introduction, it can determine whether a product is a major success or an also-ran. For example, "P&G's launch of Ultrathin diapers in the mid-'80s was supposed to give it a three- to five-year lead-time, but Kimberly-Clark caught up in months."[2]

In fact, in many cases, time has become more than a scarce resource; it has become a competitive weapon. First, companies speed new products to market to gain a competitive advantage. For example, "General Electric used to take three weeks after an order to deliver a custom-made industrial circuit breaker box. Now, it takes three days. AT&T used to need two years to design a new phone. Now, it can do the job in one. Motorola used to turn out electronic pagers in three weeks after they got the order. Now, it takes two hours."[3]

Second, time can be used to differentiate products and improve service delivery, increasing customer satisfaction. For example, at Aetna Life & Casualty, "A customer whose car has been stolen receives information about where to pick up a rental car by calling the company's 800 number, receives the name of the representative who will handle the claim, and is given an appointment date—all in one call. This used to take two to five days."[4] Speed of service is being used by Aetna as a major selling point; this forces its competitors to invest in additional technology to meet the level of service Aetna is providing. Another example of differentiating a product through speed is seen in the eyeglass industry. "Eyelab sought to reduce the long waiting time (normally one week) required to deliver custom-finished eyeglasses to consumers. It did this by transferring manufacturing from a single, centrally located laboratory to mini-laboratories at each of its retail outlets. Today, every Eyelab store has lenses, frames, grinding equipment, and technicians who are able to provide customers with eyeglasses within one hour."[5] Unfortunately, the advantage they gained was short-lived. Today, every mall has two or three companies providing the same speedy service.

Picking Up the Pace

Time compression in producing goods and services is having widespread effects. One area where the demand for speed is felt is distribution; after all, customers aren't happy if you make something quicker if it isn't delivered to them faster. This particular challenge pertains to products that go out of stock before demand is satisfied. Buyers who resent the lost sales caused by waiting have forced clothing manufacturers to find innovative ways to overcome this problem: "The Levi Strauss Company knows each night which style and size jeans have sold that day throughout the country. Levi uses this information to manufacture replacement stock and order replacement material. Other clothing companies such as

Benetton and The Limited have also adopted Quick Response Systems that link their suppliers, manufacturing plants, distribution centers, and retailing outlets."[6]

Speed, however, is only the latest method of gaining competitive advantage. Over the years, companies have used many other methods to gain an edge. At one time the primary form of competitive advantage came from price; those who made goods and services cheaper through mass production techniques were the first winners. The next generation of winners were victors because they offered choice by designing their products differently than their competitors. The emphasis then turned to making products better. In this stage, manufacturing prowess and the ability to enhance quality brought rewards. In the 1990s, companies will learn to make and deliver products and services faster and better in order to succeed. They will reduce the time between anticipating a need and meeting the expectations of the customer.

The growing importance of speed is clear. In fact, according to a McKinsey and Company study, "Products that go to market 6 months late, but within their expense budgets, earn 33 percent less than expected. Products that go to market on time however, even if 50 percent over budget, will still earn only 4 percent less than expected. The implication is that a premium can be paid for ideas that accelerate the attainment of objectives."[7] Moreover, people are willing to pay for speed. A perfect example is Federal Express, which "is the result of Fred Smith's recognizing the importance that households and businesses place on fast and reliable delivery services....[Even the] Postal Service admits that Federal Express users are willing to pay 25 to 40 times more for this service."[8]

The question is, How can we take advantage of everyone's desire for speed, for ways to save time? To start with, it is essential that we look at time as a valuable and limited resource. Time cannot be grown, expanded, or changed; it is a constant. Unlike money, which flows in and out, and earns different rates of return, time is finite. Although you cannot get more time, the time you have can be better and more effectively utilized. Today, when success often equals the efficient use of time, we must modify the way our organizations are run, rethink our management practices, and challenge the way we allocate our personal time.

Organizational Effectiveness

> Large companies need to be protected all right—from themselves....Large companies have proven willing to cut bodies to reduce expenses, but are more recalcitrant to replacing bureaucracy with entrepreneurship....Thus in the now-classic words of the cartoon character Pogo, "We have met the enemy, and he is us." Or, more accurately, the enemy is complacency supported by bureaucracy—the proliferation of unnecessary rules, cumbersome procedures, and non-value-adding administrators that strangle potential innovators with red tape....Bureaucracy was designed for repetition, not innovation; for control, not creativity.—ROSABETH MOSS KANTER[9]

No one would argue that organizations need administrative and policy-making guidance—the original meaning of bureaucracy. The problem is that bureaucracies tend to grow, expanding layer upon layer, becoming, as they increase in size, roadblocks to success. Bloated bureaucracies crush aspirations, stifle creativity, suppress ingenuity, and slow responsiveness. They create a thirst for power, leading to personal ambition over team gains, and put paperwork before people. And this happens because bureaucracies respond to power, to those who are bigger, tougher, and stronger. It happens because in bureaucracies individual employees and individual customers do not matter—their voices are never heard by the people who determine policy. It happens because in bureaucracies everything is done by committee, constructing such strong barriers to responsiveness that even those who hear do not answer.

Examples of bureaucratic excess are easy to find. General Electric, in its 1991 *Annual Report,* admits that "unfortunately, it is still possible to find documents around GE businesses that look like something out of the National Archives, with five, ten, or even more signatures necessary before action can be taken."

The report goes on to explain that the problem with so many layers of approval is that "layers insulate. They slow things down. They garble. Leaders in highly layered organizations are like people who wear several sweaters outside on a freezing winter day. They remain warm and comfortable but are blissfully ignorant of the realities of their environment. They couldn't be further from what's going on."[10]

In organizations that are heavily bureaucratic, procedures are designed to meet internal requirements rather than the needs of the customer; politics—who said what to whom, who is gaining power, who gets the credit, and who to blame—overshadows everything, from clients' needs to inroads made by the competition to overall organizational performance. When promotions are earned through political savvy rather than performance, people choose the political solution rather than the best answer; the "show" becomes more important than content; and rumor becomes the primary form of communication. The result is an organization that focuses inward and looses touch with reality.

The truth is that companies cannot compete in a fast-paced world with shackles around their ankles. "It's amazing that Bob Frankenberg ever got anything done at all. Until last year, the Hewlett-Packard Co. general manager dealt with no fewer than 38 in-house committees. They decided everything from what features to include in a new software program to what city would be the best for staging a product launch. Just coming up with a name for the company's New Wave Computing software took nearly 100 people on nine committees seven months."[11]

Bureaucracies Are Not Biodegradable

The worst aspect of bureaucracies, however, is that they are tenacious; they never seem to go away. In fact, once bureaucracy takes root, it is as difficult to control in business as crabgrass is on a suburban lawn. But in today's world, where speed and efficiency are the difference between success and failure, we must replace bureaucratic obstacles with speed, simplicity, and continuous improvement. Operational units must be allowed to remain small. People must get out of their offices and in front of customers. Ad hoc task forces, composed of multifunctional groups, must be set up to tackle issues; ideas must be chosen based on merit rather than an individual's place in the pecking order; and activities that do not add value to the client must be eliminated.

Since no bureaucracy will dismantle itself, it is up to management to change the organization. As Michael Dealey said in *Fortune* magazine:

> The great pyramids of ancient Egypt have withstood the test of time; historic reminders of an era long gone by, they have remained steadfast against the elements down through the ages. Unfortunately, the same cannot be said for a different, more modern pyramid—the traditional structure of the 20th-century multinational corporation....
>
> [It may be time for corporate structures] to look less like a pyramid and more like a spider. This spider has a multitude of legs that are often in motion—sometimes very fast motion. Think of these legs as the corporation's direct contacts with the environment, quickly sensing conditions and adjusting course to stay on track. These "legs" receive, interpret, and deliver information based on their direct interaction with environmental elements, whether they be customers, suppliers, or regulators. The power and strength of the spider lies in its ability to use these interactions not merely to maintain its present equilibrium, but also to influence and clear its path for future success. While many legs may appear to be going in several directions at once, they are all guided by a central nervous system—top management.[12]

Becoming more spiderlike will not be easy for most corporations. The bureaucratic culture is deeply ingrained, a model that permeates government as well as business and thus is a part of all our mind-sets. To overcome this way of thinking, it will be necessary to pinpoint particular elements of bureaucratic behavior and find ways to eliminate them.

Removing Red Tape

When people spend all their time on paperwork and reports, reviewing work with superiors, sending copies of everything to everybody, or getting multiple approvals before action can be taken, important activities that make the organization more competitive are put on the back burner. As a result, the organization's ability to respond quickly suffers. General Electric's 1990 *Annual Report* also said that the company wants "to liberate employees from the cramping artifacts that pile up in the dusty attics of century-old companies: The reports, meetings, rituals, approvals, controls, and forests of paper that often seem necessary until they are removed."[13] Achieving this goal requires overcoming the activities that comprise the "red tape" of an organization.

Since there is general agreement that these activities make companies less competitive, why aren't they eliminated? A major reason is a lack of trust in the capabilities of others. Some people believe they are more competent than their coworkers, or have better business judgment than their colleagues. Others believe that being directly involved in final decisions increases their personal visibility and power. Thus, part of the solution for overcoming red tape is to search for and hire excellent people and then invest in them by enhancing their skills through training. This will make everyone more comfortable with the competency levels of their colleagues and less determined to oversee every aspect of their work. Employees must also be imbued with a common purpose and rewarded for team gain.

Moreover, hiring the best and brightest people and then developing and retaining them result in increased company loyalty and personal confidence. Employees feel better about their own abilities and know that the organization believes in and supports them. When employees have this kind of confidence, they are not afraid to make bold moves and rarely second guess their own decisions. Ross Perot once said, "At GM, if you see a snake, the first thing you do is go hire a consultant on snakes. Then you get a committee on snakes, and then you discuss it for a couple of years. The most likely course of action is—nothing. You figure, the snake hasn't bitten anybody yet, so you let him crawl around the factory floor....I come from an environment where, the first guy who sees the snake kills it."[14]

Rules and Procedures That Create Freedom

Many people find routines irritating because they stifle creativity and create inflexibility, but they can also be timesaving devices that minimize mistakes. For example, doctors put their patients through diagnostic routines, and airline pilots go through routines prior to takeoff. Edward de Bono explains in *Six Action Shoes* that "in some ways routines provide freedom. If we had to think about every action we take, then life would be very slow and very complicated. Following a routine actually frees us to attend to matters that really need our attention....Instead of having to analyze each new experience, we simply recognize the situation by using a perceptual pattern."[15] In other words, routines save us time by allowing us to do by rote those things that simply have to be done.

Problems arise, however, when we fail to look at routines and policies to see if they are providing value. Often procedures that were once designed to expedite a special task become ingrained in the company's operations, remaining in place long after they are needed. *The Wall Street Journal* reported, for example, that IBM cut 34 items from the information required to justify an engineering change. The story went on to report that when the engineers investigated who had needed the information, they "couldn't even find anyone who knew....That's the crazy thing. Nobody even remembered."[16]

There is a tendency to ignore the fact that programs or procedures that were effective yesterday may no longer apply today. We continually add new procedures, but seldom eliminate old ones. The reason we do so is simple: people are rewarded for new programs, not for getting rid of old ones, even when they clearly have become unnecessary.

Streamlining the Business Process

Things don't move more quickly simply because you demand they be done faster. Organizations can achieve "order of magnitude" improvements by setting overly ambitious goals that force people to rethink things—and thus help them find new and more effective ways to accomplish their objectives. One way to streamline an organization is to redesign and improve the processes by which work is done. An emerging management practice shown to improve efficiency involves setting up teams that work across functional areas. The problem, today, is that "most companies organize themselves into vertically functioning groups, with experts of similar backgrounds grouped together to provide a pool of knowledge and skills capable of completing any task in that discipline. This creates an effective, strong, confident organization that functions well as a team, eager to support its own mission. Unfortunately, however,...a horizontal work flow combined with a vertical organization results in many voids and overlaps and encourages suboptimization, negatively impacting the efficiency and effectiveness of the process."[17]

Organizing along vertical lines slows speed. Companies not only waste valuable time, but ideas become compartmentalized, information is not shared, and optimum solutions are not found. A good illustration of this is the contrast between running a 100-yard race as an individual and as part of a relay team. The members of great relay teams are not only concerned with their own performances, but with properly transferring the baton to their team members. In fact, it is possible to have the four fastest runners in the world on the team yet lose the race because the baton transfers take too long. Therefore, everyone has to expand his or her thinking from improving personal performance to improving their skills as team members.

Unfortunately, studies have shown that "95% of the time it takes to produce a product adds no value."[18] By establishing teams to improve their business processes, organizations can channel their efforts toward adding value to the customer. The road to organizational efficiency requires exposing and then eliminating the nonessential activities that delay or interrupt processes. There are six ways to improve a business process:

The first method is to eliminate the task altogether. The second is work simplification, the elimination of all the nonproductive elements of a task. The third is to combine tasks. The fourth is to change the sequence to improve speed. The fifth is to simplify the activity, and the sixth and last is to do things simultaneously. Activities such as gathering information, transporting a product, inspecting it, correcting mistakes, and storing it until something else happens to it do not add value.

Politics Don't Promote Speed

How much time and effort is wasted due to internal politics? How much time is wasted grandstanding during meetings? How many memos do people write to cover their behinds? Someone once said to me, "I don't mind the amount of work I have to do in my job, in fact, I thrive on it. But the politics are draining and debilitating." How much time is spent justifying yesterday's actions rather than making today's decisions? How much time is wasted trying to rise in the corporate hierarchy? How much time is wasted by employees trying to impress their superiors? How much time would be saved if that same time was spent working for the good of the organization? Organizations that want to eliminate the time wasted playing politics must instill a common sense of purpose; a working environment of openness, of trust, of honesty; a climate in which playing politics is a losing game.

Territorial Barricades and Independent Fiefdoms

Organizations also suffer from inefficiencies caused by the segregation of people into functional or operational groups or the creation of other artificial boundaries. The desire to be considered independent from the rest of the organization leads to numerous problems. Sometimes it results in knowingly sabotaging another part of the organization to make one's own group look better; other times it results in misunderstandings or lack of communication. For example, a department at a slow point in its business cycle won't volunteer support to a department that is swamped because the department heads are in competition with one another.

Organizations also suffer when yearly departmental budgets are based on past expenditures instead of on future needs. When organizations operate in that manner, it encourages individual departments to spend money frivolously at the end of the year rather than helping another part of the organization desperately needing the money.

Lack of communication between departments also creates inefficiencies and the duplication of efforts. In one case, a marketing department bought and maintained a database of Fortune 500 companies representing its target audience, while unknowingly, another department had the same list because it tracked financial information for sales purposes.

Working at Cross Purposes

Another source of waste in organizations occurs when parts of the organization work at cross purposes with one another, each pursuing independent goals regardless of how they impact others. For example, the research and development group insists on increasing the testing time of a new product launch at the same time the marketing department argues for launching the product immediately. Marketing believes the delay will cost them the window of opportunity in the marketplace, while the research and development group is anxious to ensure a 100 percent fault-free product. To make matters worse, performance evaluations and compensation programs encourage this kind of thinking.

Resisting Change

One of the biggest wastes of precious time is resistance to change. When management develops strategic plans in isolation or with the help of outsiders, ignoring the employees who will be responsible for implementing the plan, it becomes more difficult and costly to introduce change. The need to manage change and ensure employee acceptance and commitment is discussed in Chapter 6, which sets forth a detailed new philosophy for change.

Simple Means Swift

Measuring ideas by their complexity rather than their merit is inefficient, wasting time and money. And yet, all too often, for example, the more convoluted reports are, the more profound they are considered. They are often measured by their bulk rather than by the soundness of their recommendations. *The Wall Street Journal* reported the story of "Bob Aguire, owner of Eastern Reproduction Corp. of Waltham, Mass., [who] handed some paperwork in a sealed envelope to a state environmental regulator. 'He hefted it and without opening it, handed it back....He said it wasn't heavy enough.'"[19] Among the other forms of needless complexity are convoluted and inefficient communications. Organizations should encourage people to first consider the needs of their audience and then communicate clearly, avoiding acronyms, jargon, and buzzwords.

The virtue of clear and simple communication is evident in the complexity of the following documents:[20]

Lord's Prayer	57 words
Ten Commandments	71 words
Gettysburg Address	266 words
Declaration of Independence	1,300 words
U.S. Government Contractor Management System Evaluation Program	38,000 words

The Technology Investment

Speed can be gained through technology. Many companies spend millions of dollars on everything from mobile phones, voice mail, CAD/CAM technology, faxes, and personal computers. Few too many organizations, however, make full use of the technology they invest in. Unfortunately, they fail to introduce it into the organization properly, and their employees are not trained to make the best use of it. One example is the publishing firm that bought all its employees desk top computers to use, but left it up to each individual to learn how to use them. While some ambitious people made the personal investment to teach themselves, others let the technology sit idle. Those companies that bring in the right technology and introduce it the right way, achieve an order-of-magnitude of savings in time and increased productivity.

Planning with a Purpose

Proper planning must be deeply ingrained in organizations that want to become world-class competitors. Unfortunately, even when companies believe in the importance of planning, they fall into many traps that cost them valuable time along the way. For example, some organizations have analysis paralysis: They spend all of their time setting up task forces and committees to analyze problems, but then never act on the recommendations. Take the example of a company that hired a consultant to conduct new product research. When the company was asked by the consultant, "How will you respond if the research points in this direction?" they said they did not know. They were then asked how they would respond if the research pointed in the opposite direction, and the answer was the same. The consultant explained that they were wasting their money conducting research without having a plan in place for acting on the recommendations: Research is not an end in itself, but a means to an end that can only be achieved through action.

Other problems include falling into the trap of saying, "There is a window of opportunity—forget planning—we must *act now!*" Many companies that claim they don't have the time to plan always find the time to do things over again when their initial actions fail. Other companies are afraid to take a firm position on an issue and end up setting vague goals that can be interpreted many different ways; then they wonder why their employees are working at cross purposes. Furthermore, there are companies that are unfocused, and don't know how to say no. They try to accomplish everything with limited resources—and never end up accomplishing anything.

Organizations that are successful in their planning efforts have common attributes. They make sure the people responsible for implementing plans are highly involved in the planning process. They develop cross-functional teams to ensure input is received from employees with different perspectives and experiences. They prioritize activities when resources are scarce, and they concentrate their critical resources in those areas that provide the greatest returns.

External Relationships Are Critical

World-class organizations know that, in today's fast-paced environment, spreading your resources too thin places you at a competitive disadvantage. It is time for companies to focus their attention on those areas that are most critical to their business success and to tap external sources to supplement their efforts. To do this successfully requires, as discussed in Chapter 8, building win-win relationships with their suppliers. Today, there is no time for mistrust, for law suits and squabbles, for formalities and long, drawn-out negotiations.

Management Style— Getting the Most from Others

> Perhaps the most insidious and costly form of waste stems from underestimating, underutilizing, and misusing the organization's most important asset: the knowledge, skills and positive attitudes of its people.—ARMAND FEIGENBAUM[21]

Organizational waste and inefficiency comes in many shapes and sizes, some visible and some invisible. Managers must find new ways to change the organization. They must overcome the cultural behaviors that prevent progress, and help employees function as efficiently as possible. Good managers are like good farmers: they invest in the future by planting seeds and then nurturing and cultivating them; they know that that is the only way to reap a harvest. And just as good coaches know the best way to utilize their players, management must build on the strengths of their employees.

In many organizations, however, management does not operate efficiently. For example, some managers make their motto, "Ready, Fire, Aim"; they act before they think. Because they do not take the time to organize themselves, they waste valuable time running around in circles, putting out fires instead of lighting the fires of innovation. Other managers believe that nothing gets done unless everyone is frantic. They have never learned the difference between motion and movement. Motion is when individuals actively move from point *a* to point *b* accomplishing their goals; movement is when everyone runs around, chasing their tails, never getting anything accomplished. Those who manage this way need to learn the difference between urgent and important.

Learning to Communicate

The absence of communications, which creates many inefficiencies in organizations, is discussed thoroughly in Chapter 4. Managers waste valuable time by not explaining their priorities, by not taking the time to communicate with those around them, by failing to listen to the needs of their people or answering their questions fully, by using words that are misunderstood, or by sharing information only when it is critical that people have it. This causes people to feel isolated, work at cross purposes, and duplicate the efforts of others. Employees, uncertain of which direction to take, move cautiously instead of charging ahead.

Managers should make sure that all employees understand the importance of time and how much delays cost the company. They should foster an environment of open and honest communication, where feedback is welcomed. After all, constructive feedback leads to continuous improvement and strengthens employee confidence.

Managing Information

According to studies, "searching for, and handling, information occupies up to 20 percent of your time"; therefore, it is critical that you think carefully about the kinds of information the organization really needs.[22] Moreover, according to another study, "the amount of paperwork that travels across a desk has increased by as much as 600 percent....The average person wastes 45 minutes a day searching for some item on his desk."[23]

The problem with paperwork is that it often keeps employees from accomplishing important activities for clients. Of course, some paperwork is necessary. The question is, Which reports are really needed? By whom? For what purpose? Is the information ever acted on? How often should the information be collected? Which reporting should be eliminated altogether? Managers who examine their paperwork requirements with those questions in mind will probably find that much reporting is unnecessary.

Learning to Make Decisions

Some decisions require spending time evaluating alternatives, while others can be made quickly. If you can learn to spot those that can be handled quickly and act on them, you can save a great deal of time. An article in *The Journal of Management* notes that researchers have found "that decisions [are] made faster when their consequences [are] more important." The same article notes that "contrary to intuition, decision makers [take] longer to make a decision with a problem when several alternatives [are] easily rejected, leaving just two, than when all four alternatives [are] of equal quality."[24]

Meetings—the National Pastime

Meetings raise many of the same issues. According to an article in *Business Week*, "the average senior executive spends four hours a day in meetings."[25] It is important to determine which of them are necessary. You may find many decisions could be made during conference calls or else require no more than a brief discussion in the hallway.

Managers should ask themselves how much time is wasted when meetings are called at the last minute, requiring everyone to drop what they are doing or reschedule planned events. How much time is wasted when meetings are called without having an agenda beforehand, when meetings drift into irrelevant discussions, or when meetings are allowed to drag on endlessly? Managers should ask why people are allowed to waste others' time by showing up late, why people are allowed to grandstand or railroad their ideas through, or why people stand around chatting when the meeting is over instead of attending to business.

Another way that meetings waste time is through the preparation that goes into them. In some organizational cultures, there is more emphasis on the "show" than on the content. When that happens, tremendous time is spent preparing materials, rehearsing, and revising presentations for an internal audience. For example, *The Wall Street Journal* reports that "Richard Flaherty, manager of the supplies operation, says he used to make 'thousands of foils at IBM to get 20 that the VP would show at the corporate strategy session. The preparation would start in November, the big presentation would be in March, and it'd be obsolete by April 1.'"[26]

Dealing with Fear and Insecurity

Employees cannot do their best work when they are worried about their future, when they are not allowed to think for themselves but are treated like children, when they know their recommendations aren't respected, or when they don't feel in control of their destinies. People can't perform at their best when they feel that every decision will be scrutinized and second guessed, and every mistake will be ridiculed; they waste more time trying to impress people internally than getting their job done; they play Monday morning quarterback and second guess each other rather than make innovative suggestions.

Confidence and security increases employee efficiency and effectiveness. Fear and insecurity have the opposite effect. They cause employees to take on more and more work trying to look busy so they won't get fired (and then they do the work poorly because they don't have enough time to do it all well—if at all). They lead employees to spend their time concentrating on things that they know well, not because they are priorities, but because they feel secure doing them. And they lead employees to ignore problems, waiting for them to go away by themselves rather than correcting them, or looking for someone to blame when they surface.

These problems will only be overcome when people have confidence in themselves and their organizations. The result can best be illustrated in a story of a problem in a Japanese company. The first department head looked within his group to see whether his employees were at fault. He was happy to find out they did not play a role. The second department head also looked within his department and found out that his employees were at fault. He was happy too because he was able to identify the cause; the problem could be fixed and the company's customers would never be inconvenienced again.

Learning to Delegate

Trying to do everything yourself is not good management; it is an addiction. Walter Kiechel III noted in an article in *Fortune* magazine that "if everybody is clamoring for your time, that time is a precious commodity, and by scheduling yourself into too many things, you show everybody how important you are."[27] To overcome the tendency to "do it all," managers must keep in mind that the cost of hiring talented people and then looking over their shoulders every step of the way destroys their confidence and creativity. Micromanagement—requests for daily itineraries, endless memos, and detailed sales call reports along with an insistence that five approvals be obtained before action is taken—creates an environment of mistrust. Some managers fear that they will not be recognized and rewarded if they aren't personally involved in every activity, if the function isn't housed within their department, or if the activity is not conducted within their sights. Those who don't delegate spend their time doing work for others as their own work piles up in their in-boxes. They think they are making themselves invaluable when they actually become bottlenecks and waste precious time for the organization.

Good managers increase their efficiency by learning how to trust. They realize that they cannot be everywhere at the same time or be the best at everything. They learn how to delegate internally to their colleagues and develop strategic alliances with outside organizations.

Acquiring the Art of Decision Making

Learning to empower your employees can save valuable time for your organization. For example, think about the time wasted by cumbersome review processes. Individuals with new ideas first have to build a case for their recommendations, preparing a written proposal or presentation for management to review. Then, they must set up a meeting, often involving multiple individuals whose travel schedules have to be coordinated, which may take days or weeks. There is often internal posturing before the meeting; time spent studying the issue. And then the meeting takes place. When all is said and done, the decision ends up being made in 20 minutes by people vaguely familiar with the situation. The individual who initially made the recommendation was probably closer to the situation, spent weeks or months thinking it through, put tremendous effort into selling it internally, and could have acted on the recommendation by the time the idea was even placed on anybody's calendar.

The problem is that many managers don't believe people should think for themselves. Robert Waterman, Jr., makes just that point in *The Renewal Factor* when he tells the story of "a General Motors executive [who] says that H. Ross Perot saw something that needed doing inside GM and told a GM manager to do it. The man replied that it was not part of his job description. 'You need a job description,' fumed Perot, 'I'll give you a job description: Use your head.' The bemused GM executive said, 'Can you imagine what chaos we'd have around here if everybody did that?'"[28]

Providing Training

Managers waste precious time by not making the proper commitment to and investment in training. Even when some people know they can't do all of the work themselves, their jobs often keep them so busy that they don't have the time to train anyone; this creates a vicious cycle. Or they are apprehensive about taking their best salespeople out of the field and sending them to additional training because their absence would lead to a short-term decline in sales; then they end up promoting them to sales manager, knowing they never received management training. Or they send employees through training programs, never reinforce the training, and then are disappointed when the employees can't do the new job well.

Controlling Expectation Levels

When managers make impossible demands on others, they get less than satisfactory results. For example, I know a manager who not only asks his employees to take the red eye from Los Angeles to New York, arriving at six o'clock in the morning, but then wants them to come to work directly from the airport. When employees haven't gotten more than a couple hours of sleep, how productive can we expect them to be the next day? Just because they put in the time does not make them productive.

On the other hand, managers whose expectation levels are too low get as little as employees know they will accept. Furthermore, correcting mistakes made by employees without explaining how they should have done the job, avoiding confrontation by asking subordinates for less than possible, or allowing employees to escape from their responsibilities all lead to mediocrity.

Dealing with Pressure

Managers must learn how to handle pressure themselves and how much can be productively applied to those who work for them. Managers who don't deal well with stress must learn that losing control and ranting and raving do not accomplish what rational discussion does; worse, it creates an atmosphere in which employees spend countless hours measuring their actions to avoid explosions. Furthermore, working under pressure does not always increase productivity. *The Journal of Management* reported that experts studying "the productivity of NASA scientists and engineers...found that productivity increased as time pressure increased (deadlines shortened)—up to a point. After deadlines became too short, performance declined....Thus, they suggest that the overall relationship between deadline length and performance may be an inverted U-shaped one. Performance increases as deadlines shorten, but beyond some limited increased reductions in deadline length, pressure reduces rather than increases performance."[29] The article also noted that "as time pressure increased (the time available to make the decision becomes shorter) and greater emphasis [was placed] on negative information, information about what could go wrong or bad."

Personal Time Management

> The average American will, in a lifetime, spend five years waiting in line, one year searching for belongings at home or office, three years attending meetings, and eight years opening junk mail.—MICHAEL FORTINO[30]

Time is short! Where did the time go? The time just seemed to slip away. If I only had more time! We all have heard statements bemoaning the fact that there isn't enough time to do what we have to do or want to do. In most cases, if we look back, it isn't that there wasn't enough time, but that the time needed was spent doing something else.

Unless we learn to treat time as personal capital, investing it wisely, we will never have enough of it—and never achieve the rewards we seek. Given the speed of today's world and the demands we face daily, if we want to accomplish specific business and personal goals, we have to learn to manage time (for example, become more organized, stop procrastinating, learn how to make decisions quickly). The problem for many of us is that time management, like every other form of management, requires discipline and changing lifelong habits.

Placing a Value on Time

The first step in learning to manage time is recognizing that time has value. Adia Personnel Services, based in Menlo Park, California, discovered that employees spend the equivalent of a three-week vacation chatting by the water cooler. In a nationwide survey of 1104 personnel decision makers, it found that average employees probably spend 30 minutes or more [each day] "shooting the breeze" with their coworkers.[31] If employees thought about how often they had to stay late to finish something because they wasted time, they might respect and value time more.

Overcoming Bad Habits

Time management is not only about saving time, it is about changing personal habits. How successful you are depends on your ability to discipline yourself on a constant basis. For example, think about how many people go on diets only to gain the weight back later; they did not change their long-term behaviors, but tried to loose weight as quickly as possible so they could go back to eating the way they always had. Another habit that needs to be controlled is mentally replaying events that took place in the past or worrying about things you can't do anything about. If you can do something to make the situation better, do it. If you can't, then don't worry about it. Furthermore, people waste a lot of time complaining to others. These behaviors not only waste time, but sap energy. Unlearn bad habits. Look for ways to use your time more effectively and learn new ways to conduct business. For example, a two-minute telephone call can often replace writing a detailed memo or walking to the next floor to ask a question. Go out to lunch five or ten minutes before or after the lunch rush and avoid waiting in line. Confirm appointments rather than arriving at your destination only to find out your appointment had to leave town at the last minute.

Learning to Prioritize

As Peter Drucker said, "It is more important to do the right things than to do things right." Some people work hard at things that they enjoy and that keep them busy, but have low payoff. They bounce from city to city attending meetings even though it isn't necessary for them to be there, maintain very elaborate to-do lists, but then don't prioritize the items on the list or they put aside the most difficult, challenging chores in favor of those that can be finished quickly.

The problem with this behavior is that it doesn't reap rewards. In contrast, proactive people tackle one thing at a time, focusing on what is important but not necessarily urgent. They avoid getting caught up in busy work, buried in minutiae. In order to be sure that you "do the right things and do them right," set milestones for yourself, plot your progress toward your company's long-term goals, and establish and reestablish priorities.

Avoiding Procrastination

Procrastination becomes a major problem when you find it easier to explain why the job isn't done rather than doing it, when you spend more time focusing on why the work will be hard to complete rather than getting down to it, when you spend more time complaining about the work you have to do than doing it. In the *Baylor Business Review*, Joe Cox and Raymond Read catalog the reasons why people procrastinate. Included in their list are such items as:

> *Fear of failure or rejection:* Procrastination allows persons to avoid risk while still protecting their self-worth...by never attempting a task, I cannot fail....*Low self-concept or image:* Many people see their worth only in the ability to perform well. By procrastinating, no effort to perform has been extended; thus there is no danger to self-worth....*Peter Pan Syndrome:* a childlike world without responsibilities or the necessity of doing unpleasant tasks....Hoping someone else will do it...*Wishing for things to happen*...if you put it off long enough, it no longer has to be done....*Perfectionism:* this is the unrealistic attitude that if a person cannot complete a task perfectly, there is no reason to start the task....*Inability to say no:* With an overbooked agenda, something must wind up on the back burner....*Adrenaline addiction:* some people like the rush of a last-minute deadlines....*Fear of success:* Some procrastinate because they fear successes. If they succeed, they must continue to accomplish. And, since the pressure to accomplish and beat the previous record is constant, it is thought that success should be avoided. *Lack of skill:* Not having the appropriate expertise or learned skills to effectively handle one's job....*Decision Making:* the difficulty some people encounter when trying to make tough decisions causes them to simply avoid making those decisions....*Too little to do:* A person learns to accept boredom

and inactivity as a lifestyle....*Authority resistance:* Procrastination can be a way of expressing hostility or anger at a superior or an organization.[32]

Almost everyone puts off doing something at some time or another. The problem comes when procrastination becomes a way of life. To succeed, you must find ways to break the pattern, choosing specific goals to meet. If you attempt things in small steps, tasks become less overwhelming and you will gain the confidence to stop putting off until tomorrow what should be done today.

Becoming Organized

One of the reasons why people accomplish far less than they should is that they are disorganized. They do not plan, they run from crisis to crisis, and they can't find things when they need them. An advertisement in *Today's Office* reported that "managers and clerical staffs often spend 25–40% of their time searching for information that is misfiled or missing."[33]

Unfortunately, anyone trying to challenge people to get more organized runs up against a bias—organization implies rigid behavior that precludes creativity and innovation. It is only when people believe that being organized buys time for thinking and creating that they overcome this prejudice.

Controlling Information

When was the last time that you cleaned up your files? It seems as though people would rather do anything than deal with the old things they have accumulated. If you play pack rat, never weed out your files, never cancel publications you no longer read, or never ask to have your name taken off distribution lists, you won't have enough space to store everything and will waste endless time searching for what you do need.

There are three sources of information that have to be managed: daily operating information, general reading information, and miscellaneous information. To control all three requires periodically reviewing the information you receive to see whether it still meets your needs, organizing the information so you can find it easily, deciding whether it is important (for example, for legal purposes), and deciding whether it should be passed on to others in your organization.

Taking Time to Plan

Planning for the future saves time. It allows you to consolidate activities, thereby saving time, money, and annoyance. Instead of making several trips to buy office supplies, let everyone know that you make one trip on the fifteenth of every month; instead of stopping at a convenience store every night because you run out of something, try to arrange to make one stop. Failing to plan leaves you with constant annoyances and problems, with little time or energy for cultivating important relationships, motivating employees, or making sure that activities are done right the first time.

Avoiding Distractions

"Do you have a minute? I have a great idea." "I have to turn this project in in half an hour. Can you take a look at it for me?" "So, what did you think of the ballgame last night?" "I'll call when I have a really strong investment recommendation, OK?" These are examples of the distractions that people face everyday.

Remember you have a choice. You can permit salespeople to walk in unannounced, you can let others control your time by dropping everything when they need you, you can be distracted by those who don't value their time and try to steal yours, or you can put your nose to the grindstone and concentrate on priorities that help you accomplish your goals.

Utilizing Small Blocks of Time

Just as it is important to manage large blocks of time, it is also important to watch how you spend small increments of time: they add up. How many times have you been kept waiting 10 minutes for a meeting, 15 minutes for the dentist, 20 minutes for a luncheon companion, 30 minutes because a flight is delayed, or 45 minutes commuting on a train? If you added up all these small increments, you would realize how much time you waste.

Make a conscious effort to invest your minutes wisely. For example, always carry reading material, keep a notebook with you to outline that speech you were asked to give, bring along stationery so you can write notes to family and friends. If you use the time that most people seem to waste, you will accomplish more—and spend less time and energy fuming over inconveniences that often cannot be avoided.

Employing Technology Time-Savers

Learn how technology can help you become more productive. Then use it. Turning on your answering machine when you are in the middle of an activity, learning what new computer software is available to make you more productive, and using voice mail rather than playing phone tag are all ways to save time.

Conclusion

> You know, people are constantly looking at their watches, but they don't really see them. [They are] too busy regretting the past or worrying about the future. So they miss the beauty of little things and, before they know it, the seasons have changed, the children have grown up, and life is almost over. Then they blame me [father time]. "Time went too fast" they say. But I'm here now.—Paul Hellman[34]

Don't think of managing time only in terms of excelling in your career and being efficient in business. It also affects your personal life, allowing you to enhance family relationships, improve yourself, become fit, pursue hobbies and cultural activities, find your spiritual side, and give back to the community. Rather than living your life on a treadmill, take the time to smell the roses.

In *Fortune* magazine, Walter Kiechel III says that "what the workaholic has forgotten, and the would-be manager of time should always keep in mind is what one might be doing outside the office. Possibilities include walking out in the weather of sunlit days and storm: watching the seasons change; seeing children grow and maybe even helping the process along; talking in candlelight, perhaps over a meal, with attractive persons, possibly including one's spouse; and being there to solace a troubled friend, or child, or aging parent. If you consistently choose work over these alternatives, then you really have a problem managing time."[35] I tell people to learn from those less fortunate than themselves: those who might only have a year to live. What are their priorities and what can you learn from them? Imagine that you are at the end of your life. What would you have done differently if you only had the chance to do it over again? Maybe it's time to start acting on that now!

8
Partnering—
Entering the Age
of Cooperation

Building
a Flexible Organization

*Reflecting on the "old days"—all of five
or six years ago—a Chicago area supplier...sarcastically recalls how one of his
big customers used to treat its suppliers.
The strategy was: "Line 'em up and beat
'em up—until you get 'em to a point
where they can't make money any more.
Then you've got the best price."*

JOHN SHERIDAN
Industry Week[1]

In today's competitive environment, companies are going outside more and more often to complement their internal
resources. This allows them to concentrate their limited
resources on their core areas; it allows them to access specialized skills that their regular employees don't have or to add
extra people during peak periods; it provides them with objec-

tive viewpoints from people with multiclient experience; and it alerts them to new trends that may affect their businesses. These arrangements take many forms, ranging from outsourcing to alliance partners to external consultants (such as advertising agencies and public relations firms) to third-party contractors to free-lance personnel.

In order to optimize any form of partnership, you must learn how to forge strong bonds and build lasting relationships with your partners. The key to doing this is to keep in mind that formal contracts don't make successful relationships; people do. It takes people to create a foundation on which trust, loyalty, and commitment can be built.

When dealing with relationships remember that each one is unique and must be treated as special. There isn't a single set of rules for doing this, but there are certain behaviors that you must avoid. For example, partnerships cannot succeed if one partner is kept in the dark; if one member of a team isn't kept up-to-date, the result is likely to be failure. Partnerships cannot succeed when one partner attempts to gain the upper hand; when a partner discovers selfish motives, the result is likely to be failure. Partnerships cannot succeed if they involve scapegoating; if one partner demands that the other perform work a certain way and then blames them because the effort fails, the result is likely to be failure.

The basic rule, whether you invest in a smaller organization to gain access to new products and services, develop licensing agreements to take advantage of a strong distribution capability, hire an agency to create a promotional campaign, or bring in a free-lancer to help write a speech for a senior executive, is that in the long run you get from these partnerships what you put into them. A partnership is successful to the degree that it replaces the traditional "we versus them" mentality with a new "us" that allows everyone involved to grow and to reach their full potential.

In the past, conventional wisdom said that multiple vendors increased competition and enhanced performance, that playing one supplier against another was good business. Today, however, the trend is quite the opposite. An article in *The Wall Street Journal* explained that companies around the country are cutting back the number of suppliers they use...by as much as 90%. They are demanding higher levels of service and product quality from the survivors. And are willing to pay a premium on the theory that getting things right initially is cheaper in the long run....The impetus for much of the change is Japanese competition. A decade ago, corporate executives and consulting gurus noticed that Japanese companies often had just a few hundred direct suppliers while their U.S. counterparts often had thousands. And the Japanese tended to have much closer and longer-term relationships with their suppliers, often owning a piece of them.[2]

Another article in *The Wall Street Journal* pointed out that "competition is one way to increase the efficiency of outside vendors, but many in-house lawyers are trimming the list of law firms that they use. Some general counsel say they get higher quality at lower cost by building relationships with fewer law firms."[3] Experience has shown them that the only way to build lasting relationships is to start with honorable intentions, make a commitment, and spend the time and effort building solid relationships with a select few.

General Electric's Jack Welch said it best in GE's 1989 *Annual Report:*

Our dream for the 1990s is a boundary-less Company, a Company where we knock down the walls that separate us from each other on the inside and from our key constituencies on the outside....A boundary-less Company will level its external walls...reaching out to key suppliers to make them part of a single process in which they and we join hands and intellects in a common purpose—satisfying customers.

Welch is not the only leader sensing the need for strong partnerships. An article in *Small Business Reports* notes that

as we move into the 1990s, it will not be sufficient to be big and multinational with the advantages in costs, finance, distribution, and service that large companies possess. Nor will it be enough to be small and entrepreneurial, with the advantages of innovation and rapid customer responsiveness. Our organizations, large and small, will have to increasingly "network"...to achieve success. What are the advantages of networking? "It's like having a fighter who can move like a lightweight and hit like a heavyweight," claims an IBM director. Networking firms will be able to effectively bring both the economies of scale and customer responsiveness to the marketplace—like a battleship surrounded by PT boats, with both power and speed of attack.[4]

What Causes Relationships to Fail?

According to the Association of Advertising Agencies, the average length of an agency and client relationship is 7.2 years. But at the same time:

> Unilever has had an uninterrupted union with J. Walter Thompson Co. for 85 years. AT&T has worked with NW Ayer for 80 years, the first 75 without a written contract. Sunkist Growers, the marketing cooperative that first brought a brand name to grocery produce departments, has been with Foote, Cone & Belding (and the forerunner, Lord & Thomas) for a similar eight-decade stretch....*Advertising Age* estimates there are as many as 60 relationships between advertiser and agency in the United States that have lasted more than 30 years.[5]

Clearly, there are some relationships that last. The difference between an average relationship of 7.2 years and ones that last more than 30 years sounds a little like the dichotomy between couples celebrating their golden anniversaries and the grim fact that one in two marriages end in divorce.

The question is, What can you do to ensure that your relationships lead to golden anniversaries? One way to discover what makes relationships work is to learn what causes them to fail. When you understand why something went wrong, you are in a better position to set out on the right course next time.

Relationships fail for many reasons; some important ones are:

- *Lack of Commitment.* Relationships fail because both partners are not equally committed to the venture or to building a lasting relationship. The result is that one partner resents doing more work or committing greater resources and getting little back in return.

- *Cultural Differences.* Relationships fail when partners, particularly organizations, are unable to adapt their work styles to fit one another's culture. For example, an entrepreneurial organization that thrives on its flexibility may have trouble working with a large established organization where several layers of approval are needed before decisions can be made.

- *Poor Management.* Relationships fail because management does not value the relationship and make the personal investment needed to grow it. Unless management encourages such relationships, they will not flourish.

- *Poor Communication.* Relationships fail if organizations inhibit the transfer of information. Unless there is a philosophy of open and honest communication, the rationale behind decisions may not be fully understood, causing errors, redundancies, and misunderstandings.

- *Failure of Individual Relationships.* Relationships also fail because the individuals responsible for maintaining them either lack interpersonal skills or because personal chemistry is missing.

These problems are potentially so damaging that they are worth further analysis. None of them can be cured by applying Band-Aids; the underlying damage must be properly treated if the wounds are to heal with as little scarring of the relationships as possible.

The Level of Commitment

In the challenge and excitement of courting a new client, claims and promises may be made that cannot be kept. This trap occurs when people go after new business with such a vengeance that they promise potential clients far more than they can realistically deliver. Then, even though no one pushed them to make concessions, they start out with chips on their shoulders, resenting their new partners for taking advantage of them. This is similar to the feelings people sometimes have after an auction when they paid far too much for an item because they kept bidding in the excitement of the moment.

To avoid these problems, make certain both parties benefit from the relationship, whether benefits are realized in the form of profitability, increased market penetration in a new area, or the prestige of working with a particular client. One of the most important questions to ask yourself is how much your business will mean to the other organization. In searching for the right partner, don't look only at organizations that are well known, experienced, or leaders in their fields—you don't want your opportunity to be a drop in the bucket financially. In choosing a strategic alliance partner, ask yourself whether the venture will be a priority for them. Is the venture the mainstay of their business? Given the relative importance of your account, you can judge the amount of time and attention you can realistically expect them to devote to the relationship.

Partnerships get into trouble when one partner fails to pay attention to the other once the relationship is under way. It is often ironic to remember how hard you worked to secure a relationship only to let it fall apart afterward because you took it for granted. Although one never forgets large gestures, relationships are built on small actions that are demonstrated everyday; saying thank-you for help given, properly managing expectations, lending a hand when it is most useful, or being there when you are most needed.

When you fail to consciously nurture relationships, you may miss signs that they are slowly deteriorating. For example, a supplier's growth rate may slow, raising doubts about the supplier's ability to maintain the same level of service as before. Or some partners experience so much success and grow so fast that they believe they have outgrown their other partners. If either side paid attention to the small things, the shift would have been noticed and an effort made to save the relationship.

Commitment also suffers when one partner feels he or she isn't getting the proper amount of attention. A client sees the successes other clients experience and becomes jealous; in these situations, explanations and renewed expressions of commitment can be useful. Product conflicts can also destroy a relationship. This occurs when you have clients who compete with each other and one of them resents the fact that you are also working with their competitor. Clients are less likely to have such reactions when they believe you are committed to them.

Commitment is also important when one organization receives negative publicity and its image begins to tarnish. The other organization may worry about being associated with that organization out of fear of being perceived in an equally poor light by the public, but if there is a longstanding commitment between them, the partner will try to withstand the strain.

Culture

Another major challenge between partners is cultural differences. For example, in a strategic alliance, a relationship may falter because the organizations don't have a common vision or share similar goals for the relationship. One organization may be interested in profiting from the venture today, even if that means jeopardizing tomorrow's benefits, while the other is interested in building a lasting relationship. The organization willing to make the long-term investment is likely to be disappointed with the myopic, uncaring, selfish approach of the other. Furthermore, if the organizations are different sizes, the larger organization may have a different investment philosophy than the smaller partner, who is willing to forsake next quarter's financial results in order to secure long-term growth.

The speed with which companies make decisions may also become a problem. For example, if a small organization's success is attributable to its ability to act quickly, it may run into problems dealing with a large bureaucratic organization. Large organizations can often smother smaller entrepreneurial organizations' innovative approach.

One General Electric venture, with Huntsman Chemical, was born over lunch and immediately spurred more projects between the firms. Glen Hiner, head of GE's plastics and materials business, believes that under the old GE culture, marked by a centralized management system, such an alliance would not have developed: "By the time the proposal had gotten through the process, someone else would have done the deal ahead of us."[6]

Management

Management should not force its own views or management style onto new strategic alliances. In such situations, it should consider creating brand-new organizations to manage the relationship or appoint an individual—a champion—who will be sensitive and responsive to the needs of the other organization, and have responsibility and accountability for the venture.

Another potential obstacle is raised when management neglects to secure buy-in across the organization: "We thought the deal was great, but we couldn't convince our offices of that." If the partnership is created at headquarters without the support and buy-in of their local offices, they may not support the venture. When headquarters is the catalyst for the relationship, it will only succeed if close working relationships are developed at the local level.

Once relationships are established, partners should understand their responsibilities as well as their rights. All too often one partner asks the other to do the impossible, and then asks them to reduce their bills because they haven't budgeted the extra costs incurred by their extra demands. A client should be willing to pay for services received.

Furthermore, partners must avoid haggling. Trust and loyalty are damaged when the agreed-upon fee structure is questioned every time they find a similar project performed for a lower price. One partner cannot ask the other to hire people, and then threaten to give business to another supplier, ignoring their earlier commitment. Lastly, management must also be willing to alter policy when working with a small business that can't wait 45 days to get paid. Although the smaller organization may be afraid to jeopardize the relationship, sensitivity to their needs brings partners closer.

Expectations.   It is important that organizations set realistic goals for themselves from the outset. Partners often get so caught up in the honeymoon period that they think no challenge is too big to overcome. Then they become so preoccupied with their own problems that they fail to live up to commitments they have already made. Or partners may underestimate the time and effort needed to get to know each other. When unrealistic goals are established from the outset, both partners are setting themselves up for disappointment—and giving naysayers in their organizations an easy opportunity to attack the relationship.

Some relationships fail because partners are unable to set priorities. They are so excited about working together that they run around trying to accomplish everything at once, but never end up completing anything. Then when it comes time to tally wins, there are no points on the board.

Furthermore, rather than putting all of your eggs into one basket, with one large activity, the risk to the relationship can be minimized by starting a few projects at a time. It is also important to balance activities so that some projects come to fruition on a short-term basis, and others bring major benefits long term. The small wins maintain momentum. Many relationships fail because management loses interest or cuts off funds because it takes too much time to realize the benefit.

Some relationships fail because one partner makes unrealistic assumptions; for example, it takes the position that because it is the client, it has certain privileges, including the right to demand whatever it wants. It acts as if it is the supplier's duty to serve, no questions asked. If partners don't view themselves as equals, the end product may be compromised because "subservient" partners fail to express their true feelings about an issue or problems they see looming.

Knowledge.   Another factor that damages relationships is the inability to learn enough about an account to properly service it. This can take a number of forms. They may not be familiar with the industry, the client's organization, or the culture in which the client operates. Sometimes one partner may not have the knowledge to perform the job adequately; for example, an advertising agency without adequate knowledge of the airline industry might discuss flight safety records in an ad. Because that would violate an industry "silent agreement," their recommendation would be inappropriate. And even when a partner has adequate knowledge to start with, in a fast-paced industry, one partner may outgrow the other. If managers don't continue to develop their people and keep up with the latest changes taking place, they risk damaging their relationship.

Communication

Some organizations have layers of personnel that act as filters of information. If you don't have access to the information that you need to do your job effectively, you will never be able to satisfy your client. They, in turn, will wonder why they spend so much time providing directions and proper action is not taken. They may feel the people handling their account are either not capable or do not listen. They don't realize that getting information third hand, from someone who does not fully understand the situation, is not helpful.

In other cases, information is held back, either consciously or unconsciously. When two groups have different frames of reference, they are bound to make different assumptions, and take actions the other disapproves of.

Lastly, people are obligated to use discretion in a relationship. When partners comes in contact with sensitive information, such as new product designs or strategic plans, it is their obligation to keep the information confidential. Leaks can cause serious damage to the relationship.

Individual Relationships

Changes in personnel have to be handled with particular care, because partnerships grow through personal relationships. If the client "bought in" because of their belief in one individual, finding the right replacement is critical if that individual leaves. Whenever you lose continuity, either by promoting an individual who was managing the relationship or when an individual leaves the organization, not only do you lose the knowledge that the individual has built over the years, but you also lose the bonds that they have built with the client. These kinds of problems can be minimized in the case of a promotion or retirement if the individual continues to keep in touch.

Personality clashes may also occur between individuals in a relationship. When problems arise, it is in everyone's best interest to resolve them, but sometimes they cannot be fixed satisfactorily. In such cases, as a last resort, someone on the account may have to be replaced. Obviously, this can be better accomplished in a large organization that has deeper "bench strength" than in a smaller organization where the choices may be limited.

Another challenge caused by such changes is the time required to bring new personnel up to speed—only to repeat it all over again because of high turnover. When an organization starts to lose business or doesn't grow as fast as others in their industry, one may wonder whether they will be able to retain their people or whether the services they provide will begin to deteriorate. If that perception is allowed to continue, clients may look to others to handle their accounts.

The Anatomy of Relationships

What is a good relationship? Roger Fisher and Scott Brown said in their best-selling book, *Getting Together:*

> From a dozen officers at the same bank we received definitions of a "good" relationship as diverse as: "A long-standing pattern of doing business." "We have made a lot of money dealing with them." "Great financial potential." "Our president plays golf with their chairman of the board." "They pay their bills; we can trust them." "We have to do things for them in return for past favors."...One management consulting firm, for example, keeps track of its clients in terms of the length of the relationship, the amount of money at stake, the number of people involved on each side, and the frequency and extent of communication....For some, the goal of a good relationship is a make-believe world without differences: "We have a marvelous relationship: we agree on everything."[7]

All of the things just mentioned are ingredients of good relationships. People who are good at building successful alliances work very hard to structure win-win relationships. One key element is searching for overlapping areas of opportunity where both organizations gain. For example, if one organization has an excellent product and the other an excellent distribution capability, the relationship offers both an excellent opportunity. In this example, both organizations have a vested interest in ensuring the success of the venture.

A partnership will succeed in the long run when both organizations work for their common good rather than each trying to gain the upper hand. When that happens, they spend all of their time trying to outnegotiate each other and both end up losing. Moreover, in these situations, one of the organizations is likely to come out noticeably ahead of the other, ultimately causing jealousy and resentment.

Furthermore, in good relationships everyone works hard to understand each other's needs and desires and then satisfies them. For example, it may involve an advertising agency that pursues a client not because the account offers an immediate profit, but because it gives them an entrée into an important new industry sector. In turn, the client selects the agency because they will receive a level of experience the company could not normally afford.

Good relationships are also built by establishing specific goals and objectives. Problems arise when a relationship drifts along aimlessly. For example, when organizations decide to collaborate on "some sort of a venture" because each admires the other, they are unlikely to accomplish anything meaningful. A specific venture must be selected—and objectives assigned—to achieve results.

For a successful venture to occur, everyone should get along with the people involved, inspire one another to a new level of creativity, and support one another when the going gets rough. These are the kinds of responses that do more to ensure success than anything else. It is also important to recognize that no relationship—personal or business—can be successful if forced. Relationships do not bring immediate returns. They require long-term investments of time, money, and effort if they are to grow and produce meaningful results.

When Does the Relationship Begin?

Relationships begin long before the papers are signed and the work starts. They begin with impressions generated during preliminary conversations. That is the courting phase, the time when promises are made and expectations established. Never promise more than you can deliver, and be certain that you don't build unrealistic expectations about what the relationship will bring.

The courting phase is a time for a meeting of the minds. It is important to be honest in establishing expectations with your partner. Although such honesty raises fears about whether an agreement can actually be reached, this is when both organizations must think beyond their immediate goals and look to the future of their relationship.

Although exaggerating your capabilities, your expertise, your resources, or the number of people who will be assigned to a project may seem harmless, doing so provides grounds for resentment the moment the relationship begins. To avoid this situation, remember that although you may feel good bringing in the business, overstatement will cause more anxiety in the long run than it is worth. This means that everything must be made clear from the beginning. For example, it means explaining that although the principals of the organization were involved in the business development, they will not be involved in the day-to-day work.

The courting period should be long enough to help you decide that a lasting relationship is desirable, that you have more than an infatuation that will lead to eventual divorce. A successful relationship means more than performing satisfactory work or delivering the goods and services requested.

Before entering into a more formal relationship, take the time to understand your partners' needs. Spend time learning their inner workings, understand the vantage point from which they see things, discover their priorities. Take the time to learn your partners' strategic direction, culture, product, client needs, and the rationale for past decisions. You must be curious, get to know the people, their backgrounds, interests, experiences, and regional differences. And finally, you should try to learn why their other relationships have succeeded or why they failed.

Although relationships thrive on good intentions and mutual trust, to be sure that there is no room for dispute later on, a letter of understanding or contract should stipulate all the parameters of the relationship, including all financial arrangements, and other promises made.

Creating the Right Environment for Growth

There are two elements of a relationship that must be balanced to ensure its success. The first is the content side—the goals, objectives, and strategies that have to be achieved. The other is the process side—the way those activities are accomplished and how everyone relates to one another. Very often people overemphasize the importance of the content side of the relationship as compared with the process. That is clearly a mistake because the success of any relationship should not be evaluated solely on meeting specific goals; it lies in the strength and durability of the relationship that is built between the partners.

One way to develop lasting relationships is by creating a working environment where people are well-treated, where integrity, sensitivity, humility, and patience are valued, and where commitments are honored even if circumstances have changed since the promise was originally made. In this kind of environment, people do more than strive to reach common goals, they learn from one another, and they treat people with dignity and respect even during heated disagreements.

The partnership should reach beyond the formal bounds of the contract signed. People should enjoy the company of those they are working with and be free to extend themselves with greater time and effort than originally planned. The working environment should promote the idea that the relationship was not developed for a single purpose, but for the long haul. This may mean doing things that do not immediately benefit your organization, or helping your partner in ways that are tangential to the relationship; in the long run, these are all beneficial because they strengthen the relationship. In the right environment, people know there will be good times and bad times, but normal setbacks are accepted and people are willing to go the extra mile for each other. For example:

In the mid-1970s, Mattel teetered near bankruptcy. Unable to pay its advertising bills from TV stations and magazines, longtime Mattel agency Ogilvy & Mather took the unusual step of handling those obligations for the client. O&M had little hope of getting its money back any time soon, but the agency decided to play the odds, believing the toy marketer would eventually make good its debts and that the relationship would endure.

The gamble paid off. Mattel is still around and still with Ogilvy & Mather after 33 years.[8]

Working Together

In every successful relationship, explicit goals and objectives are developed and bought into by everyone involved in ensuring the venture's success. Then, the goals are clearly articulated to others in the organization, making it easier for everyone to get behind the project and to work together as a team.

Bill Fox, division manager at Bell Communications Research, uses the following sports analogy to explain the concept of teamwork:

> The 10,000 runners in the New York City marathon race have a common goal or purpose. However, they are not a team. They are, in fact, in competition with each other. Teamwork requires interdependence—the working together of a group of people with a shared objective. More specifically, the only way the runners can reach their goal is by competitive efforts....Using another track example, Fox argues that a relay team is a good example of a real team. Each member of the team shares a common goal and they must work together to achieve it.[9]

In many failed ventures, teamwork breaks down; senior managers involved in initiating the relationship "disappear" once the agreement is in place. It is as if a coach were to assemble a team and then tell everyone to manage themselves. It just doesn't work that way. Relationships not only require the involvement of top management from both organizations, but they require top management building peer relationships with each other. Unfortunately, people often rush right into work because of a short-term orientation and a desire to increase productivity. Remember that the time spent getting to know your peers on a personal basis is not wasted time; it enables you to avoid obstacles down the road or second guessing a partner's intentions. It is important to note, however, that in the long term, successful partnerships are built on accomplishments achieved, not on the strength of personal relationships.

In order to facilitate the process of working together, there should be a champion who is responsible for working with the other organization. The champions must be cheerleaders or catalysts, but not the sole owners. They should build grass-roots levels of support for the relationship and ensure that necessary resources are available. They should work to extend the relationship to all levels of the organization so that it receives and is given the support and commitment necessary for its success.

To sum up, the champions have four primary functions:

1. They must serve as catalysts, ensuring that bonds are built between various members of their organization and the client. They must be willing to bring others into the relationship instead of maintaining tight control over the flow of information and doing everything themselves.

2. They must disseminate success stories about the relationship throughout their organization.

3. They must see to it that the needs of the client are heard and the resources required to meet those needs are made available.

4. They must simplify the approval process. This can be done by explaining how decisions are made in their organization and introducing their partner to individuals in their organization who can help them.

Maintaining the Relationship

Building Understanding

Knowledge and understanding underlie all successful relationships. In order to work together successfully, everyone must be kept informed and made to feel like equal partners in the relationship. In his book *Information Anxiety* Richard Wurman reminds us:

Once you see or understand something, you cannot conceive of what it was like not to have seen or understood it. You lose the ability to identify with those who don't know....If you could remember what it was like not to know, you could begin to communicate in terms that might be understood more readily by someone who doesn't know.[10]

One way to ensure that both partners have the information they need to carry out their responsibilities is to maintain open lines of communication. It is important to issue timely information about major events, policy changes, or changes in management. It is also important to inform your suppliers of new activities in your organization at the same time you discuss them with your own employees. By opening lines of communication, you make it easier for people to work together toward a common goal.

An environment should be created where new ideas are encouraged, and people are free to express their opinions. Moreover, they must feel comfortable taking risks, failing and then accepting the responsibility for their mistakes and learning from them. In such organizations, debate is welcomed and questions are encouraged, not ignored or dismissed without discussion.

If you create a supportive environment, constructive feedback will be welcomed and not construed as criticism. In the right culture, everyone listens to the problems of others and makes suggestions—and no one feels hurt when the advice they offer is not acted upon.

Being Prepared for Problems

No matter how well partners communicate, there are times when relationships experience setbacks and misunderstandings develop. That is not a time to point fingers, or reassess the value of the relationship. A method for dealing with sensitive issues or differences should be put in place as soon as a partnership begins so that these problems can be dealt with as soon as they occur. If you accept the premise that problems are natural in every relationship, you will find it less troubling to deal with them when they emerge. But remember that, as Fisher and Brown have said:

> Giving in does not build a good working relationship. It may avoid arguments, but it also eliminates the opportunity to learn how to talk through problems and to become skillful at reaching solutions. Without such skills, a relationship will be too weak to survive problems that are bound to come along. It is not enough to solve the immediate problem. We have to think ahead to the effect that this transaction will have on the next one, and the one after that.[11]

Both organizations must feel comfortable raising and discussing difficult issues before they turn into major conflicts; dealing with problems expediently will even help strengthen the relationship in the long run. Debate must be encouraged and problems brought out into the open rather than swept under the rug.

When trying to resolve problems in a relationship, keep in mind that force or pressure tactics should never be used to resolve problems. Diplomatic skills should be used instead. For example, an attitude of "take it or leave it" often results in someone who "takes it" only until they can find another partner. It is impossible to maintain a solid, lasting relationship if partners threaten to walk or to find another partner or to go over a partner's head to a superior whenever a problem arises.

Furthermore, when arguments turn into personal attacks, working together in the future becomes difficult. In addition, trying to wear someone down, by behaving like a child who wants his own way, erodes respect. And playing games—or allowing them to be played—is always destructive. While these tactics may bring victory today, the price of victory is lasting resentment. The proper way to resolve issues is through discussion and persuasion.

Tearing Down Walls

Customers and suppliers must be willing to tear down the walls between their organizations and share the information necessary to get the job done. The more that organizations think of themselves as one rather than "us" and "them," the more successful they will be. Colgate provides an excellent example of how this is done:

> All U.S. employees of the two agencies who work on Colgate business, in whatever capacity, have been inducted into the same Colgate stock plan in which all Colgate employees participate. Every year, each agency person is awarded the same number of Colgate shares that our people get. As shareholders, they also receive annual and quarterly reports. In addition, we make a personal, "Colgate performance report" each year at each agency to let everyone know how their company is performing, and the important role each of them is playing.[12]

Colgate has found a way to ensure that everyone at the agencies they deal with devotes themselves to the Colgate account. After all, the agencies know that the success of their client is unmistakenly tied to their own success.

Decision Making

There are two rules that are critical in decision making. The first is to avoid making unilateral decisions; the second is to avoid forcing your decisions on to your partner.

There are a number of reasons why people violate these rules. The decision makers feel that the decision that they are making is in the best interests of their partner; they may believe that they are best qualified to make the decision; they may believe if they don't seize the moment, the opportunity will be lost; they may have convinced themselves that their partner would have agreed with them anyway; they may believe that the decision is insignificant in nature; or they may be so excited that they blindly plunge ahead without thinking.

Remember that unilateral decision making is always a mistake. When one partner learns that the other made a unilateral decision, no matter how insignificant it is, they will wonder whether other decisions were made without them. Remember no matter how exciting an opportunity seems to be, if it is entered into without commitment from everyone, the benefits will be minimized. Furthermore, no matter how small the decision, and how busy the other partner, no one can determine what is best for someone else.

Handling Transitions

Continuity is such an important ingredient in relationships that managing transitions when an individual leaves must be a priority. If relationships are not built across several levels, employee turnover can bring partnerships to a premature end. When a new person is brought in to manage a relationship, the client should be involved in the selection process or at the very least notified of the change before it takes place. Furthermore, the replacement should be brought up to speed and taught the nuances of the relationship before assuming the role so that the client doesn't lose time while the replacement learns on the job.

There are a number of things that you can do to help ensure continuity in a relationship:

- Choose individuals with long tenure to be the chief liaisons with other organizations.

- Insist that those individuals have a right-hand person who is well known to the client and intimately familiar with the relationship.

- Set up a transition period when individuals are promoted or rotated into other positions: See to it that they remain in contact with the client after the transition is made.

- Make sure the new individual honors all the predecessor's commitments.

Making It Happen

Today's lean organizations cannot survive without strong alliances to supplement the capabilities of employees working to their fullest. The result is an age of cooperation, which often brings unexpected rewards. For example, world-class companies try to improve their partners' operations by allowing them to attend internal training programs or helping them benchmark themselves against other companies—to ensure continuous improvement. The same is true on an individual level, where cooperation offers individuals opportunities to explore new areas. But cooperative arrangements also bring responsibilities; for example, partners must work to grow and expand their abilities so they can support their clients now and in the future.

In the final analysis, the value of any partnership depends on the nature of the relationship the partners have built. Good relationships don't just happen. They are the result of partners that share a combination of individual attributes such as honesty, integrity, respect, commitment, trust, confidence, and openness. They develop an environment that encourages continuous improvement, risk taking, a long-term perspective, and, of course, win-win relationships. Clearly, the more apparent these characteristics are, the more likely it is that enduring partnerships will be forged.

9
Trust Me…
Trust Me Not

Building
a Trusting Organization

*Trust is the ultimate intangible. It has
no shape or substance, yet it empowers
our actions. And its presence or absence
can govern our behavior as if it were a
tangible force. The belief that we live in a
reasonably predictable world is the cor-
nerstone on which cooperation is built,
and the basis of our planning and action.
Would you cross the bridge, mail a letter,
confide in a friend, or work at a job without some trust that the bridge will hold,
the letter will be delivered, the friend will
keep confidence, or you will get paid for
your efforts? Living without some measure of trust would consign us to perpet-
ual fears, paranoia, inefficiency, and even
inaction.* GORDON SHEA[1]

Trust is the fabric that binds us together, creating an orderly,
civilized society from chaos and anarchy. If we can't trust our
husbands or our wives, if we can't trust our children, if we can't
trust our boss or our colleagues, if we can't trust our preacher

or our senators then we have nothing on which to build a stable way of life. Trust is not an abstract, theoretical, idealistic goal forever beyond our reach. Trust—or a lack of it—is inherent in every action that we take and affects everything that we do. Trust is the cement that binds relationships, keeping spouses together, business deals intact, and political systems stable. Without trust, marriages fail, voters become apathetic, and organizations flounder. Without trust, no company can ever hope for excellence.

There has, however, been a deep, fundamental change in the way we view the world today, and, as a result, trust is no longer fashionable. Few adults can remember a world without cynicism. Where "death do us part" once had meaning, today one of two new marriages ends in divorce and countless others exist in name only. Politicians who were once solid members of the community are dropping out of campaigns due to scandals and irregularities. Employees who once believed in devoting their entire working lives to one organization have seen so many colleagues tossed out in the restructurings of the 1980s that they try to remain emotionally uninvolved in their jobs. In fact, according to an *Industry Week* survey, "workers simply don't trust management. While 87% of the workers polled think it is 'very important' that 'management is honest, upright, and ethical,' only 39% believe that it is."[2] Furthermore, *The Wall Street Journal* reported "that more than 78% of American workers are suspicious of management and develop an "'us against them'" syndrome that interferes with their performance.[3]

This is a sea change from the period where a person's word was his bond, where employees worked for one company until they retired, where business deals were made on the basis of "I know your father" or "We've worked with your company before." They were all ways of saying we recognize your values, understand how much your reputation means to you, and know the way that you conduct business. The former values resulted in increased business, stronger customer loyalty, better employee morale, reduced turnover, and higher profit margins.

The old values also decreased the cost of conducting business because people who trust one another share information, listen to one another, and are more likely to accept criticism instead of instantly defending themselves in the face of any feedback. They waste little time playing politics; they put forth new ideas for discussion; and they help one another in order to improve the organization.

If businesses are to thrive in the global marketplace, trust must be more than something that is talked about; it must be at the core of everything that is done. Organizations cannot be jungles where only the fittest survive, living in a state of battle readiness in order to meet the grueling tests of everyday corporate life. If companies are to motivate employees and win their loyalty, they must change the way relationships are constructed. All too often, "we spend a lifetime building a trusting relationship with our friends and families, but we spend thirty minutes in an orientation session with our new employees and expect to have a successful and productive employee. For employees to trust the management, they must know that the management shares the same basic goals in the long run...and [that] each will behave in ways that are not harmful to the other."[4]

Just as high levels of trust reduce friction among employees, bond people together, increase productivity, and stimulate growth, low levels of trust adversely affect relationships, stifle innovation, and hamper the decision-making process. Employees in organizations marked by low levels of trust usually operate under higher levels of stress. They spend a great deal of effort covering their backsides, justifying past decisions, and conducting witch hunts or looking for scapegoats when something doesn't work out. This prevents them from focusing on the work they should be doing and the free exchange of ideas that results in innovative solutions. The constant need to prove one's worth promotes short-term fixes rather than long-term solutions.

Low trust in organizations also pushes people to operate with incomplete information, to come up with the most favorable interpretations, and to treat other people's suggestions with suspicion. As a result of limited discussion and feedback combined with the speed at which everything moves today, problems are not clearly defined and situations are not thoroughly examined. This means that, all too often, decisions are made out of context, and they are based on inaccurate views of reality and without an awareness of risks.

Furthermore, in organizations marked by low levels of trust, employees have so much difficulty exploring the full range of options or responding creatively to problems at hand that new challenges are avoided. Employees are so afraid of being reprimanded for failure, or torn down and ridiculed by their colleagues, that they shy away from new activities that will require new ways of thinking. Their defensiveness and mutual suspicions limit them to the restricted set of alternatives they have all agreed upon, which are designed to minimize their vulnerability. Exploration, innovation, creativity become dangers in this kind of environment.[5]

Of course, this slide into low levels of trust—with all its associated costs in loss of loyalty, productivity, and innovative thinking—did not happen overnight. However, companies are often slow to see the warning signs because, during boom times, it is more difficult to notice low trust levels. In periods of dramatic growth, promotions are often given to people who achieve goals, without regard to the long-term implications of how they achieved those goals. This mentality encourages employees to solve problems with quick fixes and then maneuver for a promotion before their actions have an affect on the people around them.

Moreover, during high-growth periods, people often focus on the short-term objective of making deals and then moving on. They do not have to worry about taking advantage of a supplier or overselling a customer or misleading an employee because, by then, the problem will not be theirs; they will have moved on to something else. This misguided thinking leads to many of our long-term problems.

Trust—the Miracle Ingredient

According to Gordon Shea, trust can be described as the "miracle ingredient in organizational life—a lubricant that reduces friction, a bonding agent that glues together disparate parts, a catalyst that facilitates action. No substitute—neither threat nor promise—will do the job as well."[6]

In organizations, trust is like love in a marriage: it bonds people together and makes them strong and effective. Trust in a relationship increases security, reduces inhibitions and defensiveness, and frees people to share feelings and dreams. Trust makes you free to put your deepest fears in the palms of your colleagues' hands, knowing that they will be treated with care. Trust allows you to be yourself and maintain your own values without worrying about acceptance. Trust makes colleagues willing to spend time together and make sacrifices for one another. Trust is an expression of faith that makes it easy for colleagues to have confidence in one another's ability to perform well and to know that they will be there if needed. Trust means that promises made will be kept, and it also means that when a promise is not kept, it was probably for good cause. And finally, trust means that a relationship will last not because it is good business, but because the relationship itself is valued.

The dilemma is that to be able to trust, you must be willing to accept the risk associated with trusting. When reaching out to people, we always risk the chance of being wrong, but if we never try for fear of failing, we may never experience the satisfaction of being in a trusting relationship.

The Parameters of Trust

Trust is generally defined as a belief in the integrity of another individual. But clearly, there are different kinds and degrees of trust; for example, there are some people you trust enough to confide in, some you may trust with your material possessions, some you trust with a project, others you may trust with your personal safety. But even in these categories there are levels of trust; for example, you may feel comfortable loaning a friend $10 knowing he or she will pay you back, but you may be less inclined to loan that friend $10,000. And there are people you trust in one area but not in another. For example, while you may trust the mechanic to work on your new car, you may not trust him to baby-sit your children; while you trust your wife enough to confide your deepest secrets to her, you may not trust her to pilot you in an airplane.

It is also important to recognize the line between liking someone and trusting them; as Dale E. Zand points out in *Information,
Organization, and Power,* "You may have affection for another
person but still not trust them. For example, a parent may love a
10-year-old child but not trust him to drive the family automo-
bile. Furthermore, you may trust another and have no affection
for them. For example, a passenger in a commercial plane may
trust the pilot but have no affection for him."[7]

Winning Trust

Understanding the meaning of trust allows you to work toward
being a trusted and trusting person. The truth is that trust is
never guaranteed, and it can't be won overnight. Trust must be
carefully constructed, vigorously nurtured, and constantly reinforced. Trust is established over time, gradually, through a long
chain of successful experiences. In the early stages of relationships, whether personal or business, we extend ourselves in
small ways and observe the responses to our actions. Then we
take appropriate action, withdrawing, maintaining our behavior, or extending ourselves a bit further each time until trust is
established.

Although trust takes a long time to develop, it can be
destroyed by a single action. Moreover, once lost it is very difficult to reestablish. Our reactions to the betrayal of trust are not
very different than our reactions to a death in the family. When
trust is violated, the hurt is long and deep. And it is only after
forgiveness is truly granted, which happens at the end of a long
agonizing process, that trust can be regained. But it is a necessary process because the alternative, repressing these feelings,
ensures that you will feel the trauma again and again over the
years and not know why. Forgiveness allows you to let go of
the past and move on to the future.

The destruction of trust does not happen without warning: A
friend who was always there for you when you needed her
begins to return calls sporadically; a spouse stops confiding in
you bit by bit; a company communicates with its employees less
frequently, providing less information or holding back information. In the case of the corporation, the reactions may be a high

degree of fear, suspicion, absenteeism, low job satisfaction, decreased commitment, and high turnover. People become risk averse and withdraw into themselves. More time is spent justifying previous actions than adding value to the organization, more time is spent figuring out how to get things approved than completing the work at hand, and more time is spent figuring out the political implications of doing something than doing what is best. These warning signs are important because the sooner the decline in trust is recognized, the better the chances of rebuilding it.

The Rings of Trust

Building trusting relationships is a process that can best be described as adding layers around a center rod one at a time in such a way that each one bonds to the prior one before another layer is added.

In a world where time is a precious resource, where we must often move quickly without having the time to explore all the options, we use shortcuts to circumvent the process. For this reason, an individual's or organization's history or track record is often evaluated to gauge how we may be treated in a relationship. The rod, the center of the ring, represents the beginning of a relationship and depicts the history of those involved. We generally start off with some preconceived notion about others. We meet and develop impressions about people through the friends we have in common; the things they talk about in meetings, while commuting, at parties; and general observations during work. We learn about the companies and organizations we buy from or deal with by consciously talking to people, reading about them, or through the myriad references we have.

The first ring around the rod is made from the characteristics that lead to trust. They are the attributes, such as integrity, reliability, and openness, that allow us to build trusting relationships. Once these characteristics are demonstrated, they become part of a person's or organization's track record. When those actions are repeated time and time again, the relationship is strengthened and becomes the foundation of the next phase.

THE RINGS OF TRUST

CENTER ROD: HISTORY

THE FIRST RING: THE TRAITS ON WHICH TRUST RESTS

 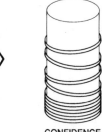

INTEGRITY	CONFIDENCE	RELIABILITY
DOING THE RIGHT THING	SAFE	OPENNESS
STRENGTH OF CONVICTION	COMPETENCE	COMMUNICATION
	FAIRNESS	

THE SECOND RING: CONSISTENCY

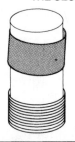 

THE THIRD RING: FROM PREDICTABILITY TO FAITH

The second ring, consistency, allows us to anticipate probable actions. It provides a certain degree of comfort that helps us to maintain the relationship even through difficult times. The third ring is faith; as it is added to the other two rings, everything that came before it is strengthened. This ring, which does not adhere to the others, but rather encompasses them, is the stage at which actions are so predictable that we don't consciously have to think about the relationship. Trust has become so integral a part of the relationship that we expect it to work. At their peak, relationships imbued with trust are welded together by a faith in one another so strong that it is very difficult to destroy them. It is at this stage that people allow themselves to become entirely vulnerable to others.

The Center Rod: History

The past is often the best indicator of the future; we all look for precedents, assuming that they are a key to anticipating behavior. We want to know how someone acted in the past when faced with a similar situation. Last time I confided in her, was she able to keep a secret? Last time he promised he would deliver it on time, did he keep his word? Last time I loaned him money, was I paid back? Last time they sold me a product, did they stand behind it? Last time there was a downturn in the economy, how were employees treated? Last time we presented an idea to management, who took the credit for it? Last time there was a problem in the department, did management support its people or look for a scapegoat? Last time we faced tough times, did management stand behind us or fend for themselves?

Whether you are an organization trying to gain trust in the marketplace or a salesperson trying to gain the trust of a consumer, keep in mind that trust is not something that is built in an instant; rather it is earned by actions repeated over time. And organizations are not perceived as trustworthy only because of what they are doing now, but because of their actions over the years. Organizations that institutionalize the value and the importance of life-long customer relationships over immediate sales know that winning the immediate sale is not as important as exceeding customer expectations over time. They know that the signing of a sales agreement is not the end of the sales process, but the beginning of the next sale. They know that the minute a purchase is made, and the consumer has placed trust in both the product and in the organization, they must work hard to maintain that trust.

Acting to build a history of trust can become part of the way that an organization differentiates itself and its products from its competitors. For example, in the late 1970s, Xerox Corporation ran an advertising campaign saying that "We won't love you and leave you," inferring that its competitors sometimes sold copiers and then were never heard from again.

Organizations that adopt a philosophy focused on building long, trusting relationships are rewarded in numerous ways. There is potential repeat business: loyal customers come back when they need more of that product and even look for other available products from that company. And once their trust in your organization grows, they may reward you with larger purchases or by increasing their personal risk by recommending a product to senior management that is strategic to their organization. Finally, long-term relationships may lead to a base of satisfied clients who tell their friends or colleagues about the service and the excellent products that they are receiving from you.

Reputation. The most tangible form of history is reputation. An individual's or organization's reputation is often a key to their probable behavior toward a friend, a client, or an employee; it indicates how they might treat others both now and in the future. That is why, before we enter into a relationship, we ask ourselves if the person or organization is respected as a trustworthy individual or a good corporate citizen. It is why we want to know how they have treated others when the chips were down or when they were backed into a corner.

An impeccable reputation reduces the time that it takes to build trust with a new client or sales prospect. By reducing selling time, a good reputation can give an individual or organization an added competitive advantage. Being referred to a company or told how satisfactory a product is by a credible individual builds trust; so do testimonials either in the form of letters or advertisements. Indeed, anything that enhances an individual's or organization's reputation is a shortcut to building trust.

But just as reputations are built over the years, they have to be protected and earned again each day or they will soon be lost. Expressions such as "No one ever got fired for buying IBM," "It's as good as a Cadillac," and "It's as safe as money in the bank" not only enhanced the sales efforts of the organizations they were attached to but also allowed them to attract new employees. People placed their trust in the product or in the organization because others did so in the past and never lived to regret it.

This means that individuals and organizations must be careful to act in ways that enhance their reputations. For example, an organization whose business is centered in a community or tightly knit industry has a vested interest in upholding its reputation. This gives people who deal with them confidence that they will work harder not to tarnish their reputations.

Both individuals and organizations must also be very careful to avoid any impropriety. If they become involved in something questionable, they must clear the air honestly and quickly. Unfortunately, even if someone distances themselves from an unwholesome situation, if it is learned that they were involved in any way (or if closure is never achieved), a cloud of doubt will shadow them forever.

The First Ring: The Traits on Which Trust Rests

At the start of any relationship, people consciously or unconsciously examine actions rather than words to begin to measure trustworthiness. As time goes by, the more that such traits as integrity, fairness, and reliability are demonstrated, the more people learn to trust one another. The more such qualities are recognized, the deeper the trust and, as long as nothing happens to change those opinions, the stronger the relationship grows. This applies to relationships between individuals, between individuals and organizations, and between organizations. The man and woman trust one another and commit to marriage, the job hunter accepts the new position offered by his future employer, the customer buys the product that the organization sells, and the supplier enters into a deal with the buyer. Relationships are built on the traits discussed below.

Integrity. There are a number of questions you ask yourself when assessing people's integrity. Do they have a good value system? Are they honest, straightforward, and nonmanipulating? Do they tell the truth and keep their promises even if circumstances have changed since they gave their word? Do they avoid even the appearance of impropriety, and are they aware that the company they keep can be a reflection on their own integrity? Do they pay as much attention to the spirit of the law as they do to the letter of the law?

The same questions apply to organizations. Do they stand behind their products? Do the senior people who sell themselves to you as part of the service actually do the work? Do they pay their bills when they say they will? Do they give back to the community or try to get around zoning laws or recycling and dumping ordinances?

Doing the Right Thing. Another characteristic we look for when building relationships is whether the people or organizations do the right thing not because they're afraid of being caught if they don't, but because it's the right thing to do. Do employees do what is politically expedient and beneficial for themselves or what is in the best interests of their companies, their clients, or their colleagues? Do they exaggerate to win the sale, or present the benefits as well as the pitfalls?

One good way to look at this is to follow the golden rule: "Do unto others as you would have them do onto you." Doing the right thing may include giving of yourself even if you don't have anything to gain at that moment, or serving an existing client above and beyond what is necessary even if there is no potential for additional business. It may mean addressing a problem before it becomes public or you are asked to correct it by the government, even if it leaves you with financial exposure.

A good example of the way organizations handle a crisis can be found by examining the actions of Johnson & Johnson during the Tylenol poisonings and the actions of Exxon after the *Valdez* oil spill. Johnson & Johnson's credo says that its first responsibility is to the people who use its products. As soon as it was informed of the possibility that Tylenol had been tampered with, it launched a public recall and pulled the product off the market; it then developed new, safer ways of packaging it, including warning labels, all at an enormous cost. Exxon made promises about cleaning up the spill and did spend resources to try to repair some of the damage, but it was later revealed that, after the price tag rose, management had, behind closed doors, decided to limit the effort. In the end, Exxon's decision to cut off funding for cleanup and leave the rest to "nature" to repair cost them much of the public forgiveness they achieved by their initial efforts.

People who always want to do the "right thing" sometimes face difficult decisions. For example, how much are they willing to tell a prospective client about their misgivings about their own product? Is holding back the truth to protect another individual doing the right thing? There is no set answer to these questions. Everyone has to have limits and draw the line for themselves.

Strength of Conviction.   Another set of questions to ask yourself when determining trustworthiness is: How ethical are the people or organizations you are dealing with? Do they have strong values? Do they stand up for what they believe in? Are they afraid to present their opinions to upper management? Do they feel comfortable presenting bad news when it is necessary to do so?

Basically, strength of conviction translates into standing up for the things that you believe in. This may include telling clients what they really need to hear instead of what you think they want to hear. Although they may disagree with you or even fault you for challenging them at the moment, they will respect you for speaking your mind and not being a "yes" person. It may include speaking up in your organization for the resources that you need to properly serve your clients. It may also include not selling or recommending products or services that are not in a prospect's best interests, even if you are under pressure to increase sales.

The strength of someone's conviction often poses a dilemma to individuals as well. For example, people who have strong convictions are often faced with the problem of knowing when to stick to their guns and when it is time to compromise to achieve unanimous consent. On the other hand, those who quickly compromise their ideals or who waffle all the time also cannot be trusted. Gerald Zaltman and Christine Moorman were exactly right when they wrote in the *Journal of Advertising Research* that "the dilemma is that if you always dig in your heels and fight for your ideas, you are considered arrogant. However, if you constantly back off when the client challenges one of your ideas you're considered a pushover."[8]

Confidence. It is important to determine whether the people you build relationships with are comfortable within themselves and believe in themselves enough to admit their faults and errors. Ask yourself, Do they always have to be right? Do they listen to suggestions? Are they afraid to admit mistakes? If they cause a problem, do they try to find a way to fix it or look for people to blame?

Confidence can be displayed within an organization by the management style that you choose. In *Principle-Centered Leadership,* Stephen Covey says: "Synergy results from valuing differences, from bringing different perspectives together in a spirit of mutual trust. Mistaking uniformity for unity, sameness for oneness, insecure people surround themselves with others who think similarly. Secure people, on the other hand, realize that the strength of their relationships with others lies as much in their differences as in their similarities. They not only respect individuals with different views, but they actively seek them out."[9]

In the same way, only people with a great deal of confidence in themselves and in the people they have chosen to work with can treat trust as more than just another buzzword. The following story is a perfect example of someone with the confidence to practice what he preaches:

> To trust, you must first trust yourself enough to let go....The feeling I had when I first exposed my financials to all of the employees was tantamount to jumping into Marblehead Harbor in January. I'd exposed my only

remaining secrets. I was administratively naked. I'd already decided the presidential perks I'd been raised with—like private secretaries, personal parking places, and private offices—were not my style. (In fact, Ben now shares space with three others on the management team.) So my only remaining badge of office was my financials—and I let them go....The productive powers of trust have made believers of both Ben Strohecker [founder and president of Harbor Sweets] and his workforce. So much so that when a financial consultant came in to present benefits options to the company's leader, he suggested presenting the ideas to the workers. The visitor responded by saying, "You're crazy. They'll ask for the moon." Some did ask for the moon, Mr. Strohecker acknowledges. But the other employees put them down and said, "What kind of place do you think this is? We don't want to go out of business." They came out with a recommended package that was probably more conservative than what we would have given them.[10]

Ben Strohecker's confidence in his people allowed him to trust them to a point where he could give away authority—and his trust was rewarded.

Safe. When deciding whether to put your trust in someone, you try to discover if they are calm, patient, and logical. You ask yourself whether they have a lot of emotional highs and lows. When conflicts arise do they act in a caring and responsible fashion? Do they resolve problems and make decisions based on logic, or do they make emotional judgments based on bias, residual anger, or desire to avenge the past?

Companies can demonstrate being safe by the strength of their balance sheets, by the length of time that they have been in business, and by their history as a forward-looking organization. Spending on research and development and remaining at the cutting edge over a long period send a strong signal to the marketplace. It is easy to believe that any company that invests in research and development will continue to enhance their current technology, develop new products and services, and be there to serve your needs in the future.

Companies can also demonstrate their safety by such diverse factors as the level of employee turnover (a sign of good management and employee satisfaction); whether products have been abandoned in the past, leaving customers out in the cold; or the level of product commitment demonstrated by sales support and the quality of handout materials.

Competence.   Trust is increased when an individual is believed to be competent. An advanced degree, an affiliation with a well-respected organization or an organization with a reputation for its thorough training, and professional status, all enhance the trustworthiness of an individual. They indicate that they have a limited amount of competence, but it doesn't guarantee competence. Salespeople can increase their level of trust by demonstrating their familiarity with a product, their ability to address specific questions related to a prospect's problem, their prior experience in resolving similar client issues, and their in-depth knowledge of the prospect's industry, but nothing is as useful in building trust as satisfactory work.

An organization's willingness to trust its employees depends in part on its estimate of their competence to perform specified tasks. But it is important to remember, as noted in Chapter 2, that people tend to live up to the expectations that we set for them. The more we trust people to do things right, the more likely it is they will live up to the level of competence expected of them.

Organizations that have strong recruiting and education programs have greater trust levels. When organizations are known for aggressive hiring practices and solid training, rather than throwing employees in the water and watching them swim, trust is enhanced. When employees know that their peers are well trained, they know that they can depend on them, that they will receive high-quality information, and that they do not have to solve every problem by themselves.

Fairness.   How much we trust other people or organizations often has a lot to do with our perception of their fairness; in other words, the belief we have in their objectivity, their lack of prejudice, their impartiality. Are they objective? Do they show bias or favoritism? Do they present both sides of an issue or only the side that puts them in the best light? Are they open minded and willing to listen to new ideas? Do they give everyone the time of day, or are their minds already made up? Do they give credit where credit is due, or do they accept credit for other people's efforts? Do they have reasonable expectations? Do they know when someone tried to do their best and praise them for their efforts, or do they reprimand them for failure to perform? In the face of disagreement, do they respect the opinions of others or attack them, embarrassing, reprimanding, or humiliating them in front of others?

Organizations have demonstrated their fairness by such actions as taking back merchandise with no questions asked or promising that if you find the same merchandise for less money in 90 days and can present proof, they will pay you the difference.

Reliability. Another quality we look for when deciding whether or not to trust a person or an organization is reliability. We ask such questions as: Are they dependable? Do they follow through on promises made? If you ask for something, can you consider it done? Are they careful not to overstate what they will do? Do they seem to know that even though they may not be conscious of making a promise, if someone else thinks they have, their honor is on the line? Do they exaggerate sales claims or set expectations that are not achievable? This may be the result of having little direct control over the outcome, but it still means that a promise that has been made is broken. For example, the product will be fixed by Tuesday; the service person will be there in an hour; you can expect at least a 12 percent return on your investment; even though I haven't had a chance to look at your tax return yet, you'll get about the same refund as last year; take this medicine and you'll feel better in an hour; the product never breaks down the first year.

Organizations can demonstrate their reliability by showing that their interest lies in more than selling a product and then forgetting about the customer; they can enhance your satisfaction by seeing to it that the owner's manual is clear, that the service force is well trained, that critical parts are not back ordered, and that customer complaints are handled promptly and properly.

One way in which we judge reliability is by deciding whether or not a failure to keep a promise was intentional. In *Getting Together*, Roger Fisher and Scott Brown distinguish among the different kinds of unreliability: "People can be unreliable in dif-

ferent ways. They can be erratic, ambiguous, secretive, misleading, deceptive, or dishonest, or they may weigh promises light-
ly in the face of changed circumstances....Some people run their
lives according to well-developed habits and carefully planned
schedules. Others are more spontaneous and variable. We often
think of the first type of person as being more reliable than the
second type."[11]

Openness.   Openness in relationships is built upon some existing level of trust. You feel comfortable confiding in people, knowing they would never break your confidence or use the information against you at a later date. If they respond to that openness as
expected, trust is enhanced and intimacy and honesty grow.

As Fernando Bartolome pointed out in the *Harvard Business
Review:*

> It is terribly important to get subordinates to convey
> unpleasant messages. The sooner a problem is disclosed,
> diagnosed, and corrected, the better for the company....In a
> hierarchy, it is natural for people with less power to be
> extremely cautious about disclosing weaknesses, mistakes,
> and failings—especially when the more powerful party is
> also in a position to evaluate and punish....Often the motive
> for silence is at least superficially praiseworthy: people keep
> quiet about a developing problem while trying to solve it.
> Most believe solving a problem on their own is what they're
> paid to do, and in many cases, they're right. Subordinates
> are not paid to run to their bosses with every glitch and hic-
> cup. As problems grow more serious, however, managers
> need to know about them.[12]

It is not enough to be totally open and honest with your employees. This philosophy must be demonstrated to your clients and
suppliers as well by such behavior as giving advanced previews
of future products, letting organizations benchmark their organizations against yours, or giving suppliers access to internal
training programs.

Secretiveness.   The opposite of openness is secretiveness, and
it has the opposite effects. Secretiveness is expressed by isolating
top management from lower-level employees, building barbed
wire around the boss's office, using one-way communication

(top-down), and distancing yourself from your clients by hiding in an ivory tower. Those organizations that deliberately build barriers between themselves and their employees or their clients will never develop relationships based on mutual trust.

The problem, according to Gordon Shea, is that "when an organization is secretive, tightly controlled, does not delegate authority, and sharply separates management and management decisions from employees and lower-level managers, it doesn't take much intelligence to recognize that management does not trust its `underlings' to behave as reasonable, responsible people."[13]

It is in every organization's best interest to get closer to employees, suppliers, and customers. Getting closer to clients requires such actions as involving them in the product development process, aggressively asking them for feedback on the services that you provide, and demonstrating your organization's commitment to them by involving top management with their account.

Communication. In Chapter 4, which examined communications, the importance of open and honest communication was discussed in depth. Here, communications are viewed as an essential quality that creates high-trust organizations. Lack of communications is particularly harmful when relevant information is withheld in order to maintain control or gain personal advantage.

There isn't much trust in an organization if employees have to weigh and measure everything they hear—if they can't trust the information that is given them. In an organization marked by trust and good communications, employees don't ask themselves: Am I being kept informed? Will they tell me about a decision that may affect me while they are making it? If they are unwilling or unable to live up to a client promise, will they let me know in advance so that I can inform my clients? Would they intentionally try to misrepresent what I said? Do they tell everyone the same story?

A manager displays trust when she openly communicates with her employees and reveals information that she doesn't have to. Dale E. Zand notes that "a manager shows trust when he seeks counsel from peers, superiors, or subordinates. He increases his vulnerability when he permits them to influence his decisions. He may be seen as a weak leader or some counselors may inadvertently or deliberately mislead him. A manager additionally shows trust when he delegates. He increases his vulnerability when he depends on others to analyze a problem, gather information, or implement a decision."[14]

The opposite of open communications occurs in organizations marked by low levels of trust. In such organizations, managers who do "not trust others will conceal or distort relevant information...withhold facts, disguise ideas, and conceal conclusions. [Such managers] will hide feelings that increase exposure to others. As a result, [such managers] provide incomplete, untimely information that inaccurately portrays reality."[15] The problem according to Zand is that "when managers withhold relevant information, distort intentions, or conceal alternatives, they introduce social uncertainty and increase the total uncertainty in solving a problem. Social uncertainty increases the probability that underlying problems go undetected or are deliberately avoided."[16]

These, however, are all problems that can be avoided through the careful use of communications. Effective communication can also have a great impact on levels of trust with clients. For example, trust increases when clients are given advance notice of bad news so that expectations are controlled, when the downside of a product as well as the benefits are presented, and when the competition is treated objectively and not denigrated.

The Whole Picture.   Taken together, these qualities form the foundation on which trusting relationships are built. When they become part of a person's or an organization's track record, relationships tend to grow stronger and last longer. They are the basis on which people choose friends and on which people select organizations to buy from and work with.

The Second Ring: Consistency

Once people or organizations have repeatedly displayed those traits mentioned in the prior section, we tend to increase our trust in them. But at this stage, we have not internalized that trust; it is not a part of our belief system. The relationships we are building will have to stand the test of time. For as we get to know the person or organization better, we begin to see patterns of behavior and take into account their actions toward others, actions they are likely to repeat.

Furthermore, we look for patterns that are regular and consistent because the more predictable people are, the higher the degree of comfort we have with them. In order to establish this, we ask ourselves, Do they encourage an activity one day and prohibit it the next? Do they feel strongly about their ideas today and abandon them tomorrow? Are they reliable one day and scatterbrained the next? Do they have the strength of their convictions or do their moods blow in the wind? Is it possible to anticipate their responses to a request or a new suggestion? Do you know whether your actions will win you praise or criticism? If the chips are down, will the individual or the organization be in your corner? Are their actions consistent with their words, or do they send mixed messages?

You can't beat your child one evening and expect that acting with tenderness in the morning will erase all the memories of the night before. If you say things you later regret, for example, attacking the individual rather than debating the issue, excusing yourself does not make up for it. "I was angry at the time, I didn't mean it, I had other things on my mind" does not suffice. You must be consistent in your behavior to maintain and grow trusting relationships.

Organizations demonstrate consistency by treating clients and employees in the same way and by standing behind the products and services that they market. They do not introduce a new product with a splash today only to abandon it tomorrow, nor do they buy and divest themselves of businesses so fast that consumers hesitate to buy products from them because they are afraid they won't be around to service them tomorrow.

Consistency is also demonstrated by continuous product quality. One organization that has competitively differentiated themselves in this way is McDonald's. You know that when you have a McDonald's hamburger anywhere around the world, it will taste the same, and you will feel at home eating it.

There is a caveat here. Companies must grow and change to be successful. Indeed, it is often critical that a company introduce new and better products to stay ahead of the competition, which seems antithetical to consistency. In cases like these, the way that product transitions are managed is critical. The public's investment in a product must not be lost overnight; for example, when Sony converted its Betamax video recorder format to VHS, the investment that its customers made in tapes was lost. Nintendo lost a lot of consumer trust when it introduced new game software that required a new machine. Similar games should have been made for the old machine at the same time as a phaseout was announced, or the old machine should have been upgradable. After a while, the consistency that the individual or company exhibits becomes expected. We assume it will behave in a certain way each time. Our trust grows and the ring is added to the one before, becoming, again, part of the history of the relationship.

The Third Ring: From Predictability to Faith

Now that consistency is established and bonded to the earlier attributes, becoming a part of an organization's or a person's history, we have a strong sense that we can predict what the person or the organization will do in the future. As a result, we do not question and worry about promises made: we trust them and are comfortable with our own belief in them.

The problem is that any time an organization or an individual makes claims, no matter how small, and then does not deliver, they shatter the comfort zone created by our trust in their predictability. In fact, as Fisher and Brown have pointed out, "If conduct is unpredictable, we may think the person is untrustworthy. If a person is untrustworthy, we begin to question his honesty. Once we have thought in terms of honesty, that concern spreads to other areas....A company that has been (perhaps unavoidably) late in shipping its products finds that customers begin to suspect the quality of the products themselves and sometimes the integrity of the company's personnel."[17]

Once the comfort zone is challenged, anything someone thought of as predictable in the future may be treated as suspect. A claim not fulfilled can impact people's impressions in totally unrelated areas. For example, your company may announce that a new product will be out in May, only to announce in April that there has been a product delay and that the product won't be available till the fourth quarter. At the same moment, a salesperson may be making claims to an individual who read about that product delay in the paper that morning. The person asking the question will then wonder whether the new claims are misstated as well.

However, it is unusual for an individual or organization that has a history of trustworthiness, consistency, and predictability to make claims that fail to materialize or make promises they don't keep. What is far more usual is that they become so predictable that you stop evaluating their actions and allow your faith in them to take over. That decision is often made unconsciously. This ring, which is less defined than the inner rings, is like a web of fine golden cords that makes the structure within glow.

Faith enables you to go beyond facts and still feel secure about another person or even an organization. Faith is often a result of someone motivated by unselfish reasons caring about your interests above their own. It is a result of people responding supportively. It is a result of empathy, of showing that you care. It is knowing that someone would never try to hurt you, take advantage of you in a pinch, or criticize you in front of others. It is knowing that your organization will support you, be available if you need them, coach you, encourage your ideas, and take an interest in your career and in your life.

Faith is strengthened when you put customers' interests in front of your own, not only meeting, but exceeding their expectations. It is strengthened when an organization is clearly more interested in helping prospective clients resolve their business issues than in selling them additional products. It is strengthened when you keep clients informed about new developments that may affect their organization even though the work that you performed has been completed.

Conclusion

Trust is in as much need of protection as the air that we breathe or the water that we drink. It is easily squandered and hard to regain. According to Tom Peters, "The essence of managing any company, whether it's IBM or Joe and Harry's Grill, is about caring, listening, trust, respect, and dignity. We talk about international competition, world-class quality, competing in time, quick turnaround, fast response, innovation, and that's the right stuff to talk about. But the other side of the coin is that all of that comes from people who give a damn, who care, who are committed, and who are cared about."[18]

The heart of the matter as Shea noted is that "it's time to think of trust as an asset—money in our pockets or in the organization's treasury. We can grasp the real utility of this resource if we view trust as a miracle currency: either it can be accumulated and spent without necessarily depleting our reserves—or it can be lost so that we become destitute."[19]

10

Following Your Conscience

A Recipe for Peak Performance

This book began by stressing the importance of intangible factors such as empowering your work force, creating an environment that encourages risk and discourages fear, improving business processes and eliminating waste, promoting continuous education and the personal and professional growth of employees, communicating in an open and honest manner, building trust among employees, nurturing long-term relationships with suppliers and clients, working hard to develop an impeccable reputation, living according to sound business ethics, and unifying your organization around a mission and shared values. While many believe these factors are critical for competing in the next century, others consider them "soft" issues.

Intangibles: Difficult to Quantify but Vital to Success

The Industrial Age brought us products such as cars, heavy farm equipment, refrigerators, washing machines, and computers—equipment that could be seen, touched, and demonstrated. The Information Age, in contrast, is characterized by intangibles—resources that involve the intellect and the ability to gather, analyze, transmit, and synthesize information. In fact, today, such intangibles form the basis of some of the most successful companies. According to an article in *The New York Times Magazine*, "Microsoft's only factory asset is the human imagination."[1]

Just as you cannot measure liquids in pounds or nuclear fusion in quarts, you cannot use yesterday's measurements of success to gauge the importance of a knowledgeable, experienced, and committed work force, a creative working environment, brand awareness, or reputation. As Tom Peters said in *Liberation Management*, "In the 'soft' world where the human imagination is all (and 90 percent of stock market value), even a huge corporation with a billion-dollar price tag) can literally turn to 'nothing' overnight. How much would Microsoft be worth if something happened to founder Bill Gates? Several billion dollars less than yesterday."[2]

There is a tendency in this country, however, to believe that if something cannot be quantified, it does not exist. It brings to mind the eighteenth-century question "If a tree falls in the woods, but no one is there to hear the sound, did it make a noise?" To put it another way: If someone enhances performance in an organization using an approach that cannot be quantified, did the improvement take place?

You won't find these soft attributes in an annual report, because they are intangible and difficult to quantify. But that doesn't make them any less important to an organization. These soft issues are all very like the tree that falls in the woods. In the Information Age, however, if we don't believe that there was a noise, maybe it's time to get our hearing checked.

The Vision, Values, and Beliefs Must Reach Peak Importance

It is time for a new style of leadership. Workers do not respond well to micromanagement or to being treated like cogs in a wheel. In order to increase work force productivity, management has learned various theories, techniques, and approaches that are believed to motivate employees. But they are all based on the fundamental premise that it is management's role to do the motivating—that is, it is up to management to push employees toward certain behaviors or to control them in a certain way. Management can reward employees by giving them a promotion, a raise, or a pat on the back; they can reprimand, discipline, or fire them. Management can create rules and procedures that give selected individuals the authority to make decisions over a minimum threshold. Or, managers can earn the respect of their colleagues through their expertise, their personal integrity, and their ability to foster trust. While reward, punishment, and authority come with an individual's position, the most effective forms of management—respect, expertise, and trust—reside in the person and are earned over time.

Furthermore, it is possible—in fact, desirable—to gain employee commitment through a leader's vision or the organization's beliefs and values. According to research conducted by James C. Collins and Jerry I. Porras, faculty members at Stanford Graduate School of Business, "If you take the visionary companies that we studied going back to 1926—or whenever the companies were first listed—and let's say you had a chance to buy a share of stock in something called 'Visionary Companies, Inc'—the visionary companies have outperformed the general market by 55 times!"[3] Successful leaders know that today's motivational techniques may only satisfy employees long enough to achieve short-term goals. If you supplement today's forms of employee motivation by instilling a belief in your organization's mission and stress the importance of every employee's contribution, you bring about commitment that motivates people forever.

Companies Must Match Individual Needs and Corporate Values

For tomorrow's employee, being part of something special and making a difference in the world are much more important than the rewards sought by yesterday's "me" generation. *The Wall Street Journal* noted that "in a recent study conducted for Hilton Hotels Corp., 50% of 1,010 people polled said they would sacrifice a day's pay for an extra day off each week. And given the choice of eight goals for the future, 77% said spending time with family and friends was a priority compared with 61% who cited making money and just 29% who said they will put more emphasis on spending money on material possessions. Furthermore, 74% of those surveyed said that they want to improve themselves intellectually, emotionally or physically."[4]

The new breed of employee wants to work for an organization that they can feel proud of—that contributes back to society; an organization that has values and viewpoints compatible with their own; an organization that is oriented toward the long haul, working toward the prevention of ills, not only curing the symptoms; an organization that cares about morals and ethics and doing what is in the best interests of its clients; an organization that doesn't dominate employees lives and allows them ample time to spend with their families; and one that cares about the impact that it has on the environment. Employees want this because they recognize that such an organization will also care about them.

What is the impact of such a philosophy? What happens when you really love what you do? When you really believe in a cause? When you really care? When you feel part of something special and are doing something good for people? When you know every action that you've made has had an impact? And when you know your efforts won't be forgotten? You become passionate about what you are doing, you can't wait to get out of bed and go to work in the morning, and you feel good about other people's successes. This generates a spark, an excitement, and an energy that becomes contagious. Employees become so committed that friends talk to them and their minds drift to work, they come in to work on the weekend to pursue their ideas, and they tirelessly fight for causes they believe in—not because it's in their own best interests, but because it's right. This kind of commitment is happening, and those organizations that unleash it are winning.

When there is a crisis, companies can count on everyone pitching in. When sacrifice is needed everyone is willing to step forward. When management needs that little something extra, people can't wait to help. People don't have to be cajoled, they don't have to be threatened, and they certainly don't have to be bribed. They only have to be asked.

Being All Things to All People Is a Guaranteed Recipe for Mediocrity

Everyone talks about sticking to their knitting, but many companies don't know what their knitting is. According to a *Fortune* magazine article, "Focus means figuring out, and building on, what the company does best. It means identifying the evolving needs of your customers, then developing the key skills—often called core competencies—critical to serving them. It means setting a clear, realistic mission and then working tirelessly to make sure everyone—from the chairman to the middle manager to the hourly employee understands it."[5]

If Your Organization Isn't Focused, Someone Is Probably Undoing Something You Just Completed

In order to be successful, an organization must focus its efforts on those factors that are critical to its success. If you randomly select fifty people in your organization and ask them basic questions about the direction and priorities of the company, how similar would their answers be? When employees don't know where the company is heading, they can't be expected to sacrifice themselves for the benefit of the organization. They won't get excited about what they're doing, or put down their swords and stop the political bickering, and they won't be passionate about their careers or the future of the organization. Unless you can get common answers to the most basic questions, you foster waste, redundancies, inefficiencies, confusion, and anxiety.

When you look at successful small corporations today, many of them have something in common. People have a common sense of purpose, and believe in the founder's vision. They maintain their individuality, but strive for team gain. People care more about the organization winning than who gets the next promotion, and they know that resources are limited, so they concentrate those resources on critical areas rather than squander them.

There Is a Difference between Motion and Movement

Once you have determined the critical success factors that will lead you to your destination, you must set milestones to ensure you keep heading in the right direction. You should always keep in mind that there is a difference between motion and movement. Motion is getting from point *a* to point *b*—working on those things that will do the most to help you achieve your goals. Movement is recklessly expending time chasing your tail, working hard at things that keep you busy, but have low pay-off; maintaining very elaborate to-do lists, but never looking to see which activities are important to the success of the organization; trying to accomplish so many things and spreading yourself so thin that your actions don't have a meaningful impact. Ask yourself whether those activities that are closest to you at the moment are the most important or just the most urgent. Otherwise you will spend all of your time putting out fires rather than lighting them.

Flexibility Is Critical— Organizations Should Be Boundaryless

Organizations must remain flexible in order to succeed; they must create an organizational structure and operating style that permit the company to take advantage of new opportunities. Many companies, for example, go outside more and more often to complement their internal resources, accessing specialized skills that their regular employees don't have or adding extra people during peak periods; gaining objective viewpoints from people with multiclient experience; and discovering new trends that may affect their business.

In the past, conventional wisdom said that multiple vendors increased competition and enhanced performance, that playing one supplier against another was good business. Today, conventional wisdom is quite the opposite. As organizations focus more of their efforts on the things they do best and those that are critical to their success, they will rely more and more on external resources, outsourcing, strategic alliances, and building strong external relationships. The only way to ensure that those relationships will last is to start with honorable intentions, make a commitment, and expend the time and effort so that everybody wins.

If Everyone Spends Time Trying to Gain the Upper Hand, Everyone Loses

Optimizing partnerships requires building balanced relationships. To do this, keep in mind that formal contracts don't make successful relationships; people do. A partnership is successful to the degree that it replaces the traditional "we versus them" mentality with a new "us" that allows everyone involved to grow and to reach their full potential. People who are good at building successful alliances work very hard to structure win-win relationships. One key element in this effort is the search for overlapping areas of opportunity where both organizations gain. For example, American Express announced an agreement to put its magazines into a joint venture with Time Warner. American Express would retain full ownership of the publications and Time Warner would operate them.[6] A partnership will succeed in the long run when both sides work for their common good rather than trying to get the upper hand. When greed takes over, supposed partners spend all of their time trying to outnegotiate each other and both end up losing. Moreover, in these situations, one of the organizations is likely to come out noticeably ahead of the other, ultimately causing jealousy and resentment.

Plantation Management Destroys Productivity

It is vital that treating people fairly extend beyond your suppliers to those who work with you. Every individual should be given the opportunity to reach his or her full potential. When managers don't abide by this philosophy they find employees show little initiative on the job, but are highly motivated outside of work; they put in time but no energy; they spend more time working on their résumés than on the activities at hand. According to a survey conducted by *Industry Week*, "Nearly 63% of the respondents say there's no joy in jobsville for them."[7] A management style that produces these results obviously won't be enough to compete successfully in today's global economy.

In fact, the result of this plantation-style management is already causing a disastrous collision between the needs of businesses and the demands of today's work force. According to an *Industry Week* survey, "Asked if there is more or less loyalty between company and employees today than there was five years ago, 87.7% of those who answered say 'less.'"[8] They want to work someplace where they can make a meaningful contribution; where procedures, policies, and protocol are never more important than results; and where building bonds between people is considered as important as the bottom line.

According to W. E. Odom, chairman of the board of Ford Motor Credit Company: "Today, the good managers are doing everything that they can to tear down the walls and destroy boxes. Today, they try to manage through empowerment, not intimidation. Not by seeing people as problems, but by getting people to solve problems. Not by telling people what to do, but by enabling people to make decisions. Not by devising elaborate financial models, but by providing people with the tools and incentives to think. Not by demanding allegiance, but by treating people with respect and dignity. In other words, managers today are placing an increasing amount of trust in their employees, and earning trust in return."[9]

People Will Live Up or Down to Your Expectations

Companies that search for the best and brightest people must learn that their efforts shouldn't end when those people join the organization. To retain these employees, companies should invest heavily in them, both personally and professionally. Today, employees demand trust and respect. They want their input solicited, their strengths utilized, and their contributions valued. Furthermore, they want and should be given challenging new responsibilities that stretch their potential.

Managers who act in this way are far more likely to achieve superior performance from their employees. In fact, "formal psychological research as well as a large amount of casual empiricism by others leave no doubt that the power of expectation alone can influence the behavior of others. This total phenomenon is called the Pygmalion effect....Studies have shown that the IQ scores of children, especially on verbal and information subjects, can be raised merely by expecting them to do well....A study showed that worker performance increased markedly when the supervisor of these workers was told that his group showed a special potential for their particular job."[10]

The opposite is also true: Employees who feel like helpless drones perform that way. Employees who believe they are essential to the success of the operation, will always rise to the occasion by accepting greater responsibility, ultimately increasing their productivity.

There Is a Direct Correlation between the Way Employees Are Treated and the Way They Treat Customers

As a leader you must keep in mind all the costs, including the hidden ones, of mistreating employees. Among those costs are employee resignations with the accompanying loss of important skills and client knowledge; voicing discontent, thereby hurting morale; using every possible "sick day" or constantly showing up late; or becoming apathetic, producing only enough to avoid being fired.

Moreover, dissatisfied employees who spend much of the workday expressing their dissatisfaction and unhappiness create an air of dissension, depressing those around them, hindering concentration, and lowering everyone's spirits. Apathy is often so subtle that you may not even realize the problem exists. When investigators examined this phenomenon, they found the number of American workers who said they were currently working to their full potential was shockingly small—23 percent. The researchers also discovered in their random sampling of American workers that "nearly half (44%) say they do not put any more effort into their jobs than is required to hold onto them. The overwhelming majority, 75%, say that they could be significantly more effective on their jobs than they are now."[11] The implications of these findings are dismaying, and the ramifications for productivity and on service quality are even more disheartening.

For Every Action There Is a Reaction

Not only is it important to recognize that every action toward a given employee inspires a reaction, but that actions toward employees rarely impact only those directly involved. If you think of the corporation as analogous to the human body with its complex and interdependent systems, you will understand why change in one area affects the whole. Every action provokes a reaction, especially when people have long-established relationships with others in the organization.

Just as Capital Equipment Requires Maintenance to Protect Its Value, Creativity Requires Nurturing

Creativity makes a difference at every level and in every type of organization—whether in the creation of new products and services, managing an advertising relationship, or finding ways to solve longstanding problems that seem unsolvable until someone with imagination throws an old ball with a new twist.

This means that organizations must first analyze the internal climate, norms, and personal biases that inhibit creativity and then create an environment where new ideas are welcomed and allowed to flourish; where ideas are evaluated on their individual merits rather than the status of the person introducing them; and where people look for "the good" in every idea, trying to add value to it rather than shooting it out of the sky.

An article in *Industry Week* noted that organizations that understand the need to foster creativity, "regard new ideas as wild flowers. They know you do not plant seeds for wild flowers; you find them by searching in many places. They concentrate on preparing the conditions for wild flowers to grow as they push for incremental change everywhere."[12]

Progress Requires Mistakes

According to an article in the *Harvard Business Review*, "Wise executives worry more about invisible mistakes—failing to take risks, failing to innovate to create new value for customers."[13] They know that when people aren't making mistakes they're probably not trying anything new. Everyone should recognize that being right all the time is an enormous barrier to innovation. When organizations foster a risk-averse climate, creativity will be stifled. Making mistakes, and then learning from them, is an important stage in the learning process. Employees need confidence and assurance that experimentation resulting in failure won't have repercussions.

Organizations Succeed Because of the Efforts of Many, Not the Strengths of a Few

In the past, the role of senior management was to make decisions and the role of employees was to implement them. Today, however, the world is quite different. According to William J. O'Brien, chief executive officer of the Hanover Insurance Co. in Worcester, Massachusetts, "The fundamental movement in business in the next 25 years will be the dispersing of power, to give meaning and fulfillment to employees in a way that avoids chaos and disorder."[14]

This will be particularly necessary in a world of rapid change, in which large bureaucracies with multiple levels of approval delay the rapid response needed to succeed in an ever-changing world. Change is fast and fierce. In fact, according to Tom Peters, "It's getting ludicrous! One hundred and four new cereal products came our way in 1991, not to mention 574 new varieties of cookies, 316 fruit and vegetable juices, and 463 salty snacks. All in all, 16,143 new drug and grocery store consumer products joined us, up from 2,689 in 1980. The average super-market now carries 30,000 items vs. 9,000 in 1976. And the non-prescription Drug Manufacturers Association says there are now 200,000 brands, varieties, and sizes of over-the-counter drugs. Between 1980 and 1990, the number of mutual funds grew from 568 to 3,347. We've got 70 cable networks in the U.S., up from 27 in 1980."[15]

If the Organization Doesn't Live in the Hearts and Minds of Its People, It Does Not Exist

Titles should all but disappear in organizations. Organization charts in a company neither define relationships as they actually exist nor direct the lines of communication. They build walls between people, stifle communication and creativity, and are often the cause of internal politics, jealousy, and resentment. No chart can fix that. An organization's function is simple: to provide a framework, a format, a context in which people can effectively use resources to accomplish their goals.

Everyone Can Make a Difference: Caste Systems Stifle Excellence

"'Oh, come off it,' you say, 'a business enterprise needn't be one happy family to succeed. Aren't plenty of slave ships making good time?' Some are. But companies seething with class discord pay penalty in drag," according to David Sirota of Sirota Alper & Pfau.[16]

It is important that employees at all levels communicate, share innovative ideas, and solve problems together. Caste systems create obstacles to success. When people only socialize along status lines, when they use jargon their colleagues can't understand, when management distances itself by creating impressive executive floors and establishing perquisites such as parking spaces, private dining rooms, and flying first-class, its actions lead to suspicion, increase personal distance, and create an air of unapproachability.

Bureaucracies Are Not Biodegradable

Peter Drucker once said, "Elephants have a hard time adapting. Cockroaches outlive everything."[17] Bloated bureaucracies crush aspirations, stifle creativity, suppress ingenuity, and slow responsiveness. Unfortunately, once bureaucracy develops, it is as difficult to control in business as crabgrass is on a suburban lawn. It causes people to thirst for power, value personal ambition over team gain, and put paperwork before people.

In bureaucracies, the individual employees don't matter because they are single voices, and individual customers don't matter because their voices are never heard by the people who determine policy. People choose the political solution rather than the best answer. Promotions are earned through political savvy rather than performance; the "show" becomes more important than content; and rumor becomes the primary form of communication. This causes organizations to focus inward and loose touch with reality.

To succeed, bureaucratic obstacles must be eliminated, and speed, simplicity, and continuous improvement emphasized. Operational units must remain small. People must get out of their offices and in front of customers. Ad hoc task forces, composed of multifunctional groups, should be set up to tackle issues; ideas should be chosen based on merit rather than an individual's place in the pecking order; and activities that do not add value to the client should be eliminated.

Waste Not, Want Not

Today, a minute can be a lifetime. Time is a precious resource that cannot be replenished: it is a constant that cannot be changed. Unlike money, which flows in and out and can earn different rates of return, time is finite. You cannot get more time, but you can manage the time that you have better. In the 1980s, resources were abundant enough that we seldom had to face the consequences of waste. Today, this isn't true; we can't make up for lost time by throwing resources at problems. Your organization will not be competitive in the 1990s if your competitors build products, using 20 percent fewer people, and aggressively market their products while yours are still in the testing stage; if innovative ideas are tied up in the approval process; if creativity is stifled by procedures; if people are more comfortable procrastinating than working; and if precious time is wasted in countless meetings.

People are not willing to wait when they can get what they want from someone else, they won't pay more to make up for ineptitude, and they won't be patient or sympathetic when their success depends on your efforts. Just as car manufacturers design aerodynamic racing cars with as little wind resistance as possible, companies that want to finish first have to expose and then eliminate all of the nonessential business activities that add drag rather than value.

If You're Not Moving Ahead, You're Falling Behind

In a world in which change is an everyday occurrence, business as usual is a guaranteed recipe for failure. To succeed, tomorrow's company must go beyond coping with change; it must embrace it. Rather than react to change; it must learn to anticipate it. Those who cling to the past will meet change with apprehension and anxiety; those prepared to meet new challenges will be rewarded with unparalleled opportunities. The rewards will go to those employees who are not only committed, but ready to lead the effort.

According to the 1990 Coca-Cola *Annual Report,* "We don't view the future as preordained, but as an indefinite series of openings, of possibilities. What is required to succeed in the middle of this uncertainty is what the Greeks called 'practical intelligence.' Above all else, this 'practical intelligence' forces adaptability and teaches constant preparedness. It acknowledges that nothing succeeds quite as planned, and that the model is not the reality. But it also teaches that choice and preparation can influence the future."[18]

It is very easy to look at a situation and determine that since nothing is obviously wrong, it should be left alone. After all, inertia creates comfort, and changing requires breaking old habits, which creates discomfort. Businesses must seize change for the opportunities it offers. As part of that effort, they must encourage learning and continuous improvement through experimentation, making it clear that there is no disgrace in trying and failing. This will require fostering an environment of trust, loyalty, and commitment; those qualities that free people to devote time and attention to their work instead of covering their tracks and hiding errors.

Everyone Is Responsible for Leading Change

Because change is no longer an occasional but rather an everyday occurrence, companies can ill afford the length of time between the development of an idea and its implementation. As soon as new ideas are introduced, they become obsolete. Just as manufacturers search for faster ways to bring new products to market, companies must search for better and faster ways to foster change in their organizations. They must create a working environment where employees change and renew themselves everyday. Second, in an age in which the work force is becoming empowered and layers of management are being dismantled, companies can no longer afford to have a few select people make all the decisions for the company.

The reality is that people don't resist change; they resist being changed. Executives should aim not at changing their employees, but rather at fostering a spirit that it's everyone's responsibility to change the organization. In addition, in the past, management made decisions and employees were expected to conform. Companies wrongly assumed that while participation was nice, it was not critical. Today, such attempts will cost the commitment of employees, something empowered companies cannot afford.

The Only Thing We Have to Fear Is Fear Itself

Just as pollution damages the environment, an air of fear is toxic to companies. When people believe they lack control over what happens to them, they become fearful. And whether their fears are real or imagined or whether they arise over things that are concrete and immediate, such as loss of a job, or over things that are more ephemeral and long term, such as personal embarrassment or damage to personal credibility or career mobility, the results are still the same: inaction, withdrawal, hiding mistakes, misrepresenting facts, and procrastination.

Unfortunately, the "overwhelming majority of Americans (85 percent) are reactive and static, not action- or dynamic- or instinct-oriented as a result of this desire to play it safe."[19] This response is brought on by a sense of powerlessness and fear; it makes people less likely to challenge the status quo, confront issues, or openly question things they feel are wrong. A survey of employees in twenty-two organizations around the country revealed that "70% of them say they 'bit their tongues' at work because they feared the repercussions of speaking out. And 98% of their responses indicate that fear has negative effects on them or their work."[20] In a time of constant change, fear must be eliminated so that all employees feel absolutely comfortable making suggestions that will better the organization.

**Unless You Learn Something
New Everyday, You're
Becoming Obsolete**

Learning is not only an important catalyst for organizational change, but according to an *Industry Week* study, "There is a direct relationship between the amount of training the work force receives and how committed that work force is."[21] People today understand that they must accept responsibility for their destinies. The days are gone where it was possible to stay with an organization for life. Employees only have job security to the extent that they continue to grow, providing more value to their current employer and becoming more marketable should they decide to leave. Thus, employees believe that the company that invests in them cares about them. As a result, training provides double value, making the organization more competitive and building employee commitment.

Internal Communication Is
Not a Luxury; It Is a Necessity

Since open and honest communications are essential to creating a climate conducive to learning and change, management must accept responsibility for fostering this kind of environment. Changing to a more open and trusting environment requires letting go, unlearning many management practices of the past. But that is not easy, and it does not happen quickly. It requires that managers leave behind many skills, sources of status and power, and implicit assumptions about the workplace that were formulated during past experiences. In the past, leaders assumed the role of controlling the information employees needed to make day-to-day decisions. Leaders who continue along that path will become frustrated as they lose the confidence of employees whose desire for timely, customized information is not satisfied. Leaders must view communication as an avenue to release the creative genius of an organization, not as a bothersome chore. After all, communication acts as a powerful agent of change, a source of continuous improvement, and a catalyst for moving the organization forward.

In an age of rapid change and abundant information, employees can't be productive by waiting till the end of the month to get a generically written, watered-down newsletter that doesn't provide relevant information. While that may have been satisfactory yesterday, when everything wasn't so time sensitive, in today's global economy, it just isn't enough. Employees are saying that they need information today, because it will be obsolete tomorrow; they are saying that it must be customized to meet their specific needs or they're just not interested.

Where employee communication was once produced by the professional, it will now be developed by the layman. Where it was once broadcast from the ivory tower, it will now be transmitted through the grapevine. Where the purpose of internal communications was once to report on the completion of an event, it will now plant seeds that will grow into new ideas. Where communication was once infrequent, it will now become constant. Where there was once lag time in reporting an event, communication will become instant. Where formal mass communication was once commonplace, customization and personalization will become the norm.

Compartmentalization of Knowledge Builds Walls between People

Employees must know and understand how their actions affect others in the organization, and they must be held accountable for the impact their decisions have on other parts of the organization. Problems occur when employees become so focused on achieving their own departmental goals that they optimize their own personal interests at the expense of the organization. When employees don't share information, efforts are duplicated, deadlines are missed, redundancy occurs, rework increases, and interdepartmental relationships deteriorate.

It is everyone's job to encourage communication to flow freely in an organization, breaking down the compartmentalization of knowledge. Communication cannot be stifled because of organization charts or other artificial boundaries created by management. Employees must feel free to contact anyone who has information that can help them accomplish an activity. Management must actively develop forums encouraging employees to get to know people, build shared values, discuss emerging issues, and solve joint problems.

There Is No Substitute for Open and Honest Communication

Access to information is so fundamental to doing our jobs properly that it must be considered a right, not a privilege. At a time when we must encourage creativity from all of our employees, the information that we give them serves as the fundamental building blocks and catalysts to stimulate those new ideas.

According to Henry Stimson, U.S. secretary of war in World War II, "The only way to make a man trustworthy is to trust him."[22] But if this rings true, according to an article in *The Wall Street Journal*, "nearly 70% of more than 200 employee communication managers polled by consultant William M. Mercer call their messages to workers 'attempts at truth'; fewer than 15% say they reflect the whole truth."[23] To ensure that people are not kept in the dark, even unwittingly, management must be committed to open and honest communication throughout the organization. That openness is part of the nurturing environment that spurs creativity, an environment in which there is little distrust, one in which everyone pulls together to achieve a common end. In this environment, new ideas are challenged and constructive feedback is offered.

Organizations Must Become Obsessed with Listening

Many management groups spend so much time talking among themselves that they lose sight of reality. Organizations must become obsessed with listening to both their customers and their employees. Many managers isolate themselves from those who have daily contact with customers and, as a result, lose touch with client needs. Some CEOs appear in their offices infrequently because they spend so much of their time serving on boards or making appearances. Other managers isolate themselves by spending time in meetings with other managers. When employees don't have access to management, when they have to go through two secretaries to make an appointment that is later canceled and rescheduled, saying that the company has an open-door policy is meaningless.

Clients Must Be the Centerpiece of Your Attention

Due to global competition, companies have placed so much emphasis on, and have made such great strides in, the production process that it will be very difficult in the future to differentiate products solely on the basis of workmanship. Now, much more is needed to win the loyalty of the marketplace. Overcoming the tendency to treat customers poorly—and the costs of doing so—will require a greater focus on the customer. In fact, intangibles, such as quality service, have been shown to lead to market expansion and even to make premium pricing possible.

The change in emphasis is much more evident in the services industry, where products are often intangible, precise specifications cannot be set, and production and consumption of many services are inseparable. There, quality will be defined universally as meeting and exceeding the expectations of customers— that is, everything leading up to, during, and after the sale.

Furthermore, clients must not be viewed as isolated sales transactions, but by the potential lifelong relationship that they represent. Every client deserves to be treated as your organization's only client. Companies cannot afford to spend the time and effort it takes to develop new business only to lose clients shortly thereafter. In fact, companies should be so outraged when they lose an existing client that they immediately search for ways to improve themselves so it never happens again. Think about the effort of bringing in new clients; the way they are courted; how you accommodate their every whim. Then when they become clients, the honeymoon ends. Think about your major clients. When they call, everything else is dropped; when they make suggestions everyone listens; and when they need something done, everyone responds. Now think about all of your other clients. We can't accommodate them because it's against company policy; we don't listen to their suggestions because we know better than they do; we can't take their calls because we're in meetings; everything that takes a little extra effort is a bother.

Since superior client service is as much a mind-set as it is an activity, it is important to understand the culture that produces excellent service. Such a culture is built on the belief that policy changes should be made to make your client's life better, not your own; that your employees do their best work because they care rather than because the competition is making inroads; and that your company's employees know their first and foremost job is to service clients, never taking their business for granted.

Unless You Listen to Your Clients, You'll Be Making Today's Decisions Based on Yesterday's Information

Just as you cannot develop a long-term friendship with someone you don't know well, you cannot develop relationships with clients unless you understand their needs. And that won't happen by magic. Ask yourself if you spend your time dominating discussions or actively listening. Do you understand your clients' political sensitivities? Are you flexible in responding to clients or set in your ways?

Because giving customers what they want is the only thing that matters, it is very important to understand what customers consider excellent service. You can accomplish that by providing such opportunities for feedback as conducting account reviews, periodically meeting with your clients to discuss the relationship and how it can be improved; holding focus group sessions; conducting surveys; establishing dealer councils; setting up 800 numbers.

In fact, in today's competitive business climate, responding to clients' needs isn't enough; you must anticipate them. Thus, one of the best ways of improving client service is to actively search for new ideas both from inside and outside your industry, and then find ways to adapt those ideas to your organization.

Talk Is Cheap

Having integrity means sticking to your principles, no matter what. It means making sure that your actions are consistent with your words. If it's the last day of the sales month, and the numbers look lousy, are employees still encouraged to do what is in the best interests of the client or asked to sell something for immediate gain? Are managers rewarded for the development of their people as well as for the bottom line? Is a promise made to a client kept even though circumstances have changed in such a way that the agreement is now less profitable? The answers to these questions will tell you whether your company values ethical behavior over short-term business.

Take the Short-Term View if
You Plan to Be in Business
Only for the Short Term

Real leaders provide a legacy for those who follow them; they don't focus only on today's results. They build organizations that deliver service excellence and train employees to recognize the value of building long-term relationships. They help employees learn to see themselves through their customers' eyes rather than focus inwardly. They teach employees to go beyond the selling role, offering advice and information that provides added value to the buyer and recognizes their ongoing needs. They concentrate on building ongoing relationships with a few clients instead of endlessly searching for new prospects and then losing them as they focus on yet new leads.

Quality, Training, and Internal Communication Must Be Integrated into Everything You Do

Employees shouldn't think about quality only when participating in a quality meeting, they shouldn't think about learning only when attending a seminar, and they shouldn't think of communication as a series of activities such as newsletters or brochures. Quality, training, and communication must be as much a mindset and a way of conducting yourself as they are an activity.

Honesty Isn't the Best Policy—It's the Only Policy

It takes a long time to win confidence and trust, but both can be quickly destroyed if you do not live up to your claims. People do business with those who have a high degree of integrity. They avoid organizations that charge different prices for the same merchandise. They avoid organizations that have a reputation for talking about other clients with outsiders, whether that involves disclosing confidential information or just not speaking well of them. They avoid organizations that claim other people's ideas as their own or that take advantage of a relationship by overselling.

Know When to Walk Away from Business

There are many times when the best thing for you to do is walk away from a sale. Don't accept business unless you can handle it properly. Don't sell your services if you are not 100 percent sure that you can satisfy your customers' needs. Never perform a service when you feel that clients won't receive sufficient value for their money. Lastly, never give away business just to get your foot in the door: the long-term costs may lead you to resent the client later.

Trust Is the Miracle Ingredient

The importance of trust cannot be overstated. Remember these words from Chapter 9; keep them in mind when you have difficult decisions to make:

> Trust is the fabric that binds us together, creating an orderly, civilized society from chaos and anarchy. If we can't trust our husbands or our wives, if we can't trust our children, if we can't trust our boss or our colleagues, if we can't trust our preacher or our senators, then we have nothing on which to build a stable way of life. Trust is not an abstract, theoretical, idealistic goal forever beyond our reach. Trust— or a lack of it—is inherent in every action that we take and affects everything that we do. Trust is the cement that binds relationships, keeping spouses together, business deals intact, and political systems stable. Without trust, marriages fail, voters become apathetic, and organizations flounder. Without trust, no company can ever hope for excellence.

Trust is like love in a marriage: it bonds people together and makes them strong and effective. Trust in a relationship increases security, reduces inhibitions and defensiveness, and frees people to share feelings and dreams. Trust makes you free to put your deepest fears in the palms of your colleagues' hands, knowing that they will be treated with care. Trust allows you to be yourself and maintain your own values without worrying about acceptance. Trust makes colleagues willing to spend time together and make sacrifices for one another. Trust is an expression of faith that makes it easy for colleagues to have confidence in one another's ability to perform well and to know that they will be there if needed. Trust means that promises made will be kept, and it also means that when a promise is not kept, it was probably for good cause. And finally, trust means that a relationship will last not because it is good business, but because the relationship itself is valued.

There Is a Direct Correlation between Integrity and Bottom-Line Performance

All too many people lose sleep because of an unfocused anxiety. They are worried about the future. They don't know if this is the last round of layoffs, whether their suppliers will make good on their promises, or if their clients will continue doing work with them. We no longer trust people to tell us the truth, to do what is right rather than what is politically expedient, to live up to their commitments, or to care about living up to a code of honor. In a labor-intensive society, hard work resulted in tired bones and muscles. In the Information Age, our bodies tell us that enough is enough by reacting with stress-related ailments ranging from headaches to backaches to anxiety attacks.

In fact, according to an article in *The Wall Street Journal:* "What makes an ethical executive tick? Nobody knows for sure, but London House [a consulting firm] thinks they may be happier, less tense and more responsible than people who are more willing to tolerate unethical behavior....The most striking finding: The more emotionally healthy the executives, as measured on a battery of tests, the more likely they were to score high on the ethics test. High-ethics executives were also less likely to feel hostility, anxiety and fear."[24] The costs to society of everyone acting like random molecules bouncing off of one another is just too great. We have no time to think about what is important. We judge someone's worth by what we see on the outside rather than what's on the inside. We envy someone who has achieved success without thinking about what they did to earn it. In business, the new bottom line means you don't jump down peoples' throats when they make mistakes; you make it clear that you know they are trying their best—and they will respond in kind. It also means you don't hire bodies—you seek valued employees to join your business family. You invest in your people. You are not out to sell to your customers, but to service them now and in the future. Your responsibilities go beyond the next quarter's financials to build a legacy for those who follow.

Being true to ourselves does not mean harming or even ignoring others; honesty has to be more than obeying the letter of the law because it is too easy to pervert the legal system to avoid acting the way we know we should. Being loyal to others means assuming that they will keep their word and letting them know that we will keep ours. In the past, we assumed that people had integrity. Their actions rested on a foundation of values that made it very unlikely that they would act dishonorably. We need not try to re-create the past, but we ought to work toward a better future, keeping in mind that everyone can make a difference and that we can't wait for the next person to make the first move. In our complex society, contracts are needed to formalize arrangements, but they should not substitute for honorable relationships. We lose something very tangible when we abandon such intangibles as loyalty, trust, and honor.

Notes

Chapter One

1. Nancy Ten Kate, "Brand Names Can Be Prime Assets," *American Demographics*, December 1991, p. 20.
2. Robert Fulghum, *All I Ever Really Need to Know I Learned in Kindergarten* (New York: Ivy Books, 1991), p. 4.

Chapter Two

1. Ken Shelton, "Plantation Management," *Executive Excellence*, vol. 7, no. 2, February 1990, p. 11.
2. Stephen R. Covey, *Principle-Centered Leadership: Teaching People How to Fish* (Provo, Utah: The Institute for Principle-Centered Leadership, 1990), p. 139.
3. Jack Gordon, "Who Killed Corporate Loyalty?" *Training*, March 1990, p. 29.
4. Amy Saltzman, "The New Meaning of Success," *U.S. News & World Report*, September 17, 1990, p. 57.
5. Ken Matejka and Jay Leibowitz, "A Commitment to Ex-S," *Manage*, February 1989, p. 3.
6. Saltzman, p. 56.
7. Alan Deutschman, "What 25-Year-Olds Want," *Fortune*, August 27, 1990, p. 44.
8. Thomas F. O'Boyle, "Fear and Stress in the Office Take Toll," *The Wall Street Journal*, November 6, 1990, p. B1.
9. Laurence Kelly, "Understanding Absenteeism," *The Worklife Report*, December 1989, p. 8.
10. The Wyatt Company, "Wyatt Work America Survey of Workers Attitudes," in *Boardroom Reports*, September 15, 1990, p. 15.
11. William L. Ginnoda, "How to Build Employee Commitment," *National Productivity Review*, Summer 1989, vol. 8, no. 3., p. 251.

12. Tracy Benson and Robert Haas, "Vision Scores 20/20," *Industry Week,* April 2, 1990, p. 23.

13. Robert Howard, "Values Make the Company: An Interview with Robert Haas," *Harvard Business Review,* September–October 1990, p. 139.

14. Charles O'Reilly, "Corporations, Culture, and Commitment: Motivation and Social Control in Organizations," *California Management Review,* Summer 1989, p. 12.

15. Robert H. Waterman, Jr., *The Renewal Factor* (New York: Bantam, 1987), p. 71.

16. Covey, p. 260.

17. Ibid., p. 261.

18. Ibid.

19. Ibid.

20. Ibid., p. 262.

21. Max De Pree, *Leadership Is an Art* (New York: Dell, 1989), p. 22.

22. Thomas A. Stewart, "New Ways to Exercise Power," *Fortune,* November 6, 1989, p. 52.

23. Ibid., p. 53.

24. Ron J. Markin and Charles M. Lillis, "Sales Managers Get What They Expect," *Business Horizons,* June 1975, p. 52.

25. Ibid., p. 53.

26. Stanley Modic, "Whatever It Is, It's Not Working," *Industry Week,* July 17, 1989, p. 27.

27. Jim Braham, "A Rewarding Place to Work," *Industry Week,* September 18, 1989, p. 16.

28. Holly Rawlinson, "Make Awards Count," *Personnel Journal,* October 1988, p. 140.

29. Morton Grossman and Margaret Magnus, "The 2.1 Billion Rash of Awards," *Personnel Journal,* May 1989, p. 72.

30. Braham, p. 17.

31. Fran Tarkenton, "The Big Boss Is Dead," *Fast Track,* March 12, 1990.

Chapter Three

1. Roger von Oech, *A Whack on the Side of the Head* (New York: Warner Books, 1983), p. 30. See also von Oech's *A Kick in the Seat of*

the Pants (New York: Harper & Row, 1986) for valuable insights on creativity.

2. Von Oech, *A Kick in the Seat of the Pants,* p. 14.

3. Thomas Osborn, "How 3M Manages for Innovation," *Marketing Communications,* November–December 1988, p. 19.

4. Larry Reibstein, "For Corporate Speech Writers, Life Is Seldom a Simple Matter of ABCs," *The Wall Street Journal,* June 30, 1987, p. 33.

5. Russell Mitchell, "Masters of Innovation: How 3M Keeps Its New Products Coming," *Business Week,* April 10, 1989, p. 59.

6. Jack Adamson, "The Art of Managing Creative People," *Executive Excellence,* September 1989, p. 9.

7. R. Donald Ganache and Robert L. Kuhn, *The Creativity Infusion* (New York: Harper & Row, 1989), p. 25.

8. Robert H. Waterman, Jr., *The Renewal Factor* (New York: Bantam, 1987), p. 91.

9. Deborah Dougherty, "The Trouble with Senior Managers on Product Innovation: A View from the Trenches," paper published by The Wharton School, August 1988, pp. 11–12.

10. David Placek, "Creativity Survey Shows Who's Doing What," *Marketing News,* November 6, 1989, p. 14.

11. Dougherty, p. 8.

12. Von Oech, *A Whack on the Side of the Head,* p. 49.

13. Mitchell, p. 58.

14. Waterman, p. 85.

15. Reibstein, p. 33.

16. Ganache and Kuhn, p. 34.

17. Dougherty, pp. 14–15.

18. Mark Frohnan and Perry Pascarella, "Achieving Purpose Driven Innovation," *Industry Week,* March 19, 1990, p. 20.

19. Stratford Sherman, "Eight Big Masters of Innovation," *Fortune,* October 15, 1984, p. 84.

20. Mitchell, p. 58.

21. Alicia Johnson, "3M Organized to Innovate," *Management Review,* July 1986, pp. 38–39.

22. Dougherty, p. 22.

23. Edward de Bono, *Lateral Thinking* (New York: Perennial Library, 1973), p. 108.

24. Dougherty, p. 7.

25. Ronald A. Mitsch, "Three Roads to Innovation," *The Journal of Business Strategy*, September–October 1990, p. 8.

26. Vic Sussman, "To Win, First You Must Lose," *U.S. News & World Report*, January 15, 1990, p. 64.

27. Gary Meyers, "How to Nurture Creativity," *Public Relations Journal*, November 1988, p. 45.

28. Art Fry, "The Post-It Note: An Intrapreneurial Success," *SAM Advanced Management Journal*, Summer 1987, p. 6.

29. Osborn, p. 20.

30. Von Oech, *A Whack on the Side of the Head*, p. 105.

31. Placek, p. 14.

32. Roderick Wilkinson, "50 Booster Rockets for Your Imagination," *Supervision*, January 1989, p. 25.

33. Royal Bank of Canada, "The Creative Approach," *NRECA Management Quarterly*, Winter 1988–89, pp. 39–40.

34. Ibid., p. 39.

Chapter Four

1. Richard Saul Wurman, *Information Anxiety* (New York: Bantam, 1990), p. 32.

2. Jeanette A. Davy, Angelo Kinicki, John Kilroy, and Christine Scheck, "After the Merger: Dealing with People's Uncertainty," *Training and Development Journal*, November 1988, p. 57.

3. Dunhill Personnel Systems Inc. and Columbia University, School of Business, "Workplace Issues Top On-the-Job-Stress Points for Managers," *INC*, September 1990, p. 131.

4. Alvie L. Smith, *Innovative Employee Communication* (Englewood Cliffs, N. J.: Prentice-Hall, 1991), p. 231.

5. E. Zoe McCathrin, "Beyond Employee Publications," *Public Relations Journal*, July 1989, p. 16.

6. Julie Foehrenbach and Steve Goldfarb, "Employee Communication in the '90s," *IABC Communication World*, May–June 1990.

7. Bill Lane, "Liberating GE's Energy," *Monogram* (GE Publication), Fall 1989, p. 3.

8. Robert E. Kelley, "Gold Collar Worker Survey," *News Release*, Carnegie Mellon University, November 9, 1989.

9. Peter M. Senge, *The Fifth Discipline* (New York: Doubleday, 1990), p. 150.

10. Ibid., p. 212.

11. Terrence E. Dean and Allen A. Kennedy, *Corporate Cultures* (Reading, Mass.: Addison-Wesley, 1982), p. 135.

12. Max De Pree, *Leadership Is an Art* (New York: Dell, 1989), p. 92.

13. Joanne Martin, Martha S. Feldman, Mary Jo Hatch, and Sim B. Sitkin, "The Uniqueness Paradox in Organizational Stories," *Administrative Science Quarterly*, September 1983, p. 448.

14. Ibid., p. 439.

15. Ibid., p. 144.

16. James A. Autry, *Love and Profit: The Art of Caring Leadership* (New York: William Morrow, 1991), p. 81.

17. Ibid., p. 181.

18. Frank K. Sonnenberg, *Marketing to Win* (New York: Harper & Row, 1990), p. 183.

19. Thomas Shellhardt, "Slick Annual Reports Gloss over Employees," *The Wall Street Journal*, April 29, 1991, B1.

20. "When Employees Talk," *Communication Management*, July 1988, no. 107 [newsletter]. Tower, Perrin and Company.

21. Sonnenberg, pp. 176–179.

22. *HR Focus*, May 1990, p. 7.

23. McCathrin, p. 15.

24. Foehrenbach and Goldfarb.

25. Terry Van Tell, "Communications with Your Employees and Boss," *Supervisory Management*, October 1989, p. 5.

26. McCathrin, p. 15.

27. Jay L. Johnson, "Internal Communication: A Key to Wal-Mart's Success," *Direct Marketing*, November 1989, p. 72.

28. McCathrin, p. 20.

29. Ibid.

30. John Thorbeck, "The Turnaround Value of Values," *Harvard Business Review*, January–February 1991, p. 56.

31. Valerie McClelland and Richard E. Wilmot, "Improve Lateral Communication," *Personnel Journal*, August 1990, p. 32.

32. Senge, p. 283.

33. Donald E. Petersen, speech before the Foundation for American Communications, Naples, Florida, January 16, 1987.

34. Maryann Keller, *Rude Awakening: The Rise, Fall, and Struggle for Recovery of General Motors* (New York: William Morrow, 1989), pp. 124–125, 129.

35. Johnson, pp. 68–72.

36. Dean and Kennedy, p. 86.

37. Alvie L. Smith, "Bridging the Gap," *Public Relations Journal,* November 1990, vol. 46, no. 1, pp. 20–21, 41.

Chapter Five

1. Adam Snyder, "Revolt against the Professionals," *AdWeek's Marketing Week,* February 25, 1991.

2. Leonard Berry, "The Costs of Poor Quality Service Are Higher Than You Think," *American Banker,* June 24, 1987, p. 4.

3. Ibid.

4. The Forum Corporation, "Customer Focus Research," *Executive Briefing,* April 1988, pp. 3–4.

5. The PIMS Data Base, *PIMS LETTER,* No. 33, p. 8.

6. Valarie A. Zeithaml, A. Parasuraman, and Leonard L. Berry, *Delivering Quality Service* (New York: Free Press, 1990), p. 21.

7. Carl Sewell and Paul B. Brown, *Customers for Life* (New York: Doubleday, 1990), p. 121.

8. Rosabeth Moss Kanter, "Think Like the Customer: The Global Business Logic," *Harvard Business Review,* July–August 1992, p. 9.

9. Ibid.

10. Sewell and Brown, p. 17.

11. Russell R. Miller, "Modest Alternative to Killing All Lawyers," *Manager's Journal.*

12. James Donnelly, Jr., *Close to the Customer* (Homewood, Ill.: Irwin, 1992), pp. 76–77.

13. Ibid.

14. Paula Haynes, "Seven Principles of Waiting. Hating to Wait: Managing the Final Service Encounter," *The Journal of Services Marketing,* Fall 1990, vol. 4, no. 4, pp. 20–26.

15. Donnelly, p. 21.

16. Tom Peters, *Thriving on Chaos* (New York: Knopf, 1987), p. 91.

17. U.S. Office of Consumer Affairs in cooperation with Chevrolet Motor Division of General Motors, *Increasing Consumer Satisfaction*, p. 4.

18. Frank K. Sonnenberg, *Marketing to Win* (New York: Harper & Row, 1990), p. 203.

19. Kristin Anderson and Ron Zemke, *Delivering Knock Your Socks Off Service* (New York: Amacom, 1991), p. 14.

Chapter Six

1. Robert J. Kriegel and Louis Patler, *If It Ain't Broke...Break It!* (New York: Warner Books, 1991), pp. 9, 26.

2. *Fortune*, March 26, 1990, p. 30.

3. John P. Kotter and Leonard A. Schlesinger, "Choosing Strategies for Change," *Harvard Business Review*, March–April 1979, pp. 106–113.

4. Peter M. Senge, *The Fifth Discipline* (New York: Doubleday, 1990), p. 55.

5. Alfred J. Marrow, David F. Bowers, and Stanley E. Seashore, *Management by Participation* (New York: Harper & Row, 1967).

6. Patricia A. Galagan, "The Learning Organization Made Plain," interview with Peter M. Senge, in *Training and Development Journal*, October 1991, p. 42.

7. Chris Argyis, "Teaching Smart People How to Learn," *Harvard Business Review*, May–June 1991, p. 99.

8. Kriegel and Patler, p. 128.

9. Ibid., p. 34.

10. Galagan interview with Senge, p. 38.

11. Brooks Carter, "Kicking the Habit," *Quality Progress*, March 1991, p. 88.

12. Ibid., p. 88.

13. Kriegel and Patler, p. 85.

14. Therese R. Welter, "They're Afraid of You," *Industry Week*, October 1, 1990, p. 11.

15. Judith M. Bardwick, *Danger in the Comfort Zone* (New York: Amacom, 1991), p. 36.

16. Kathleen D. Ryan and Daniel K. Oestreich, *Driving Fear out of the Workplace* (San Francisco: Jossey-Bass, 1991), p. 133.
17. Jack Welch, *1991 Annual Report*, General Electric, p. 5.
18. Richard J. Schonberger, *Building a Chain of Customers* (New York: Free Press, 1990), p. 122.
19. Walter Kiechel III, "The Boss as Coach," *Fortune*, November 4, 1991, p. 204.
20. *Vis à Vis*, March 1990, p. 80.
21. Kriegel and Patler, p. 167.
22. Richard Saul Wurman, *Information Anxiety* (New York: Bantam, 1990), p. 192.
23. Tom Peters, *Thriving on Chaos* (New York: Knopf, 1987), p. 259.
24. Dr. Tineke Bahlmann, "The Learning Organization in a Turbulent Environment," *Human Systems Management*, 1990, p. 255.
25. Alan Mumford, "Learning Styles and Learning," *PR*, March 16, 1987, p. 158.
26. Lucia Solorzano, "Helping Kids Learn—Their Own Way," *U.S. News & World Report*, August 31, 1987, p. 62.
27. Wurman, p. 172.
28. Galagan interview with Senge, p. 43.
29. Ibid., p. 43.
30. Jeremy Campbell, *Grammatical Man: Information, Entropy, Language, and Life* (New York: Simon & Schuster, 1983), p. 141.
31. Ikujiro Nonaka, "The Knowledge-Creating Company," *Harvard Business Review*, November–December 1991, p. 102.
32. Ibid.
33. Christopher Knowlton, "Shell Gets Rich by Beating Risk," *Fortune*, August 29, 1991, p. 82.
34. Ibid., p. 84.
35. Nonaka, pp. 96–104.
36. Ibid., p. 97.
37 Ibid., p. 99.
38. Thomas A. Stewart, "GE Keep Those Ideas Coming," *Fortune*, August 12, 1991, pp. 41–49.

Chapter Seven

1. Robert J. Kriegel and Louis Patler, *If It Ain't Broke...Break It!* (New York: Warner Books, 1991), p. 53.
2. Tom Peters, "Beyond Speed," *Industry Week*, June 3, 1991, p. 22.
3. Brian Dumaine, "How Managers Can Succeed through Speed," *Fortune*, February 13, 1989, p. 54.
4. Rahul Jacob, "Thriving in a Lame Economy," *Fortune*, October 5, 1992, p. 44.
5. Philip Kotler and Paul J. Stonich, "Turbo Marketing through Time Compression," *The Journal of Business Strategy*, September–October 1991, p. 24.
6. Philip Kotler, "Turbo-Marketing," *Marketing Executive*, April 1, 1991, vol. 1, no. 2, p. 24.
7. Lester R. Bittel, *Right on Time* (New York: McGraw-Hill, 1991), p. 148.
8. Kotler and Stonich, p. 24.
9. Rosabeth Moss Kanter, "Ourselves Versus Ourselves," *Harvard Business Review*, May–June 1992, p. 8.
10. General Electric, *Annual Report*, 1991, p. 2.
11. Barbara Buell, Robert D. Hof, and Gary McWilliams, "Hewlett-Packard Rethinks Itself," *Business Week*, April 1, 1991, p. 76.
12. Michael F. Dealy, "Changing Organizational Structures," *Fortune*, July 13, 1992, p. 49.
13. General Electric, *Annual Report*, 1991, p. 3.
14. As quoted in Kriegel and Patler, p. 117.
15. Edward de Bono, *Six Action Shoes* (New York: Harper Business, 1991), p. 32.
16. Paul B. Carroll, "Story of an IBM Unit That Split Off Shows Difficulties of Change," *The Wall Street Journal*, p. 1.
17. Jim Harrington, *Business Process Improvement* (New York: McGraw-Hill, 1990), p. 153.
18. Charles A. Sengstock, Jr., "Pursuing the Not-So-Elusive Goal of Perfection," *Public Relations Journal*, August 1991, p. 22.
19. Brent Bowers, "The Doozies: Seven Scary Tales of Wild Bureaucracy," *The Wall Street Journal*, June 19, 1992, p. B2.
20. Harrington, p. 153.
21. Armand V. Feigenbaum, *Empowering Business Resources* (Glenview, Ill.: Scott Foresman, 1990) p. 294.

22. Bittel, p. 5.

23. Karen Matthes, "Clean Up Your Life...Or at Least Your Desk," *Personnel,* October, 1991, p. 23.

24. Allen C. Bluedorn and Robert D. Denhardt, "Time and Organizations," *The Journal of Management,* vol. 14, no. 2, 1988, p. 310.

25. Bill Symonds, "No, They Can't Stop Time, But They Can Help You Manage It," *Business Week,* May 22, 1989, p. 179.

26. Paul B. Carroll, "Story of an IBM Unit That Split Off Shows Difficulties of Change," *The Wall Street Journal,* p. 1.

27. Walter Kiechel III, "Over Scheduled, and Not Loving It," *Fortune,* April 8, 1991, p. 105.

28. Robert H. Waterman, Jr., *The Renewal Factor* (New York: Bantam, 1987), p. 201.

29. Bluedorn and Denhardt, pp. 310–311.

30. Richard Saul Wurman, *Information Anxiety* (New York: Bantam, 1990), p. 161.

31. "Is All Time Wasted on the Job a Waste?" *Training and Development Journal,* November 1987, p. 17.

32. Joe A. Cox and Raymond L. Read, "Putting It Off 'til Later," *Baylor Business Review,* Fall 1989, p. 10.

33. As quoted in Bittel, p. 84.

34. Paul Hellman, "An Interview with Father Time," *Management Review,* January 1990, p. 63.

35. Walter Kiechel III, "Beat the Clock," *Fortune,* June 25, 1984, p. 147.

Chapter Eight

1. John Sheridan, "Suppliers: Partners in Prosperity," *Industry Week,* March 19, 1990, p. 12.

2. John Emshwiller, "Suppliers Struggle to Improve Quality as Big Firms Slash Their Vendor Rolls," *The Wall Street Journal,* August 18, 1991, p. B1.

3. "Corporations Scale Back use of Outside Counsel," *The Wall Street Journal,* October. 15, 1991, p. B1.

4. Harry S. Dent, Jr., "Corporation of the Future," *Small Business Reports,* May 1990, p. 55.

5. Jennifer Pendleton, "Matches Made in Heaven," *Advertising Age,* March 14, 1988, p. 3.

6. Jordan Lewis, "Competitive Alliances Redefine Companies," *Management Review*, April 1991, p. 15.

7. Roger Fisher and Scott Brown, *Getting Together* (New York: Penguin, 1988), p. 4.

8. Pendleton, p. 3.

9. As quoted in Glenn M. Parker, *Team Players and Teamwork* (San Francisco: Jossey-Bass, 1991), p. 16.

10. Richard Saul Wurman, *Information Anxiety* (New York: Bantam, 1990), p. 130.

11. Fisher and Brown, p. 21.

12. Reuben Mark, "Steps to Building a Creative Partnership," *Advertising Age*, November 9, 1988, p. 70.

Chapter Nine

1. Gordon F. Shea, "Building Trust in the Workplace," AMA Management Briefing, 1984, p. 7.

2. Stanley J. Modic, "Whatever It Is, It's Not Working," *Industry Week*, July 17, 1989.

3. Labor Letter, *The Wall Street Journal*, February 18, 1987, p. A1.

4. William Ouchi, *Theory Z* (Reading, Mass.: Addison-Wesley, 1981), p. 5.

5. Research has shown that "the level of trust in a relationship affects the degree of defensiveness. Gibb (1961) found that members of small groups that developed a 'defensive climate,' had difficulty concentrating on messages, perceived the motives, values, and emotions of others less accurately, and increased the distortion of messages. Other studies suggest that some interpersonal trust is required for effective problem solving in a group. Parloff and Handlon (1966) found that intensive, persistent criticism increased defensiveness and mistrust among members of a group and decreased their ability to recognize and accept good ideas. Meadow et al. (1959) reported that defensiveness induced a lasting decrease in problem solving effectiveness. They found that groups penalized for poor ideas and admonished to produce only good ideas while working on early problems produced poorer solutions to later problems when these restrictions were removed than groups that were not penalized and admonished during their early problem assignments." Dale E. Zand, "Trust and Managerial Problem Solving," *Administrative Science Quarterly*, p. 229.

6. Shea, p. 7.

7. Dale E. Zand, *Information, Organization, and Power* (New York: McGraw-Hill, 1981), p. 38.

8. Gerald Zaltman and Christine Moorman, "The Importance of Personal Trust in the Use of Research," *Journal of Advertising Research,* October–November 1988, p. 19.

9. Stephen R. Covey, *Principle-Centered Leadership* (Provo, Utah: The Institute for Principle-Centered Leadership, 1990), p. 151.

10. Tracy E. Benson, "In Trust We Manage," *Industry Week,* March 4, 1991, p. 28.

11. Roger Fisher and Scott Brown, *Getting Together* (New York: Penguin, 1988), p. 125.

12. Fernando Bartolome, "Nobody Trusts the Boss Completely—Now What?" *Harvard Business Review,* March–April 1989, vol. 67, no. 2, p. 135.

13. Shea, p. 55.

14. Zand, p. 38.

15. Ibid., p. 140.

16. Ibid.

17. Fisher and Brown, p. 123.

18. "Needed: Less Bureaucracy," *USA Today,* April 1989, p. 14.

19. Shea, p. 319.

Chapter Ten

1. Fred Moody, "Mr. Software," *The New York Times Magazine,* August 25, 1991, p. 56.

2. Tom Peters, *Liberation Management* (New York: Alfred A. Knopf, 1992), p. 12.

3. Tom Brown, "On the Edge with Jim Collins," *Industry Week,* October 5, 1992, p. 12.

4. Carol Hymowitz, "Trading Fat Paychecks for Free Time," *The Wall Street Journal,* August 5, 1991, p. B1.

5. Ronald Henkoff, "How to Plan for 1995," *Fortune,* December 31, 1990, p. 70.

6. Patrick M. Reilly, "American Express Is Said Near Accord on a Time Warner Magazine Venture," *The Wall Street Journal,* November 27, 1992, p. B5.

7. John S. McClenahen, "It's No Fun Working Here Anymore," *Industry Week,* March 4, 1991, p. 20.

8. Joseph McKenna, "What Can Restore Fading Loyalty?" *Industry Week,* February 4, 1991, p. 50.

9. W. E. Odom "Changes and Choices: The Wisdom to Choose Wisely," *Vital Speeches,* June 1, 1991.

10. Ron J. Markin and Charles M. Lillis, "Sales Managers Get What They Expect," *Business Horizons,* June 1975, pp. 52–53.

11. William L. Ginnoda, "How to Build Employee Commitment," *National Productivity Review,* vol. 8, no. 3, Summer 1989, p. 251.

12. Mark Frohnan and Perry Pascarella, "Achieving Purpose Driven Innovation," *Industry Week,* March 19, 1990, p. 20.

13. Rosabeth Moss Kanter, "Think Like the Customer: The Global Business Logic," *Harvard Business Review,* July–August 1992, p. 9.

14. Anne B. Sisher, "CEOs Think That Morale Is Dandy," *Fortune,* November 18, 1991, p. 83.

15. Peters, p. 637.

16. Alan Farnham, "The Trust Gap," *Fortune,* December 4, 1989, p. 5b.

17. Mark Skousen, "Roaches Outlive Elephants: An Interview with Peter Drucker," *Forbes,* August 19, 1991, p. 72

18. Coca-Cola, 1990 *Annual Report,* p. 4.

19. Robert J. Kriegel and Louis Patler, *If It Ain't Broke...Break It!* (New York: Warner Books, 1991), p. 85.

20. Therese R. Welter, "They're Afraid of You," *Industry Week,* October 1, 1990, p. 11.

21. Brian S. Moskal, "Is Industry Ready for Adult Relationships?" *Industry Week,* January 21, 1991, p. 19.

22. Henry Stimson, *The Bomb and the Opportunity, March 1946* (Boston: Little Brown, 1980).

23. Albert R. Karr, "Labor Letter," *The Wall Street Journal,* February 4, 1992, p. 1.

24. Amanda Bennett, "Unethical Behavior, Stress Appear Linked," *The Wall Sreet Journal,* April 11, 1991, p. B1.

Index

Absenteeism, 14–15
Accountability, 12, 116, 228
Accounting, 84
Activist learning, 125, 126, 128
Activities, 69, 152, 159–160, 162, 178
   daily, 25, 63, 158–159
   (*See also* Meetings; Presentations)
Added value, 87, 146, 147
Adia Personnel Services survey, 158–159
Advertising, 91, 105, 173, 197
Advertising agencies, 168, 176
Aetna Life and Casualty Company, 139
A. Foster Higgins & Company survey,
   73–74
Agreement, 110, 111
Aguire, Bob, 149
Allen, Thomas, 70
American Express Co., 217
American Productivity Center study, 26
Anger, 23, 98–99, 120, 161
Anheuser-Busch, Inc., 76
Apathy, 15–17, 219–220
   (*See also* Motivation)
Apologizing, 98
Apple Computer Inc., 27
Assets, 22
   (*See also* Resources)
Association of Advertising Agencies, 168
AT&T Co., 138, 168
Attitudes, 84, 116, 160
   of employees, 11–12, 38, 62, 117–118,
      213–214
   toward employees, 7, 9, 19–20, 79,
      158–159
   of management, 38
   toward management, 24, 69, 188
   toward organizations, 87, 165–166, 175
Authority, 20, 21
   delegation of, 22, 33, 155
   (*See also* Decision making;
      Management)

Bahlmann, Tineke, 125
Bardwick, Judith, 118
Bartholome, Fernando, 204
Behavior, 18, 24, 130, 189
   changing, 130, 159–163
   of employees, 11, 12–17, 62, 97–100,
      118–119, 152, 158–159
   emulation of, 27, 46, 60, 62–63, 130
   managerial, 3–4, 23, 64–66, 73–74, 114,
      116, 120–121, 169
   organizational, 4–5, 89, 119–121, 151,
      166, 188–190, 192–193, 195–197
   in relationships, 204, 206–209
Beliefs, 187, 199–200
   promoting, 59, 61–68
Benchmarking, 134, 184
Benefits of relationships, 170, 183–184
Berkeley, George, 2
Best interests, 183–184, 198, 199
Best practices evaluation, 134
Blame:
   accepting, 96, 98
   assigning, 114, 120–121, 166, 189
Boss, 65, 69
   terminology, 19
   (*See also* Management)
Bottom line, 10, 12, 57, 234
Brainstorming, 129
Brown, Paul B., 89, 90
Brown, Scott, 175, 182, 203–204, 208
Budget, 91, 140, 147–148, 172
Bureaucracy, 13, 30, 41–43, 141–144, 171,
   221–222, 223
Business relationships, 155, 172, 188–189,
   232–233
   building, 176–178, 217
   defining, 175
   environment for, 178–180
   maintaining, 2, 180–184, 191, 199,
      207–208
   problems with, 166, 171

Business relationships (*Cont.*):
  strengthening, 178–179, 209
  (*See also* Client relationships; Supplier
    relationships)

Caldwell, Philip, 40
Call reports, 103
Campbell, Jeremy, 130
Caring environment, 11–12, 16, 24, 28, 68,
  209, 210, 226
Carver, Brooks, 116
Caste system, 47, 51–52, 70, 119, 222
Catalysts, 57, 68, 112, 180
Centralization, 41
CEOs (Chief executive officers), 21, 32, 57,
  69, 73–74, 78, 229
Ceremonies: organizational, 27, 63
Change, 56, 109–110, 111–112
  adapting to, 6, 7, 81, 224–225
  agents, 57, 227
  overcoming resistance to, 4, 110–111, 135
  resistance to, 30, 35, 47–52, 111, 113–117,
    145, 148
  waste in, 36, 38
Change management, 110–111, 112,
  113–116, 140–141, 145–151
Client relationships, 6, 7, 10, 11–12, 83,
  108, 167
  building, 86–88
  problems with, 13, 83–84, 168–175,
    195–196, 229–231
  (*See also* External communications;
    Service excellence)
Clients, 3, 84, 199
  access to, 34, 46
  communication with, 73, 88, 102–106,
    205, 206
  requests from, 42
Close to the Customer (Donnelly), 92, 93,
  94–95
Clothing companies, 139–140
Coca-Cola Company, 224
Coercion, 110, 111, 116, 120, 121
Colgate-Palmolive Co., 183
Collins, James C., 213
Columbia University School of Business
  study, 56
Commitment, 28
  barriers to, 15–16, 112, 115–116, 156

Commitment (*Cont.*):
  building, 6, 19–20, 25, 58, 82, 178
  to clients, 169–171, 184
  of employees, 33, 188, 201, 205, 213, 214,
    215, 226
  to employees, 15, 17, 57
  to mission, 5
  to products, 201–202, 208
  in relationships, 7, 168–171, 183–184, 208
  to values, 62
Communication, 27, 50, 72, 110–111, 133
  effectiveness, 57, 68, 72–73, 77, 149
  failure, 18, 34, 74, 117, 169, 174
  frequency, 58–59, 73–74, 81, 104
  and treatment of people, 178, 182,
    205–206
  verbal vs. written, 39, 177–178
  (*See also* External communication;
    Feedback; Internal communication;
    Listening)
Compartmentalization, 73, 77, 87, 146,
  147–148, 228
Competence, 88, 96–97, 144, 202
Competition, 2, 85, 166–167
  learning from, 114–115, 131·
Competitive advantage, 6, 106, 115,
  132–133, 138–139, 140, 151, 196
Competitive environment, 18, 55, 85
Competitiveness, 7, 79, 108, 165
  and change, 1, 3, 29, 42, 125
  managerial, 38, 144, 147–148
Complaints:
  by clients, 96, 107, 203
  by employees, 38
Compliance, 16, 80, 112
Comprehensiveness, 72, 73
Confidence, 117, 200–201
  of employees, 24, 43, 44, 144, 154–155
  in organizations, 89, 99
  in professional institutions, 84
  reducing, 38, 59
Confidential communications, 100, 101,
  174, 204
Consistency, 34, 41, 71, 91, 195, 206–208
Consultants, 166, 175
Consumers (*see* Clients)
Contingency planning, 131–132
Continuity in relationships, 174–175, 184
Continuous change, 112, 113, 115,
  184–185, 207–208

Continuous communication, 27, 58–59, 73, 81, 104
Continuous learning, 2, 25, 97, 122–123, 127, 134, 225
Contractors, 166
Contracts, 166, 177–178
Contributions by employees, 18, 20, 43, 80
  recognition of, 12, 13, 23, 24–25, 26, 36, 45, 47, 155
  (*See also* Reward system)
Control, 205, 206
  by clients, 94
  by employees, 13, 56, 67, 95
  of employees, 17, 18, 19–20, 37, 42, 121, 141
  of information, 18, 59, 71, 79, 119, 206
  loss of, 117–118, 120
  of time, 162
  (*See also* Empowerment of employees)
Cooperation, 184–185, 187
Coordination, 73, 79
Co-optation, 110, 111
Corporate culture, 61, 63, 81, 86
  changing, 39, 50, 115, 116
  and creativity, 20, 30, 33, 47–50
  differences in, 64–65, 169, 171
  problems with, 62, 71
  understanding, 100, 106
Corporate Cultures (Dean and Kennedy), 62
Costs, 108, 111
  of absenteeism, 15
  of employee turnover, 12, 13, 25, 141
  of lack of communication, 58, 79–80, 190
  of products or services, 3, 85, 91, 105, 199
Cost-benefit analysis, 25, 84, 140, 173
Courtesy, 88, 97–99
Covey, Stephen, 10, 19–20, 200
Cox, Joe, 160–161
Creativity, 20, 29–30, 52–53
  barriers to, 35–44, 115, 141, 145, 190
  encouragement of, 5, 7, 17, 33–35, 48–49, 220–221
Creativity Infusion, The, 36, 41–42
Credibility, 72, 88, 99–100
  (*See also* Trust)
Credo (*see* Mission)
Criticism, 23, 114, 119–120, 124, 190
  accepting, 188–189
  of ideas, 37–38, 45, 118
Culture (*see* Corporate culture)

Curiosity, 127
Customers (*see* Clients)
Customers for Life (Sewell and Brown), 89, 90
Customer surveys, 5, 85, 96, 135
Customization, 58, 59, 82, 138
Cynicism, 39, 118

Dale Carnegie Organization, 28
Deadlines, 38, 39, 157–158, 160
Dealey, Michael, 143
Dean, Terrence, 62
de Bono, Edward, 145
Decision making, 31, 76, 153, 180
  by clients, 3, 94, 106
  by employees, 59, 95, 218
  fear of, 43, 118, 160
  flawed, 124, 157–158
  layers of, 41, 142, 155–156, 169
  managerial, 3–5, 38, 112, 156, 198–199, 205
  problems in, 18, 41, 142, 144, 155–156, 171, 189
  sharing, 25, 183–184, 221
Delays, 105, 140, 152
Delivering Customer Service, 88
Delivery of products or services, 42, 88, 139–140
De Pree, Max, 21, 63
Diagonal communication, 78
Dictatorial management, 9, 10–17, 35–37, 120, 217–218
Discretion, 27, 33, 36, 100, 101, 174
Dissatisfaction, 84, 85, 93, 95, 96, 104, 219
  (*See also* Satisfaction)
Distraction, 162
Distrust, 34, 46, 69, 79, 101, 105–106, 117, 144
  (*See also* Trust)
Donnelly, James, 92, 93, 94–95
Downsizing, 5, 66, 110
Downward communication, 73–74, 80, 204–205
Dress: appropriate, 89
Driving Fear Out of the Workplace (Oestreich and Ryan), 119–120
Drucker, Peter, 159, 223
Dual career ladders, 46

Dunhill Personnel System Inc. study, 56

Eastman Kodak Co., 76
Eastern Reproduction Corp., 149
Education, 53, 114, 116
  of employees, 2, 96–97, 110–111
  (*See also* Learning; Training of employees)
Employee relationships, 10, 12, 22, 78, 190, 204–205
  (*See also* Internal communication)
Employee surveys, 15, 26, 75, 77, 118, 188, 213–214, 218, 219–220, 226
Employees, 151
  reduction of, 5, 66, 110, 141
  treatment of, 6–7, 9, 10, 22–26, 64–65, 67–68, 110–111, 119, 219–220
  (*See also* Employees under subjects, e.g., Investment, in employees)
Empowerment of employees, 2, 112, 201, 205–206, 218
  and clients, 40, 95
Equality in relationships, 180
  lack of, 166, 168–169, 173, 176
Ethics, 2, 5, 11–12, 24, 67, 234
Evaluation, 156, 193
  of ideas, 34, 38, 42–43, 45–47
  of procedures, 41, 145–147
  techniques, 131, 133–135
Executive Excellence, 9
Executive surveys, 42, 47, 48, 56, 57, 58, 73–74, 158–159, 228
Executives, 60, 62, 221, 228
  personal investment by, 169, 172–174, 205
  stories about, 64–67, 156, 200–201
  (*See also* CEOs (chief executive officers); Middle management; Senior mangement)
Expectation, 36–37, 48, 202
  of clients, 85, 92, 94, 104–105, 140, 209
  managerial, 34, 157, 218–219
  in relationships, 172–173, 206
Experience, 3, 4, 105
Expertise, 21, 51
Expression: freedom of, 25
External communication, 57, 58, 81, 89–90, 102–106, 176, 180–181, 232
External environment, 81, 114–115, 129, 134, 165

External relationships, 151, 217
  (*See also* Business relationships; Client relationships; Supplier relationships)
Exxon Corporation, 199
Eyelab, 139

Facilitation, 68, 110, 111
Failure, 40, 53, 124
  causes of, 34, 38, 48–49, 166, 168–175
  fear of, 47–48, 117, 160, 190, 191
  learning from, 23, 114
Fairness, 197, 198–99, 202–203
Fear, 46, 117, 160–161, 225–226
  by employees, 14, 47–49, 50, 117–121, 135, 154, 226
  managerial, 43, 150
  (*See also* Confidence)
Federal Express Corp., 140
Feedback, 25, 27, 35, 68, 124–125, 152, 184
  from clients, 107, 205
  limited, 34, 45, 80, 123
Feigenbaum, Armand, 151
Fifth Discipline, The (Senge), 60
Firing employees, 66, 68
First impressions, 89, 176
First-line management, 68, 69, 75
Fisher, Roger, 175, 182, 203–204, 208
Flaherty, Robert, 154
Flexibility, 6, 7, 145, 169, 216–217
Focus, 215
Foote, Cone & Belding Communications, Inc., 168
Ford Motor Company, 40, 79
Formal communication, 58, 59, 81, 82, 103, 128
Formal knowledge, 133
Formal play, 130
Formal rewards, 27
Fortino, Michael, 158
Fortune, 11, 21
Frankenberg, Bob, 142
Friendly behavior, 22, 89, 90
Fulghum, Robert, 7
Frustration, 94–95

Gates, Bill, 212

General Electric (GE) Co., 32–33, 42, 134,
138, 141–142, 144, 167, 171
General Motors (GM) Corp., 79, 144, 156
Germinal phase, 30
Getting Together (Fisher and Brown),
203–204
Gifts: accepting, 100
Goals, 20, 115, 214
achieving, 17–18, 22, 116
barriers to achieving, 40, 74, 144, 148,
150
common, 147, 171, 175–176, 189, 215
reaching for, 33, 145–146, 161
and rewards, 27
setting, 13, 134, 172–173, 178
Grapevine (*see* Informal communication)
Groups, 41–42, 51–52, 58, 71, 128–129, 142
(*See also* Teamwork)
Growth:
corporate, 71, 130, 189
of employees, 124–125

Haas, Robert, 5, 18
Halpert, Jane, 21
Harbor Sweets Inc., 200–201
Harris polls, 84
Health of employees, 14, 15
Hellman, Paul, 163
Heroes: organizational, 62–63, 81
Hewlett-Packard Co., 78, 142
Hilton Hotels Corp. study, 213–214
Hiner, Glen, 171
Hiring employees, 98, 165, 172, 202
Honda, Soichiro, 124
Honesty, 72, 79–80, 99, 125, 177, 204,
228–229, 232
Horizontal communication (*see* Lateral
communication)
Horizontal work flow, 146
Human relations phase, 20
Huntsman Chemical Corporation, 171

IABC survey (*see* International
Association of Business
Communicators survey)
Iacocca, Lee, 118
IBM Corporation, 27, 49, 64–65, 76, 145,
154, 168

Ideas, 51–52
(*See also* New ideas)
If It Ain't Broke...Break It! (Kriegel and
Patler), 109, 137
Image, 13, 89, 160, 171
Implementation, 78, 134
of ideas, 31, 36–37, 76, 148, 150
of technology, 4
of vision, 60–61
Impressions, 176, 193
by clients, 87, 89–90, 100, 208–209
of management, 24
Incentives, 41, 45–47, 111, 218
(*See also* Reward system)
Incremental change, 36–37, 44, 134
Individual relationships, 169, 174–175,
179–180, 184, 196
Industrial Age, 3, 4, 211
Influence, 57, 67, 81, 97, 111, 143, 205–206
Informal communication, 35, 58, 66, 81,
84, 104, 105, 142
Informal learning, 126
Informal rewards, 27
Information, 18, 55, 56, 158
access to, 79, 81–82, 174, 181, 189
accuracy, 82, 205, 206
extrapolation of, 113
flow, 73–78
lack of, 33–34, 51, 79, 117, 124, 174, 189,
192
managing, 152–153, 161–162
protecting, 100, 101
right to, 25
sharing, 35, 78, 104, 126, 130, 133, 181,
182–183, 188
sources, 74, 161
from storytelling, 64–68
use of, 72, 111
withholding, 18, 59, 71, 77, 80, 99, 119,
146, 169, 174, 206
Information Age, 3–5, 7, 211–212, 234
Information Anxiety (Wurman), 55, 180–181
Information, Organization, and Power
(Zand), 192
Innovation, 36, 132, 145–147
barriers to, 38–39, 43, 141, 189, 221
climate for, 5, 6, 7, 32–33, 43–44
(*See also* New ideas; New products)
Innovative Employee Communication
(Smith), 56

Instinct, 3–4, 118, 133
Intangibles, 1, 3–6, 85, 105, 187, 211–212,
    229–230
Integrity, 7, 100, 197, 198, 208, 231
Intel Corp., 46
Internal communication, 35, 55–56,
    205–206, 227
  directions of, 73–78, 80–82
  effectiveness, 68, 72–73, 77–78
  problems with, 68–72, 77, 119, 148, 152,
    206
  purpose, 52, 58–59
Internal environment, 35, 227
  (*See also* Organizational climate; Work
    environment)
Internalization, 61, 62, 129, 195, 206–207, 222
International Association of Business
    Communicators (IABC) survey, 57, 58
Interpersonal behavior, 70, 119–120, 126,
    205
  (*See also* Employees, treatment of)
Intimacy in communication, 81
Investment, 1
  in clients, 171, 179
  in employees, 11, 156
  in new ideas, 36–37
  return on, 6, 7, 176
Involvement (*see* Participation)
Isolation (*see* Clients, access to;
    Management, access to)

Japan, 2, 115, 129, 132–133, 154–155, 167
Johnson & Johnson, 4–5, 198–199
Judgments, 3, 95, 144
  (*See also* Decision making; Instinct)
J. Walter Thompson Co., 168

Kanter, Rosabeth Moss, 90, 141
Kearns, David, 26
Keller, Maryann, 79
Kelley, Robert, 60
Kennedy, Allen, 62
Kiechel, Walter, III, 122–123, 155, 163–164
Kimberly-Clark Corp., 138
Knowledge, 97, 132–133, 185, 202
  lack of, 173
  (*See also* Information)
Knowlton, Christopher, 132

Kotter, John, 21
Kouzes, Jim, 123
Kriegel, Robert J., 109, 114–115, 123, 137
Krough, Lester, 46

Language use, 70, 76–77, 102–103,
    127–128, 149
Large companies, 143, 166, 171, 174–175
Lateral communication, 34, 59, 73, 76–78
Lawyers, 84, 167
Layoffs, 14, 23, 110
Leadership, 12, 17–18, 74, 112, 130, 167,
    206
  styles, 19–21, 122–123, 212–213
  (*See also* Role, of leadership)
Leadership Is an Art (De Pree), 21, 63
Learning, 97, 106
  encouraging, 2, 25, 225, 226
  organizational, 114–115, 130–135
  process, 23, 37, 122–123
  styles, 53, 125–130
Levi Strauss & Company, 139
Listening, 25, 72, 80, 107, 229, 230–231
London House, 234
Long-term relationships, 2, 102, 166–168,
    230
  building, 86–87
  failure, 168–171
  investment in, 7, 84, 176, 179, 195–196
Loyalty, 100
  of clients, 3, 85, 88, 96
  damage to, 172
  to organizations, 5, 7, 17, 25, 56, 135,
    144, 218
  to suppliers, 98

Madden, Dick, 37
Mail-in system, 76
Mangement, 19–21, 115
  access to, 25–26, 69, 74, 75–76, 97, 123,
    204–205, 222, 229
  principles, 20, 22–28, 134
  reducing, 110, 112
  (*See also* Bureaucracy; Change manage-
    ment; Executives; Leadership)
Management by Participation, 112
Management styles, 116, 120–121,
    151–158, 200–201, 205, 212–213

Management styles (*Cont.*):
 and creativity, 30, 32–33, 35–37
 (*See also* Specific styles, e.g., Dictatorial
  management)
Managers (*see* Executives)
Manipulation, 110, 111, 120, 126
Marketing, 7, 48–49
Marketing to Win (Sonnenberg), 70, 72
Market share, 1, 2, 7, 108
Matson, Jack, 49
Mattel Inc., 179
McDonald's Corp., 207
McKinsey and Company study, 140
Meaning:
 of products, 90
 in rewards, 27–28
 in work, 10, 13, 14, 22–23
Meetings, 69, 75, 76
 being on time for, 89, 92, 102
 and communication, 66, 70–71
 preparation for, 154
 wasted time in, 153–154
Mentoring, 130
Micromanagement, 17, 24, 120, 154
Microsoft Corporation, 212
Middle management, 56, 110
Military model, 80
Mission, 2, 20, 60, 71, 80, 82, 199
 (*See also* Goals)
Mistakes, 23, 99, 157, 221
 admitting, 98, 124
 learning from, 37, 45, 48, 124–125, 181
Mitsch, Ronald, 48–49
Moorman, Christine, 200
Morale, 11, 46, 108, 188
Motivation, 209
 of employees, 1, 17–20, 47, 60, 67, 213
 problems with, 10–12, 16, 42, 115, 116,
  122
Motorola, Inc., 138–139
Multidirectional communication, 72, 78, 81
Multinational corporations, 143, 167
Mumford, Alan, 125–126

Needs, 142, 149
 anticipating, 107, 140
 of business, 11, 172
 of clients, 7, 87, 90, 93, 98, 102, 104,
  106–107, 170, 180

Needs (*Cont.*):
 for information, 79–80, 81
Negotiation, 110, 111
Networking, 24, 25, 78, 81–82, 168
New ideas, 29, 47, 68, 181, 189
 barriers to, 35–39, 43–44, 46, 51
 and clients, 104, 107
 development, 30–35, 41, 225
 measurement, 148–149
New products, 46, 49, 97, 146, 207–208,
  221–222
 development, 32, 51, 132, 205
 timeliness of, 3, 42, 55, 138–139, 140
Newsletters, 58, 66
Nintendo Co. Ltd., 208
Nonaka, Ikujiro, 132–133
Nonverbal communication, 70, 71

Obedience, 16, 80
Objectivity, 72, 107, 134, 165–166, 197,
  198–199, 202–203
Objectives (*see* Goals)
O'Brien, William J., 221
Obsolescence, 112
Odom, W. E., 218
Oestreich, Daniel K., 119–120
Ogilvy & Mather Partners, 179
Open communication, 34–35, 73, 79–80,
  82, 182–184, 191, 205–206, 228–229
 and problems, 181–182, 204, 206
Open-door policy, 25–26, 69
Operational style, 39–47, 147–148
 (*See also* Bureaucracy; Corporate cul-
  ture; Management)
Oral tradition, 128–129
Organizational access, 88, 102
 (*See also* Management, access to)
Organizational charts, 68–69
Organizational climate, 44, 67–68,
  121–122, 144, 190–191, 227
 (*See also* Corporate culture; Work envi-
  ronment)
Organizational effectiveness, 141–151,
  161–162
Organizational size, 143, 166, 167–168, 171
Organizational structure, 1, 18, 39, 51–52,
  70, 112, 142–143, 167
Osborn, Thomas, 51
Out-placement programs, 66

Ownership:
of corporations, 166, 167
sense of, 17, 27

Packaging, 39, 44, 45, 51
Participation:
of employees, 40, 73, 75–76, 124
and change, 110, 111, 112, 128–129
of management, 27
and planning, 78, 150
(*See also* Decision making, sharing)
Paterno, Joe, 124
Patler, Louis, 109, 114–115, 123, 137
Pay, 13, 46
differences in, 10
importance of, 26, 45, 213
severance, 66
Peer relations, 179–180
Performance, 75, 183, 188
by employees, 6, 14, 24–25, 42, 64–65,
121, 135, 154, 219
by groups, 51–52
measurement, 2, 134, 135, 157
problems with, 142, 160–161
Perot, H. Ross, 144, 156
Personal beliefs, 61, 200
Personal bias, 45, 161, 202
Personal commitment, 33, 214
Personal distance, 69, 70
Personal goals, 77, 214
Personal growth, 124–125
Personal knowledge, 133, 185
Personal relationships (*see* Individual rela-
tionships)
Personal safety, 88, 101
Peter Pan Syndrome, 160
Peters, Tom, 209–210, 212, 221–222
Peterson, Donald E., 79
Philosophy, 59
American, 2, 118, 129
of learning, 23, 125
organizational, 171, 196, 204, 214
Planning process, 77–78, 131–132, 150, 162
Plantation management, 9, 10–12
effects of, 12–17, 217–218
Play: and learning, 130
Policies, 59, 94–95, 100, 141
Politics: organizational, 47, 49–50, 71, 79,
118, 142, 147, 189, 193

Porras, Jerry I., 213
Power, 21, 43, 66, 71, 97, 141
Practical phase (of idea development), 30,
31
Pragmatists, 126
Presentations, 34, 41, 44, 49–50, 92, 103, 154
Pressure (*see* Stress)
Pricing, 3, 85, 90–91, 100, 140, 165, 167, 172
Pride, 18, 22, 40, 89, 214
Principle-Centered Leadership (Convey), 200
Priorities, 43, 57, 73, 150, 214
identification of, 1, 6, 13, 159–160, 173
Problem solving, 35, 88, 90, 95–96, 114,
123–124, 182, 204
Problems, 11, 42, 100, 154–155, 189–190, 204
being prepared for, 105, 181–182
prevention of, 39, 206
size of, 106, 113
(*See also* problems under subjects, e.g.,
Decision making, problems in)
Procedures, 30, 40–41, 68–69, 144, 145–147,
152–153
problems with, 13, 39–40, 94–95, 142,
143–144
Procrastination, 38–39, 116, 160–161
Procter & Gamble (P&G) Co., 138
Products, 91, 201–202, 207–208
conflict in, 170–171
differentiation of, 85, 139, 140, 196, 207
knowledge about, 97, 202
returning, 203
use of, 90, 106
(*See also* New products)
Productivity, 146–147, 149, 163
effect of communication on, 57, 67, 69
effect of employee treatment on, 7, 25,
56, 189
problems with, 11, 14, 15, 16, 157–158
Progress reports, 103, 104
Project groups, 41–42
Projects, 42, 173
Promises, 91, 105, 169, 177, 178, 191,
203–204, 208–209
Promotions, 142, 190
Pygmalion effect, 24, 219

Quality, 7, 202
of ideas, 51–52
of organizations, 89–90, 115, 230

Quality (*Cont.*):
   of products, 2, 85, 89, 90, 140, 167, 207
   of service, 83–84, 85–86, 88, 91, 92–93,
      139, 167
Quality Progress (Carter), 116
Quantifiction, 2, 6, 73, 212
Questions, 181
   answering, 91–92, 96, 97, 123, 128–129
Quick Response Systems, 139–140
Quitting employment, 12–13

Read, Raymond, 160–161
Record keeping, 92
Redundancy, 131
Referent power, 21
Reflective learning, 125–126, 129
Reinforcement, 59–60, 61–62, 65, 71, 73,
      156
Relationships, 2, 220
   (*See also* Business relationships; Client
      relationships; Employee relation-
      ships; Long-term relationships;
      Supplier relationships)
Relevancy, 72
Reliability, 88, 91–93, 197, 203–204
Renewal: organizational, 29, 112, 121–122,
      225
Renewal Factor, The (Waterman), 19, 156
Reports, 103–104
Reputation, 99, 100, 202
   developing, 2, 7, 13
   importance of, 3, 188, 196–197
Research, 36, 150, 201
Resentment in relationships, 166, 168–170,
      177
Resources, 3, 6, 29
   allocation of, 1, 94, 150, 151, 165
   availability of, 13, 33, 58, 138, 180, 199
Respect, 40, 97, 121, 178, 199, 200
Responsibility, 44, 81, 150
   by employees, 12, 22, 23, 24, 40, 53, 218
   managerial, 10–20, 31, 32, 33, 60, 125,
      134
   problems with, 120, 144, 157
   in relationships, 172, 185
Responsiveness, 88, 93–96, 107–108, 137
Retraining, 66, 144
Review process (*see* Evaluation)
Revlon Corporation, 64, 65

Revson, Charles, 65
Reward system, 1, 12, 39, 40, 66
   criteria for, 26–28
   importance of, 21, 26, 46, 124, 135
Rights:
   of employees, 22–26
   in relationships, 10, 172, 173
Risk adverse, 80, 193, 221
Risk taking, 48–49, 123–125, 181, 189, 191
Rituals: organizational, 63
Role, 87, 107–108, 183
   of employees, 80
   of leadership, 59–68, 123, 231–232
   of management, 17, 34, 68, 212–213, 221
   of outsiders, 107, 165–166
   perception, 115
Role models, 62–63
Role playing, 31
Routines, 145
Rude Awakening (Keller), 79
Rules, 40, 64–65, 94, 95, 145
   (*See also* Procedures)
Ryan, Kathleen, D., 119–120

Sales, 2, 7, 86, 87, 94, 108, 139
Sales representatives, 87–88, 100, 202
Satisfaction:
   of clients, 84, 92–93, 96, 139, 167, 196
   of employees, 12–17, 45, 57, 135
   in relationships, 176
Scapegoating (*see* Blame)
Schellhardt, Timothy, 71
Scientific management, 19–20
Security, 200, 201–202, 209
   for clients, 88, 100, 101–102
   job, 120, 154, 226
Senge, Peter, 60, 112, 113, 115, 128–129
Senior management, 27, 48–49, 64–66, 143,
      153, 179–180
   problems with, 38, 65, 90
Service excellence, 3, 6, 82, 83–84, 107
   (*See also* Quality, of service)
Service industries, 85
Sewell, Carl, 89, 90
Shea, Gordon, 187, 190, 205, 210
Shell Oil Company, 132
Shelton, Ken, 9
Sheridan, John, 165
Sherman, Stratford, 46

Shewmaker, Jack, 75, 80
Short-term perspective, 115, 116, 189, 190, 213
Simplicity, 42, 145–147, 148–149, 180
Sirota, David, 222
Six Action Shoes (de Bono), 145
Skills, 60, 114, 121, 135, 160, 165, 182, 215
Small companies, 166, 167–168, 171, 172, 175, 215
Small groups, 71, 143
Smith, Alvie, 56, 81
Smith, Fred, 140
Smith, Samuel S., 84
Socialization, 70
Social motivation, 19
Socratic method, 128–129
Soft issues, 2, 7, 19, 211, 212
Solorzano, Lucia, 126
Sonnenberg, Frank K., 70, 72
Sony Corp., 208
Specialization, 51
Speed (*see* Time)
Sportsmanship, 98
Staff (*see* Employees)
Start-up companies, 69
Status, 65, 70
Stayer, Ralph, 21
Stimson, Henry, 228
Storytelling, 28, 63–68, 81, 180, 200–201
Strategic alliances, 155, 166, 170, 171, 172, 184, 217
Strategic planning, 27, 33, 78, 148, 178
Stress, 14, 56, 62, 94, 157–158, 160, 189
Strohecker, Ben, 200–201
Studies, 135
  (*See also* Customer surveys; Employee surveys; Executive surveys)
Success, 23, 50, 75, 123, 175
  achieving, 2, 8, 18–19, 107–108, 124, 216, 224
  factors, 3, 6–7, 57–58, 110, 115, 140–141, 180
  problems with, 16, 17, 48, 160
Sunkist Growers, Inc., 168
Supplier relationships, 165, 166–167
  building, 6–7, 151
  maintaining, 98
  problems with, 99, 100
  (*See also* External communication)
Suppliers, 167

Support:
  for employees, 25, 37, 65–66, 67, 110, 111, 123, 144
  of information, 72
  in relationships, 176, 179–180, 185, 209

Tacit knowledge, 133
Tandem Computers, Inc., 81
Tangibles, 88, 89–91
  (*See also* Intangibles)
Tarkenton, Fran, 28
Teamwork, 34, 58, 122–123, 133, 144, 146, 179, 201
Technological safety, 101
Technology, 7, 18–82, 89, 110, 132, 139
  use of, 4, 72, 149, 163
Telephone calls, 90–91, 95–96, 102, 139
Terminology, 3, 4, 19
Theorists, 126, 127–128
Thought processes, 3, 17, 31, 36, 50–51, 125–126, 127–129, 146
  (*See also* Creativity)
3M Company, 5, 32, 35, 40, 46, 48–49, 51
Time, 3, 6, 56, 65, 110
  and communication, 58, 59, 72, 73
  in cost-benefit analysis, 173
  and creativity, 36, 37–39, 43, 49
  and decision making, 153, 157–158, 144, 171
  to develop relationships, 172, 177, 180, 196–197
  devoted to client, 170
  importance to client of, 89, 93–94, 102, 184
  loss of, 15, 162
  as a resource, 58, 93, 111, 138–139, 140–141, 193
  and rewards, 28
  in training, 175
  use of, 11, 36, 141, 146–147, 158, 163–164
  value on, 138, 140, 152, 158–163
  wasted, 36, 104, 144, 146, 147–148, 153–154, 155–156, 223–224
Time Warner Inc., 217
Top-down communication (*see* Downward communication)
Top management (*see* Senior management)
Total Research Corporation study, 5

Trainees, 96–97
Training of employees, 2, 66, 96–97, 115,
    116, 175
  investment in, 11, 68, 144, 156, 202, 226
  in technology use, 4, 149, 184
Trust, 6, 121, 187–189, 194, 233–234
  breach of, 46, 101, 208–209
  building, 58, 82, 192, 193–195
  characteristics of, 193, 197–206
  defining, 191
  by employees, 2
  in employees, 24, 37, 189
  lack of, 42, 79, 172, 189–190, 192–193
  level of, 191–192
  in management, 24, 188
  in organizations, 67, 89, 90, 99, 105–106
  as a resource, 210
Turnover of employees, 12, 13, 25, 175,
    184, 201
Tylenol, 4–5, 199

Uncertainty, 104, 206
Understanding, 72, 76–77
  building, 72, 180–181
  change, 113–116, 125, 129
  clients, 88, 91, 102, 106–108
  employees, 67
  products, 90, 103
  in relationships, 176, 177–178
Uniformity, 200
Unilever plc, 168
Upward communication, 73, 75–76, 80
Utilicorp United Inc., 71

Values, 5, 188–189, 191
  learned, 40, 71, 195
  promoting, 59, 61–68, 82
  shared, 2, 17
Vendors (*see* Suppliers)
Verbal communication, 39, 72, 90–91,
    95–96
Vertical communication, 34, 57, 59, 73–76,
    77, 80
Vertical organization, 146

Vested interest, 175, 183
Vision, organizational, 59–61, 115, 215
Visiting clients, 98
Visual learning, 126
von Oech, Roger, 30–31, 40, 51

Waiting, 94, 139, 162–163, 224
  (*See also* Time)
Walton, Sam, 75
Wal-Mart Stores Inc., 75, 80
Waste, 36, 104, 147–148, 151
  elimination of, 2, 145–147
  (*See also* Time, wasted)
Waterman, Robert, Jr., 19, 156
Watson, Thomas J., 49, 64–65
Welch, John (Jack), Jr., 32–33, 46, 59, 110,
    121, 167
Wharton School study, 38, 42, 47, 48
Whole person paradigm, 20, 22
William M. Mercer (consultant) survey,
    228
Work: and fun, 32–33
Work environment, 8, 32
  and change, 6, 112, 225
  creating, 2, 20, 82, 122, 147
  problems in, 13, 119–122
  in relationships, 178, 181
  (*See also* Innovation, climate for;
      Organizational climate)
Work force (*see* Employees)
Work style, 169
Written communication, 39, 72, 91, 92
Wurman, Richard, 55, 127–128, 180–181
Wyatt Company survey, 75

Xerox Corporation, 196

Young, John, 78

Zaltman, Gerald, 200
Zand, Dale E., 192, 205–206
Zippel, George, 134

About the Author

Frank K. Sonnenberg is president of RMI Marketing and Advertising, Inc., whose clients include major U.S. and international companies. Formerly the national director of marketing for the Management Consulting Group of Ernst & Young, he is a nationally recognized expert in the field of marketing. He is the author of the best-selling *Marketing to Win*, as well as more than 300 articles in such publications as *IndustryWeek, Management Review, Investor's Business Daily, Entrepreneur, Adweek's Marketing Week, Sales and Marketing Management,* and *Executive Excellence.* Sonnenberg is also an expert panelist for *Boardroom Reports,* the marketing columnist for *Business Strategy,* and serves on the editorial board of *The Training and Development Journal.*